Finding
Hope
in the
Long Run

∞

Kathy Sebright

For Tony

Hope. It is the only thing stronger than fear.
Suzanne Collins

Acknowledgments

~To everyone who believed in me even when I didn't believe in myself: You have built me up when I have torn everything down in fear and frustration. You saw what I couldn't see. You have made me brave. You stood behind me and cheered me on even when I wasn't sure I could go another step.

~To the founders of Fellow Flowers - Maryellen (Mel) Charbonneau and Tori Sager: Thank you for giving the world Fellow Flowers. Thank you for being brave enough to follow your dreams. Your bravery has inspired my bravery. I hope you know the depth by which you have changed not just my life but many others. You leave bits of hope and possibility in your wake. You have challenged me to reach for the stars. This is me reaching.

~To my focus group friends - Susanna Brennan, Donna Robinson, Lacey Dembroge, Sarah Greim, Sharon Roach, Amanda Lane, Sarah Joanis, Susan Johnson, and Brandy Muth: You have provided me with insight, advice, and feedback that has made this book better on so many levels. Your words have impacted my words, so in a way, some of these very words are your own. I value you all and your loving input.

~To Crystal Fieber: The time and effort you've given me has been amazing. A thousand thank-yous aren't enough.

~To my Fellow Flowers friends, far too many to name: The bond of your sisterhood and support goes far beyond a simple flower in our hair and running. The bond of this sisterhood is too deep for mere words. I don't need to explain this to you because you already know. You have covered me in love and support. You have been a collective hum of hope in the background of some of my darkest days. You have been instrumental in my stepping out and stepping up into the life that I always wanted.

~To my amazingly loving and huge hearted family: Whether we are bound by blood or by marriage, I am incredibly blessed by all of you. Parents, sisters, brothers, grandparents, aunts, uncles, nieces, and nephews. I hit the jackpot with each and every one of you. You have made me smile when I wanted to cry. You have gone above and beyond to be everything and anything that we ever needed. You have brought love, light, and laughter into our home when we needed it the most. Thank you for being you.

~To Kristy Westrate: My chief editor, my photographer, my publicist, my agent, my head of research, my cheerleader, and above all, my dear friend. You've been instrumental and amazingly supportive in every single step of this process. I hope you know that I couldn't have done any of this without you. Thank you for responding to a thousand texts and a thousand questions without hesitation. Thank you for the incredible amount of time you have given to help me reach my dream. Thank you for your labor of love. My heart loves your heart.

~To Kelly Moore: Your calling card is rainbows, sunshine, and smiles. I have never known anyone so positive and optimistic in my life. You have been a great source of inspiration and cheer whenever I have found myself with that dark cloud hanging above my head. Thank you for supporting me every step of the way.

~To Aggie Kurzmann: resident flip-flop master and Pinterest crafter, and the best hair and wardrobe stylist one could ask for. Thank you for your time, support, guidance, and friendship.

~To my many groups of supporters and friends: My MOPS (Mothers of Preschoolers) friends, my fellow road warriors, my church family, my coworkers, my support group, and my Facebook friends near and dear to my heart but far away. Thank you for being a part of my life. Thank you for believing in me, taking an interest in me, and standing beside me. You have inspired me to love the world around me deeper because of the way you have loved me.

~To all of my dearest friends who have seen it all: You are not just my friends but my family. You have seen me at my very worst but only ever given me your very best. You have watched me fall time and time again and have been there every single time holding out your hand to me, willing to pull me back up. You are the friends that I have always wished for.

~To my son Travis: My strong, loving, and compassionate boy who has his life tailored to fit his little brother's needs. You are the most loving little boy I've ever had the privilege of knowing and the way you take care of Emmett and those around you makes me see what great things you will do in this life

~To my son Emmett: You are a miracle, not just because you have survived when they said you wouldn't, but because of the way you have touched all of our lives so deeply and helped me find new purpose in this life. You are a light in this world and I can't wait to see what you will do with it.

~To my loyal and loving husband Tony: This wouldn't be in any way, shape, or form, possible without you. Thank you for putting up with my eccentricities, for seeing through all my bravado and for taking care of me even when I was sure I didn't deserve it. You have loved me far beyond any capacity I have ever thought possible. You are my very best friend and the backbone of our family. Thank you for supporting me and my dreams in this life every step of the way.

~To God: For the amazing, overwhelmingly joyous life that You have given me. You must know I never deserved to have so much and yet here I am, humbled once again. I don't always understand, but I can always see You in the details.

Prologue

I wanted to tell a story. An inspirational masterpiece that starts with me, your heroine, who is down and out. It would be a triumphant climb out of darkness, a setback, a return to greatness with an even stronger resolve, and finally the happy ending we all knew was coming. It would be a great story: an uplifting, positive, "if I can do it, you can do it" kind of story. Oh, I had plans. So many plans and ideas about the story I could tell, a dramatization, based on actual events, made for TV kind of story. When I sat down to do it and the words stared me back in the eye, I knew I had overestimated my ability to put the truth down on paper. The words staring back at me were lovely and heavy handed with a rosy outlook and perpetual optimism but they weren't the truth. The truth of this story is not a smooth, linear timeline. It does not swell in the middle and end in a blaze of glory. It is one of deep lows and extreme highs, up and down, round and round, over and over again. It's messy. It's uncomfortable. It's embarrassing and it's true. To put the truth down on paper, out in the open makes me burn with both shame and empowerment.

So much of my life contradicts itself at times. It doesn't make sense. It doesn't fall into line with what I believe today in this moment. I'm not sure if I'm supposed to admit that or not. I can swing from holding fast to hope and trusting God, to complete and utter desperation. Depending on the circumstances and where I find myself, I can fall apart in the morning and be completely fine by the end of the evening. The mood swings were, and still are at times, so severe and so wide reaching, it seems almost impossible that I could be talking about something just days or hours apart with a completely different attitude, but I really am.

I hope, if you skip everything else in this book, if you can't even bring yourself to make it past chapter one, bored to tears or drowning in poorly written clichés, I hope you read this; I hope that you understand this: I am not sad for this life. I do not wish to change it. I have no need for re-dos in any area. I sit here, who I am today, because of these experiences and because of learning things the hard way, which is unfortunately the only way this stubborn woman before you has ever known. I'm so grateful for this amazing life. I don't ever want to give the impression that I want anyone to feel bad for me, my family, or my son. It has not been a burden to carry. It has not been tragic. It has been our life and, although hard at times, I would not trade it for anything in this world. As my wise friend Liz would say, "We are the lucky ones." What I want is for people to understand. What I want is for people to see there is always hope. This life is truly extraordinary. It just took me some time to see that fully.

Sometimes life isn't okay. Sometimes the world collapses in on you and the unthinkable happens. Sometimes there is nothing to do but hang on when it feels like you can't. I know what it's like to hurt, to grieve, to be depressed, to fake it, and to feel absolute nothingness. I have seen that door slam in my face more than once. I have been emptied of joy and happiness and filled with pain and sorrow. I have faced fears that I never knew I had. I have screamed terrible anguished screams, sure that I was going to explode if I didn't get the blackness out. I could feel it, devouring me from the inside out; taking everything good about me and ripping it into useless shreds. I have felt that weight inside my chest and inside my heart, pressing in on me until I couldn't breathe, pressing in on me until I was down on my hands and knees afraid I was losing my mind.

Somehow life goes on, day after relentless day of life, until one day, bit-by-bit, hope returns. One day, I laughed and I wasn't just pretending. I thought maybe I could really live with this. One day, I was ready to face my fears. I could see the cold, hard, scary and embarrassing truth without despair setting in. That is where I must begin my story. A random collection of our life, in bits and pieces, in no particular order. The hope that I lost and the hope that I found. The hope that was desperate and the hope that was comforting. The hope that restored and the hope that I wanted others to feel radiating from me. The hope that was there, even when I couldn't see it.

The hope that remains today.

Chapter 1

More times than I care to admit or probably ever will, I must confess I have spent time standing in front of a mirror and have seen only flaws. I have cringed, sighed, and stomped out of the room in frustration before leaving the house. *Good enough, I guess* and I'd walk dejectedly to the car. More often than not, I have been guilty of only seeing the bad. Of only seeing what I wanted to fix, what I couldn't change, and who I thought I should be. So many times I have fallen flat on my face. So far from whom I thought I was that I wanted to kick my feet like a toddler and demand someone pick me up.

I've stared into a face riddled with scars. Scars from a life that hasn't always been fair. Scars that cut deeper than just into my flesh. Scars that have seared themselves upon my very soul. I can run my hand over the jagged skin and I know. I know each scar by heart. I know where it's from, how it's been transformed, and how it transformed me.

Growing up, I was quite average looking and that was fine. I'm secure enough in myself to tell you that. Mind you, I was a bit nerdy with a head of bad hair and clothes that always were too short for me as I continued to grow taller than many of the boys in my class. When you want to blend in, a wide shouldered six foot tall frame with long gangly arms and legs is not the way to do it. Still, I was okay with what I looked like. I wasn't one of those people who were dying to change a million things about themselves. I looked in the mirror and I was proud of who I was. Average, but strong. Plain, but deep. Different than others. Of course, all these revelations were before I got up close and personal with the car windshield and I became unrecognizable to myself.

There was really nothing that registered at first. They said it was the adrenaline and shock. The pain didn't come until later when I was barefoot, covered from head to toe in blood, and screaming at the side of the road like a crazy person. If I close my eyes and think about it, I can put myself right back there. I can see it; the little gray car wrapped around the tree. I can feel it; the caustic burning feeling all over my entire face. I can sense it; the blood running down my face and down my arms. I could see a bloody trail dripping onto the pavement from me. My light purple pajama pants were stained a deep crimson red from the unstoppable flow of blood coming from my face. It was so thick; I had to keep wiping it from my eyes to be able to see straight. The color red. It was all I could see. *How did I not go all the way through the windshield? What were these physics I didn't understand? How did I not die?*

I was fifteen years old, just a week before my sixteenth birthday. I had gone to Lake Michigan for the first time the night before with some friends from school. We were driving home early in the day. The sun was shining and the sky was perfectly blue, with huge puffy white clouds. I can see it so vividly because I remember it so clearly, wondering how I'd ever feel any happier than I was in that moment. We were less than two miles from my home. I was supposed to be leaving for a Texas vacation with my family the next day. I was excited to see somewhere new.

I was kicked back in the front seat and barefoot with my feet perched up on top of the dashboard. I wearing a tank top and my favorite light purple pajama pants with little white clouds on them. My window was down just a little bit, so as to not overwhelm the girls in the back seat with a face full of wind. In what can only be described as fate, I wasn't wearing a seatbelt. I always wore a seatbelt. I wasn't a risk-taker in that area. I was the queen of safety. I always wore my seatbelt, except for that perfect morning in early June.

There I sat, without a care in the world, when everything went wrong. The tires hit gravel, the car swerved and jerked from one lane to the next, there was screaming, and then we went airborne off the side of the road. Life moved in slow motion. I was flying through the air, clawing at nothingness, and thinking a thousand different thoughts at the same time. I was desperate to grab hold of something to stop myself, to get myself back in the seat, and to stop heading toward what I was sure would be my imminent death. I looked down and saw the driver of the vehicle directly underneath me. I was going to go through the windshield sideways.

I'm not sure that I have the right words to tell you how it felt to be so powerless, to be so hopeless, to be so small and finite, and to have my life flash before my eyes. To see the culmination of just fifteen years and know there were still so many things I wanted to do. So many things I wouldn't be able to do. I was devastated as I headed toward that windshield, sure that I was about to die and miss out on a lifetime. I don't remember screaming. I don't remember closing my eyes. I can still see the windshield getting closer and closer while I seemed to float in a suspended state of fear. I remember just wishing it would be over. That's how long the wait felt while I was in the air.

Suddenly, there was nothing but blackness and eerie quiet. I thought I had died. I really honestly thought I died. It was too quiet. At that point, I had believed in God, but really wasn't sure about the rest of it. I thought that was it. The dark nothingness was death. I was gone. The first sensation I felt was strange. My hands were wet. *Why on earth?* I pulled them back to look at them and realized I had been covering my face with my hands. Pools of blood spilled out from between my fingers and onto my lap. *I didn't die?* I touched my hands to my face and let out a tortured scream when I accidentally stuck my thumb in a very nasty deep gash on the side of my face. *I was alive?* It didn't make sense. There was so much blood.

It was then that I looked at the driver who had heard me yelp in pain. She was okay but her seatbelt had locked up and she couldn't get out. In the backseat, behind the driver, another friend was unconscious but alive. I could see her chest rise and fall. Directly behind me, on the side of the car that took the brunt of the impact, was a sight that could never, ever be unseen. My beautiful friend, Christine, with her head lying awkwardly close to her knees, her jaw unhinged, and the car caved in all around her. She looked like a rag doll that someone had just tossed back there. We screamed her name over and over, but there was no response. From the way she lay there all crumpled up, we couldn't tell if she was breathing or not.

I don't know exactly how long this taking stock of the situation took, but it couldn't have been more than a minute or two. Since I was the only one conscious and free of a seatbelt, I decided I had to go get help. Thus, the only saving grace of not wearing a seatbelt; I was able to go for help for our friend in the backseat who desperately needed it. When I would later throw myself a pity party and get angry at myself for being so stupid as to not wear a seatbelt, it would be this reminder that would calm my frazzled nerves. We had gone completely off the road, down into a deep ditch, and traveled into the woods. *Would she have died if I couldn't have gone to get help right away? Would someone have seen us down there through the trees? How long would we have waited?* This was my fate. I didn't wear that seatbelt for any reason that I could understand.

It never occurred to me to grab someone's shoes. I was still barefoot when I leaned against the driver and started kicking at the window with my feet. I needed to make a hole big enough to jump out of. My door wouldn't open, the window was stuck where it was, and surprisingly enough, a good amount of glass still remained. I cleared out what I could with my feet and hands. I looked at my sunglasses that were embedded in the windshield over the top of the steering wheel. I saw where my body had slammed up against each point of that cracked and broken windshield and shuddered.

I took a deep breath to steady myself and jumped out the window feet first. The leftover jagged glass from the window cut into my arms and sides of my stomach. I landed awkwardly on a field of glass and found myself on my hands and knees, bleeding all over the place. My right ear, which had been cut clean off, was horrifyingly enough hanging on by this tiny, thin thread of skin past my shoulder. Yes. All the way down to my shoulder. I was holding onto my ear because I was afraid it would fall off and I would lose it for good. I popped back up off of my hands and knees, holding my ear, and saw even more glass sticking out of me. I pulled a massive chunk out of the bottom of my foot with a scream and stumbled up the ditch. My feet were shredded and the pressure of just standing upright, let alone attempting to run with thousands of shards stuck in them was excruciating. I tripped over a branch and went down hard, skidding across the ground, driving the glass in further to my delicate skin, inciting more blood in the field of glass. The pain made me angry. I screamed loudly and desperately in frustration.

I dragged myself back up, hobbled out of the ditch and stood on the gravel shoulder. A long lonely stretch of road spread out in front of me. There were no cars in sight. I slowly shuffled down the road, thinking I was going to have to head toward the nearest house. I left a thick trail of blood behind me. I was screaming, at no one and at nothing in particular. I don't remember if it was even words or just screams of terror, I only knew I couldn't make myself stop. I would hear the first responders on the scene later say I was in shock, but I kept screaming as a car came into view and zoomed past me. I stood staring after it and began to cry. I hadn't cried at all up until that point, but now I was hysterical. *Who was going to save us?* I stood unmoving and cried harder, gasping for air, when I noticed they were rapidly backing up toward me. They had seen me. It was going to be okay.

I sobbed and yelled incoherently by the side of the road as people came in droves. It gets a little fuzzy after they put me on the stretcher. I was lying there looking up at the sky. I remember familiar faces, but mostly I remember how much it hurt. It hurt to lay there. It hurt to breathe. It hurt all over from the top of my head to the bottoms of my feet. They wouldn't let me up from that stretcher, but I tried anyway and it hurt to attempt to move. It hurt to have the neck brace on, unable to see what was going on. I didn't want the brace. I had crawled on my hands and knees up the ditch, clearly I didn't need the suffocating brace, but they insisted and I hated it. It hurt even more to listen to the terrible screeching sound of the Jaws of Life as it sliced through the car. It hurt to not know. *Was my friend dead? Was she going to be okay?* No one would tell me anything. It even hurt to cry. The tears stung my shredded face.

A short time later, I found myself lying on a table looking up at the hospital ceiling. The lights were too bright. Everything was fuzzy. My parents were there along with my grandparents. My mom and my grandma were standing over my bedside. The pain was all I could see and feel; it makes a much stronger impression and leaves much more vivid memories than anything else did that day. My feet were horribly shredded. My skin was on fire from head to toe. Hundreds of cuts littered my entire body, all over the place, one after the other. Small thin slashes, long, deep cuts, ragged chunks of skin missing and everything in between.

As I lay half awake, half asleep on the table, they cut off my pants from my body. I was upset. The clouds made me so happy and they were taking them away. I didn't want them to do it, but they did anyhow. Someone told me that I could get new pants and I started to cry. Two nurses spent hours picking and carefully removing all of the glass chunks and shards from my body. They spent a particularly long time on my feet, which brought a fresh wave of tears. There was so much glass in my feet.

The hospital flew in a fancy surgeon from Detroit to reattach my ear. They put hundreds of stitches (non-dissolvable back then) all over the place. I was a patchwork doll. I had been ripped apart and sewn back together haphazardly. My scalp was shredded and huge chunks of hair were missing. A row of jagged staples ran across the top of my head. When they were finally done with me, I asked to be brought to the bathroom. I wanted to look at myself. I saw someone else staring back at me. I wanted to scream: I was so appalled by my reflection. That wasn't me. That wasn't what I looked like. It couldn't be. I was a vision in stitches, gauze, and thick antiseptic ointment. My entire face was tinted a light red, my hair wildly sticking out in every direction in the front where it had been hacked off by the windshield. I was a sickly pale color, shivering in response to what stared back at me in the mirror. No. Not what, but who. That was still me in the mirror, but it didn't look like me anymore.

I recovered well enough with time. I laid in bed for a lot of days at first. It hurt to do absolutely nothing and moving was ten times worse. My friend, Christine, who sat in the seat behind me, and had the car caved in around her, suffered the very worst of it. She was in the ICU and in the hospital for a very long time.

There are things by which you are never the same afterward. This was one of them. Just the sheer act of getting into a car after that made me break out into a sweat. My heart would pound and I would just hang on tightly to the seat belt. Because of that accident, I didn't get my license for nearly two years afterward. I rode the bus nearly all through high school. I was scared to go outside, scared to get into a car, and scared to let people see my face. Throughout the summer, I remained a shut in, partly because of the doctor's orders to stay out of all sunlight, but secretly I was relieved. I didn't want to go see people. I didn't want to face the world.

I went out for the first time after the accident with some friends for the Fourth of July in our super small town square. It had been only been a few weeks since the accident and my cuts were still very raw looking. I was aware that people were staring at me. I knew I stood out and people were talking about me. A group of the "popular" kids were walking toward us, including a boy I had a small crush on. With all the giddiness a group of sixteen year old girls can have, we noticed. They walked right up next to us when I heard him speak up, loud enough for all of us to hear. "Eww. It looks like someone put her face in a blender," and they laughed at his astonishing wit. I was too stunned and too embarrassed to say anything. I just stared after them. I was different now, I could see it, and so could everybody else. People thought I was ugly now, and there was nothing I could do about it.

For a lot of years, I let that hold me back. I never left the house without makeup. I carefully applied layer after layer of concealer on the worst of my scars. I spent an uncomfortable amount of time covering up every single slash and cut I could see. I became very self-conscious, seeing only what I was sure everyone else saw, a mangled face. When I looked into a mirror, all I saw were those things that were wrong with me. My deeply flawed face. Bright red raised angry scars staring back at me.

There were three different procedures to remove the excess scar tissue and smooth out my face. It made a huge difference. It gave me a glimpse of my old face and of my old self. Of course I was more than my appearance, but tell that to a teenage girl with a shredded face that has become a target. If there was any way to cover it up, I would have. I suppose its good character building. What's life without suffering to toughen you up a bit? Not that I felt I needed any more toughening up. *Wasn't there some sort of limit?* As time passed, my tormentors got bored and moved on. Still, my scarred face remained.

Sometimes I look at myself in the mirror and can see it all over again like it happened yesterday. I continued my obsessive makeup routine even into my adult years. When I first started running, before I would go to a race, I would put my makeup on just to cover my scars. Of course, I would sweat it all off in about two miles, but I still did it. Every. Single. Time. In the summer, the scars got darker, brighter red, and more noticeable. Or maybe it's because my skin got tanner and it stood out more. Regardless, the summer always had me applying and reapplying multiple times throughout the day. When I got a running partner and started running with a group, I still needed my safety net of makeup.

It took a lot of time before I could see those scars, not as an indication of loss, but an indication of triumph. I lived. I don't know how. I should have died back then. All the thick cuts I had slicing through my neck, how was I not injured beyond repair? The terrible angle at which I flew through the car and slammed back down in a pile, how didn't I come out of that paralyzed somehow? My feet on the dashboard that went through the windshield, how did I not even break anything? It wasn't my time yet. There is no reason, looking back now, that I should have survived that. People die in accidents much less severe than that, and I walked away with the scars to prove I lived.

I can look at my scars now and see them for what they really are. A badge of honor. Something that makes me different yes, but different in a good way. You see this thickened slash on the left side of my face? It was so horrifyingly deep that I accidentally stuck over half of my thumb in it while I was patting around my face looking for the source of pain. You see this thin red line on my ear? That's where my ear was sheared off and they put the whole thing back on. You see this double underline on my neck? That's where they pulled out a huge chunk of glass that was embedded in that delicate skin. You see my rough hands and knuckles? I cleared the jagged sides of a broken window with my bare hands. Of course, no one really wants to be riddled with scars, even I don't. However, instead of seeing an enemy in the mirror, I see a reminder of how I have lived and how I have survived. I see a reminder that I must be meant for something more in this life or else I wouldn't have walked away from that wreckage. It makes me see the big picture. It makes me wonder what else there is in store for me. I must have been saved for something pretty amazing.

What's the point of this little trip down memory lane? Life. Life that was given and life that could be taken away in an instant. How you see yourself is way more important than how others see you. Sometimes, you can't even see yourself anymore but you are in there, just as I was, trapped and fighting my way back out. Today, I no longer wear makeup to go running. I no longer feel the need to cover my scars in concealer when going to the pool. I even go without makeup around my close friends. I can look in the mirror and appreciate my face instead of be embarrassed about it. These scars are a map. They lead me back home.

They are the broken pieces of me that remind me I have lived, loved, and hoped.

8

#Kathyfacts

First let me explain #Kathyfacts. Hashtags scare me. I don't do Twitter at all and I don't use them on Facebook unless I'm told to, like when I am sharing a post in hopes of winning some piece of running gear or entering a contest. My husband Tony started #Kathyfacts on Facebook years ago. At first it was just a joke, for all of these random off the wall things that I have done, and for sharing embarrassing stories. Trust me on this one; I have a lot of embarrassing stories. With time, it evolved into bigger and more serious things that I have done and accomplishments that he was proud of. Eventually #Kathyfacts became something said in half jest, half fist pump when I started handing down "nuggets of wisdom." When I told the truth about something or shared something that resonated with others, someone would inevitably #Kathyfacts me.

Now that we understand the silly joke behind this and you don't think I'm some self-important woman with a huge head trying to start a hashtag movement, we can go on and get to the point.

I want to push you out of your comfort zone. If you are not a person who journals, self reflects, or has spent time thinking about how your past continues to influence your present, this is going to be a bit of a stretch for you. It may seem strange and possibly a bit hokey, but I encourage you to try answering the questions honestly and thoroughly. Write it down, think about it, or say the words out loud. Whatever you prefer, just give it a try.

#Kathyfacts

We all have scars. Some can be seen by the naked eye, others are buried so deep within the scarred person that you don't even know they are there. I have both kinds of scars. You can look at my face and see that I am flawed. Scarred. Different. You can also look at me and not have a clue what lies underneath; of the deep layers of scars I carry with me. This is true of so many of us. We are all wounded in one way or another. So often, we can't see each other's wounds or scars so we don't even know they are there.

1. Do you cover your scars up and attempt to conceal them or do you let them be seen?

2. What is one thing that has scarred you deeply others may not know about?

I spent a lot of time worrying about my scars and how different I looked. I didn't realize then that scars are stories of victory and triumph. Scars change us, yes, but scars do not define us. We can embrace our scars, our past, and the experiences that have broken our hearts or hurt us greatly. When we embrace the past and what has happened to us, we are able to let those scars heal completely. No longer do the scars need to remain raw, open, and painful to the touch. When we embrace the scars and grow from them, we are able to put them to rest for good. The scars close and heal. Although they may always hurt a little bit if you poke hard enough at them, they need not remain so tender.

Look for one scar that you can make peace with. There is a scar you carry that is not a sign of defeat but proof of overwhelming victory and survival. Look for that scar and let it be a reminder of how you have traveled through immense pain and lived to tell of it.

Chapter 2

I've been a runner since 2005, a year after I married my high school sweetheart Tony. I put on a few pounds in the happy, honeymoon phase of marriage and wanted to quickly lose them. Little did I know what a difference running would make in my life over the next ten years. I ran through all seasons, literally and figuratively. Not only was I outside running through the very real seasons: spring, summer, fall, and winter, but I also ran through seasons of darkness and pain, joy and light, and pure desperation. I ran away from my problems, ran into other problems, and found a way to thrive in the life that came after my son Emmett's diagnosis. Running embedded itself deep into my heart, deep into who I actually was, and transformed me not just on the outside, but on the inside. Running pulled me out of depression, hopelessness, and gave me focus. Running gave me the strength I needed to be brave or to at least pretend to be brave. Running saved me from myself. I found myself again out on the open road and in the dusty trails.

It all started one hot June day. Weighing about ten pounds more than I wanted to, I laced up an old pair of shoes I wore when I mowed the lawn. I wore a pair of cotton shorts that were usually worn for pajamas and an old cotton t-shirt that was officially my painting shirt. I was a vision, needless to say. I was at my in-law's house, in the tiny rural village of Hopkins, Michigan, my hometown, population six hundred-fifty in village limits.

I stepped outside, soaking in the full heat and humidity. I didn't stretch or do anything else. I probably should have. I just closed the front door behind me and set off to the point exactly one mile away from the house. Two miles seemed a doable first-day distance, I naively thought. Ten steps into my journey I knew I had been overly confident (this running thing was a lot harder than it looked). Still, being the person I am, highly motivated and ridiculously stubborn, I decided I was going to complete the two miles. I wasn't even twenty-three years old but ten minutes later, I was pretty sure I was going to have a heart attack and die. My lungs burned. My heart beat wildly out of control, desperate to catch up. I couldn't get in enough oxygen and my legs thudded heavily underneath me with a weight I didn't realize they possessed. All in all, I was absolutely, positively miserable.

My half way point was where the road split from being paved to an old gravel road. When my feet touched gravel, I contemplated just sitting down and taking a break. Maybe I could call Tony and have him come get me. Instead, I turned around and headed back to the house for what felt like the longest mile of my life. I had never run a mile before, but I was fairly certain before this endeavor that it wasn't that far. Oh, how wrong I was.

I don't know how long it took me but eventually I made it to the steps of that glorious front porch. I sat down feeling completely pained and out of my league. I promised myself I'd never do anything stupid like that again. Fate must have had a good laugh. Just a few hours later, I was already making plans to attempt my two mile trek again the very next day. Surely that's how it worked; the more I ran, the easier it would get. I couldn't place my finger on it, but I felt more alive somehow. I felt happier. I felt stronger even though it hurt all over. I felt joy. I really did. It didn't make any sense but I kind of loved it. The next day and the day after that, I continued on doing way too much, way too soon. It must have been after a week or so of this haphazard running that I got it in my head to run a local 5K that was two weeks away. I didn't want to just run it; I wanted to finish in less than thirty minutes. That seemed reasonable to me.

Tony, full of good intentions and concern, was afraid I was doing too much too soon. Although he wasn't a runner either, he didn't think the 5K was a good idea. We had agreed on so many things in our life together, it was the first big thing we butted heads on. It was important to me and I wasn't willing to back down. Multiple fights and chaos ensued leading up to the race, until I reached my boiling point. I was pretty hot tempered in my younger years and maybe I haven't outgrown that as well as I should have. Regardless, I was not accustomed to anyone questioning what it was I wanted to do. For years, I had been very independent and made up my own mind about what was best for me.

One evening, I screamed my closing argument. "Either you're with me on this or you're not! I'm doing it. You can be there to cheer me on when I cross the finish line or hear about it later." With all my snotty, overly confident assuredness, it was the very last time he would ever question anything running related I would do, even nine years later, when I was hunched over weeping like a child at some eighty plus mile mark of a hundred mile race. Even then, Tony would refuse to say anything but how he knew I could do it. He would later admit how much he had to bite his tongue and tell me to stop doing this to myself and just call it quits, but I'm getting ahead of myself.

On a very humid Fourth of July, I toed the start line with excitement mixed with fear and ran my very first race. It was both extremely hard and extremely gratifying. When I crossed the finish line in just over twenty-eight minutes, I knew this was the beginning of something big. I wanted to go further, faster, and more often. Thus began the spark that would change my entire life. At first it felt silly to admit that running changed my entire life, but it really did. It's how I survived the turbulent years. It's how I found my faith. It's how I dealt with diagnosis after diagnosis. It's how I found hope again, just a glimpse with every mile at so many different points in my life. Running helped sustain me before I could sustain myself or trust God to do the same.

After that first 5K, I was hooked. I signed up for every race I could. I steadily progressed from the 5K, 10K, half marathon, 25K, to a full marathon and everything in between. It was really good for a while. It was enough. I wasn't really interested in getting faster anymore. I just wanted to run to enjoy it. I thought about another marathon but waffled back and forth with it. I had already run a few, and I wasn't sure if I wanted to do any more. I just wanted to run for the fun of it.

That was my running mindset when I diagnosed our youngest son Emmett with Craniosynostosis, a birth defect of the skull. I went from happily running on my own for pure enjoyment to everything being completely turned upside down. Suddenly, I didn't want to run anymore at all. After all those years of finding my passion and fueling it daily, I wanted out. That's when it all came together, slowly, painfully, and with a crushing force. I had to run. I had a responsibility to run. I kept going only because I was pacing for the first time for the Fifth Third River Bank Run in Grand Rapids.

Pacing for this race meant I was able to help other runners finish their race. I was able to be a part of something bigger than me and step into someone else's journey. It is one of the largest 25K races in the world and offered a chance to make a real difference for a struggling runner on race day. I kept going despite everything inside of me that told me it was pointless, that I wasn't going to be racing again, and that I had much bigger things to focus on. I didn't really understand what it was that made me go, but something did and it made all the difference. This was the only way. It was a deep need within, a glimpse of my old self out there on the road. It was the way my heavy legs felt just a tad lighter after I ran them into the ground.

It was the way the ground beneath me became a part of me. Piece by broken piece.

#Kathyfacts

When it comes to trying new things and stepping out of our comfort zones, I think people generally fall into three camps:

~The watchers. These are the people who usually live comfortably in their safe zone. They don't really want to do big, scary things. They'd rather watch someone else do it and cheer them on.

~The waders. These are the cautious toe dippers. They aren't quite sure of it yet. They try a little bit at a time, wait, see what happens, and then decide if they should continue on.

~The jumpers. These are the people who run head first and fully commit to things before they even understand them. Some call them impulsive, I prefer the term adventurous.

1. Are you a watcher, a wader, or a jumper? What do you think has been pivotal in your life to influence how you approach new or scary things?

2. Are you happy with your current approach? If you are, have you always felt that way? If you are not, what would you like to change and why?

Do something that is out of your comfort zone. Big or small. Talk to a stranger, say yes to a party where you won't know anyone, or decide to go after a dream that feels huge and impossible. Adventure is waiting. Go find it.

Chapter 3

When our oldest son Travis was two years old, I was pregnant with our second child. I found myself crawling on my hands and knees to the bathroom in some of the worst pain of my life. The pale blue walls tilted up at me and I was spinning out of control. I desperately held onto the bathroom rug, trying to stop the momentum of my body, but it was no use. I could only scream in pain as my body betrayed me. I hated it. I willed it to stop. I begged and even prayed to a God I wasn't even sure was there. Still it didn't stop. I couldn't control it. I was a mere passenger in my own life. Then it passed. The blinding pain was gone and a blinding emptiness replaced it. I was holding a tiny lifeless baby in my hands, what would have been our second child, born much too soon, and already gone. As I stared at the tiny baby, I felt the life and hope leave my very being.

I was numb. I felt absolutely nothing, but every time I closed my eyes I saw my hands shaking with that tiny little baby in them. It haunted my dreams and kept me from sleeping. It twisted up everything inside of me and left me with just the wreckage of the person I used to be. Depression set in, although I didn't realize that was what it was back then.

I noticed things getting worse but I couldn't make myself care enough to do anything about it. Eight days after that awful night, I was cleared to run by my doctor. I laced up my running shoes. Stepping into them felt like home, even though I was sitting in the middle of my kitchen.

It was winter in Michigan, cold and frozen with lingering snow on the ground and a brisk, biting wind. I took off running down the road, not sure where I was going or how far I would go. My feet ran on autopilot. I found myself on my favorite route, standing on the outskirts of a small lake within a campground. I stopped for a second, staring out at the frozen lake, watching the barren trees with their empty limbs bending in the wind. The strong wind made the branches creak and groan, emphasizing the vastness of the missing leaves. For a minute, it was like looking into a mirror. That is who I was then. I was the tree missing the leaves. I was the lake, cold and frozen. I was the wind passing through where life used to be. I was surprised by the tears that had started to spill over. They stung in the cold air as they rolled down my cheeks. I turned away from the lake and took off running again. I wanted to make it stop. I wanted to feel free, like the old me, for just a moment. I wanted to feel anything but numb. I didn't want pity or prayers. I didn't want to talk about it. I just wanted to run.

I ran harder than I probably should have until I felt pain in my stomach. The pain seemed to radiate from my heart and cover every part of my body. It brought tears to my eyes, but not for the reason you'd think. It wasn't that it hurt that badly to make me cry. That wasn't it at all. It was that I could feel the pain. I was alive. I did not die even though I felt dead inside. I was still here. I was alive and in pain. In the weeks that followed, there were many more tear soaked runs. Each run brought back a little piece of me. I felt just a little bit better each time. It was no cure, it was no replacement for my baby, but it was an outlet. It was an outlet I desperately needed when I couldn't find the courage to speak out about the pain I was in. My running shoes knew though. My running shoes saw it all and felt it all. I didn't have to hide who I was out on the road. Of course, I didn't have to off of the road either, but I just couldn't tell the truth at that time. I wasn't ready.

My first pregnancy with my son Travis had been easy and complication free (until the car accident, of course, but I'll get to that later). Even though Travis was born healthy, now I was worried that it was just a fluke. Travis had miraculously survived my poisonous body, a body that was not conducive to growing life, only ending it. I was terrified that my body had betrayed me and I would never have another child.

A couple of months later, I was standing at that same lake again. If you can believe it, I was pregnant again, kind of. There was a baby but the baby was already gone. I was waiting for my body to reject that tiny little life I couldn't keep safe. My doctor had told me it was ok to run as long as I wasn't in pain. Bitterness rose up within me. Define pain I thought, because I certainly was in pain.

This time it was early spring. The trees were starting to bud; the ice had thawed and was just a memory. A few shreds of green were peeking through the ugly grayish clumps of dirt. It was like a slap in the face. Life. All around me. Shining through. Starting over. I turned away once again and kept running. I didn't cry this time. I was too angry. I screamed and ran, most likely frightening anyone within a two mile radius of me but I didn't care. I was filled with anger and disappointment.

If there was a God up there, what sort of God was He, I wondered? A God who wouldn't save my baby, again and again. The anger consumed me. I had to let it out or be consumed by it. I had so badly wanted these babies. I had wanted to give our oldest son Travis a little brother or a sister. I could feel we were missing a member of our family.

I silently screamed in my head and raged at everyone around me. I closed off everything about myself and dissolved into nothingness. I gave up. In so many ways, in so many things, I gave up and resolved myself to leaving Tony, taking Travis with me, and making a run for it. I was going to start all over because I couldn't bear to live like that, silently suffering alone. I didn't realize the problem was within and not something I could outrun. I saw fault in all of the circumstances and people all around me but could never see the fault in myself back then. I was blinded by anger.

That is where God threw Himself in my life in the one place He knew that I absolutely, positively could not ignore: running. I had always kind of believed in God, but that about covered my relationship with Him. I didn't go to church. I didn't pray. I didn't talk about Him. I didn't read the Bible or do any other of the things that I imagined good Christians did. Just mentioning the word God made me squeamish and uncomfortable. However, I ran. I ran with passion and abandonment. I ran like a woman with nothing to lose, like a woman searching for herself in those miles. I ran for many hours each week, five days a week plus a long run every single Sunday morning. Running was my religion then. Running was the thing I could hold onto, that didn't change in the chaos that my life had become. When everything else fell apart around me, it was running that stayed the same. I clung to that steadiness with everything I had because it was so deep in my soul. I was sure then that this passion could never be extinguished.

Shortly after I had lost the second baby, I was directing a local 5K race. I was still in the mindset of cutting and running. I had every single intention of doing so; I was just finishing up my final responsibilities. This race was one of my very final responsibilities. Our friend and daycare provider, Jodi, had suggested I bring a flyer down to her church because there were a bunch of runners there. *God? Church? Church people? No thank you.* I wanted no part of that. I didn't want to be preached at. I didn't want to talk about God. I didn't want to go to church. I didn't want any of it. I only wanted to recruit a few runners, so I sent my husband to the church to drop off a flyer instead. When Tony returned, he told me about this "nice pastor guy" who wanted to start a running group. This pastor was going to hang up our flyer. He and his churchy runners would even come to the race. Not only that, but he had even invited us to church. This was the exact reason I had opted not to go. I didn't want to go to church, but now I felt bound by a responsibility since this guy was going to drum up some business for my race. I was annoyed because now I felt like I owed this pastor and I don't like to owe anyone. I decided to go just once, out of nothing more than sheer obligation, and to say thank you to him.

The following Sunday, in a strange church in a strip mall, I sat alone in the last row of chairs as far away from everybody as I could get. I kept my head down; my arms crossed stubbornly in front of me, and avoided all eye contact in case I saw anybody I knew. The band started playing and then a strong voice rose out from that stage. Something happened that I wasn't prepared for at all. "Into marvelous light I'm running, Out of darkness, out of shame." The singing continued and it was like I had been punched in the gut. I suddenly didn't have enough air to breathe in. I started to cry. Tears that I had shunned for years, locked away in self-preservation, came.

I didn't understand it. *Why was I crying at this strange song in a strange church surrounded by these strange people?*

As I listened to those around me singing about faith and hope, it clicked. I didn't belong there. I knew I did not belong there. My life was clean out of hope. I had faith in nothing. I was so broken and these people seemed so whole and happy. I had nothing in common with any of them. My tears had turned into sobs that racked my whole body and left me gasping for air. I knew I was making a scene and I decided I had to get out of there. I had to get away from this place, away from these people, and away from it all. Forget the thank you and other pleasantries, I was not coming back. Ever.

I stood up and started to make my way for the door as the song ended, when she appeared. A woman, who I know now as Sarah, had been singing on stage suddenly stood in front of me, blocking my escape route. She looked at me in all of my disastrous glory: wads of Kleenex in my hand, black mascara pooled under my eyes, and tears still running down my face. She put her arms around me and simply said "I am glad you are here with us today, may God bless you." I couldn't do anything but nod while more tears fell.

In that split second, something happened. Something, someone, somehow got through to me. *Sit back down. Don't walk out.* What was happening? I felt myself drawn to stay. I didn't understand it. Why would I ever want to stay? I was trying to run away from this place but I couldn't bring myself to do it. I stood there for a few seconds that felt like hours. I had a decision to make here. I took two steps backwards into my seat and sat back down. When I sat down, I felt an overwhelming sense of relief out of nowhere. It was like a wave rushing over me and I sat there stunned. *You are home now.* It was a thought that entered my mind without my permission. I didn't know how or why, but I knew this was where I was supposed to be. It was the most absolute true feeling I have ever had in my life. It was faith. If I hadn't been a runner, if I hadn't been directing that race, there would have been no way I would have ever stepped foot in that church.

That was the thing that changed everything. God.

#Kathyfacts

I found God in running. I wasn't looking for Him but He came looking for me. For me, running and God are intertwined. I can feel His presence when I run. I can see His handiwork all around me. Sometimes I pray the deepest words of my soul while I run and sometimes I just pray that the run will be done soon.

1. What connects you to your sense of spirituality? Regardless of what or whom you may believe in, how to do you practice seeking out deeper meaning in your life?

2. Have you found solace in an unexpected place? If so, has that changed how you handle painful events or tough times?

3. Is there something that holds you back from seeking peace? Is there anything you could do to change that?

I believe that we are all capable of making peace and moving forward in our everyday lives. Whether you believe in God, the universe, or something different altogether, we all have a common thread that ties us together. Our life experiences. Heartbreak. Joy. Healing. Suffering. Love. No one is immune.

Do something to seek out peace for a tough situation. Practice deep breathing, meditate for five minutes, color, pray, or journal. Do whatever brings meaning and hope into your life. Try to make a habit of noticing the small but beautiful bits of life around you. Anything can be beautiful if you look at it in a certain frame of mind.

21

Chapter 4

After attending church and soaking in the messages for a few weeks, I started seeing the world differently. Instead of identifying all the bad in my life and using it as proof that no one was watching over me, I learned to say "I survived that. Someone must have been watching over me." I could see all these events and circumstances start to click together. For the first time in my life, I could see things as more than just a mere coincidence. Maybe it was something bigger than that. Fate. A plan. A purpose. God. I felt a small but significant shift in the right direction. Hope.

That hope grew rapidly each day until I wasn't sure who I was anymore. I was different. I could feel it. I felt a joy that I never knew was possible in the most mundane of experiences. It was enough of a change to convince me running away and leaving Tony was a terrible idea. I could see how wrong I was and how leaving wouldn't have changed anything. I wasn't running from him. I was running from me. I was what needed to change. Staying changed everything. Tony started going to church with me and I saw significant changes in him as well. Then one day, my hands shook as I stared at the pink plus sign. Pregnant. I was pregnant for the fourth time.

A few weeks later, I lay with my stomach exposed as the words of my doctor swirled around in my head like a slow moving poison. It was like an out of body experience. I was no longer on the table myself, but watching the scene unfold as an impassive observer. I could see myself, wide-eyed and clutching the table in fear with the compassionate eyes of a doctor that knew my reality all too well staring down at me. She couldn't find a heartbeat. The words got stuck in my throat and tears came out instead. I shook my head. *She was wrong. She was wrong. She was wrong.* Everything I wanted to say stalled out and a sob escaped. I cringed. I hated crying, and even more so, I hated crying in front of people. She kept talking, reassuringly squeezing my shoulder, trying to tell me that sometimes she can't pick up a heartbeat until later, sometimes dates were off, and sometimes these things happened.

I went home feeling utterly hopeless. I didn't believe her. I couldn't believe her. In my mind the pregnancy resulted in a happy, healthy child; there couldn't be any other outcome. I told myself I wouldn't get attached, but as I lay there with tears streaming down my face, I knew it was much too late. I was crying because I was already attached. This was my baby. I wanted my baby to live.

Just one week later, I was lying on that same cold exam table. My heart beat frantically and my hands shook in fear and anticipation. My doctor turned the monitor away from me so I couldn't see. All I could do was stare at Tony's equally frightened face trying to look reassuring for me. Seconds felt like minutes and then like hours. I searched her face and stared at her with an intensity that was probably frightening. I was studying her for a giveaway, looking for a clue, a frown, a hint of a smile, a look in her focused eyes, or anything. Her stoic poker face gave nothing away, absolutely nothing. Just when I had decided I couldn't take another second and was going to demand she turn the monitor to me so I could see the baby that was already gone, she spoke up. With one swift movement, she swung the monitor back into eyesight and I focused on it. "There's your baby, strong heartbeat."

I closed my eyes in a gratitude that defied words. Relief washed over me as I took a deep long breath and finally, gloriously exhaled. I had been holding my breath for what seemed like a week straight. I looked up at this wonderful woman who had seen me way too often crying on her exam room table with tears streaming down my face yet again. I wanted to find the words to convey to her how wonderful, compassionate and kind she had been. I wanted to tell her how great this news was when I noticed she wasn't smiling back at me. Before I could even ask her what was wrong, she pointed at something else on the monitor. A large sub chronic hematoma or more simply, a bleed, right near the baby. It was threatening this tiny, fragile little life with no regard for consequences. The overwhelming relief I had felt just a second ago vanished along with the air in my lungs. *No. Not again. No. Not again.* In that moment, I hated God. I felt pure, deep hatred for a God I had come to know, believe in, and rely on. *How could He?*

The rest of the conversation fell on deaf ears. I was there, but really I wasn't. I couldn't hear her. I couldn't believe her. I couldn't feel anything. I already loved this baby. I already wanted this baby to survive more than I wanted anything else in this world. I already was willing to die to save this baby. I already was fighting a losing battle. I already was heartbroken.

Thus began two solid months of strict bed rest with weekly appointments to check on our growing baby. I could tell you how desperate I was, but it's hard to understand it in just one sense. You have to see it as a two part process.

First, as a mother, your job, your primary duty, is to protect your children. I felt like I was failing hopelessly in my duty. My body was toxic. I couldn't sustain life, only kill it. I knew it wasn't my fault. I knew there was nothing I could do. I knew it was common. All these things you can know and not quite believe to be true in your life. I felt my body was betraying me. More importantly, God was betraying me.

Our son Travis was two years old at the time. A wildly active two-year-old and I was a prisoner on the couch, held hostage. I was feeling defeated because I couldn't play with the child that was already there; I couldn't protect the growing baby; I selfishly just wanted to go for a run. I was homesick, heartsick, and sick and tired.

Second, running was not just exercise to me at that point; it was an extension of who I was. Running gave me the strength to believe that maybe life really would be okay. Running is where I saw God. I felt His presence in the shadowy trees and the deep red sunsets. I belonged there. Now, as I lay confined to my couch in a horizontal position, there was nothing where my connection with God used to be. There was nothing to make it better. I was angry at a God that would continue to allow my babies to die one right after the other. I didn't want to see or hear Him in anything anymore. I just wanted Him to make this better.

Every day I awoke full of both fear and hope. It was a constant rollercoaster that always culminated with the weekly ultrasound. Those Mondays felt so far away yet rapidly approaching every single week. I would tell myself it was going to be okay if this baby didn't make it, but in those long seconds before the doctor spoke each week, I knew that was a lie. Three strikes and I'd be out. I would shatter. I didn't know if I would be able to try again. I didn't think I could go through it one more time. This was it. I tried to focus on all of my blessings instead of my curses. Sometimes it worked and sometimes it didn't. I felt the most selfish and guilty each time I stepped into that office and prayed fervently that God save this baby, that God give me just one last chance.

In this excruciatingly long, yet short, span of time, the 5K that I was directing rapidly approached. It was the third week in July, hot, humid, and muggy. I was still on bed rest but had gotten clearance to attend the race, as long as I stayed in the wheelchair. Tony was overwhelmed with trying to direct everything in my place, but then all of these wonderful people came to our rescue. On race morning, Pastor Scott, his wife Carrie, and my new friend from church, Azsure, showed up to help put on the race.

I sat in the wheelchair at the side of the finish line and waited for the runners to come through. One by one, they came barreling down the road towards the finish line. I watched them in wonder as I saw on their faces everything I used to feel: sheer grit and determination, joy and exhaustion, and exertion and strength. I thought I would be sad for myself in that moment, surrounded by others doing something I wished I could do, but I found myself smiling. Tears welled up in my eyes for this gift that I'd been given. I put a hand on my ever rounding stomach and felt life. Not just in my stomach where life truly lived, *but life in me.* Proof that I had not been left behind. Proof that I was still here just as much as anyone else was. I was going to be okay. I was still stumbling forward with no real finish line in sight but I was getting there. Maybe I'd get there years after everybody else but I was not going to give up.

A few weeks later, I lay once again on my old, familiar, cold exam table. I waited breathlessly for the word of the week, for the doctor to either break my heart or give me just enough hope to make it through another long week. This time the monitor faced her for much longer than it should have. Her poker face remained on, not even a line creased her smooth face. I waited and waited. Every second that passed I felt myself slipping further into desperation. *No, no, no. Please God, no. Please let me have this baby.* I had made peace with it. I understood. This was why the other babies couldn't survive. It was because of this baby. This baby was the one that had been meant to survive all along. The others couldn't. The timeline wouldn't work. *Please God, please.* I repeated it over and over in my head. The more I said it, the more desperate I felt, the more I was sure He couldn't deny me this. He had to see how desperate I was. *Please God, please.*

The monitor swung back to me with ease. Her poker face was gone. I could read her face clear as day and I knew. I started sobbing before she even spoke. An embarrassing choking noise escaped my throat as I cried even harder. Tony's grip on my arm tightened. He brushed my hair off of my face as it clung in clumps to my wet cheeks. I couldn't find the words. She squeezed my shoulder hard and smiled at me so brightly; it was like I'd been blinded. I stared at the monitor and saw only my baby, curled up into a little ball. There was no more sub chronic bleed. There was just a tiny, healthy baby with a strong heartbeat.

After being inundated with information, I felt immense hope. I wouldn't be leaving there in a wheelchair. I could sit up again. I could walk. *I could even…. I could even run, couldn't I?* I looked at my doctor, a fellow runner herself. I gathered every bit of courage I had to lay it all on the line and ask the deepest question on my heart now that I knew my baby was going to live and be perfectly safe. I tried to pull myself to a sitting position with all the grace a pregnant woman can. I threw my weight to the left, then to the right, before attempting to sit straight up when Tony gave me a nudge to help me up. I looked down at my shirt that was too small. I had been afraid of my maternity clothes, sure that I would jinx it somehow. I couldn't bring myself to put on those stretchy pants or those tent-like shirts that tie in the back. Not yet. They sat in a box in the corner of my closet. *Focus Kathy, focus* I scolded myself.

I stopped thinking and just went for it. "Do you think I could run again?" I asked trying to keep my voice calm and even. I was tempted to get down on my hands and knees to beg for her blessing before I realized if I got down there, I wouldn't get back up so easily. She smiled at me. "I remember when you asked me to do the 5K while nine months pregnant with your first," she said with a chuckle. "If it were anyone else, I would have told them no but I knew that you knew what you were doing." Her words hung in the air. *Was that a yes or a no?* "So…." I prompted. She laughed again. "Yes. You can run all you want. Go slow, drink lots of water, and be careful. Have fun Kathy." I had to restrain myself from squealing with joy and clapping my hands together like a two year old.

I set out for my first run of that pregnancy with a barely restrained glee. I was bouncing on the balls of my feet like a child circling the tree on Christmas morning. I ran slowly, getting the feeling back in my legs and lungs. I hadn't run or even walked for over two months straight. I moved steadily and confidently towards my destination, the lake. Of course it would be the lake. I stopped to take in the scenery. Lush, green grass and trees surrounded it. There were flowers nearby and the sun glistening off the top of the water in picture perfect form. I exhaled loud and long and closed my eyes to take in the moment. I heard people laughing in the distance, children screaming, a pontoon boat slowly going by, and a dog barking. When I opened my eyes, the tears continued to pour out. I was overcome with gratefulness for this beautiful life. I could see it now. The way it was supposed to be. I had to believe this was where God wanted me to be. This was it.

I accepted the heartbreak within the hope. I saw the beauty and the pain along with the devastation and the joy. They were but one single strand, woven so intricately and delicately I couldn't have one without the other. People were always talking about God's plan. I couldn't see it for so long because I had my own plans. I was so focused on the way I had wanted things to go.

I could see a plan and a purpose for this pain, full of hope for tomorrow.

#Kathyfacts

So much of my life has revolved around being in control. I could tell you silly little stories about being a control freak but that's not all of it. I sought out control when my world was spinning desperately out of control. To be helpless and out of control was the worst place that I could think of to be. I don't like to be helpless. I don't like to have no options. I want to DO something. I want to FIX it. I want to CONTROL it.

1. Have you ever found yourself in a situation completely out of your control?

2. Do you believe there is anything you can do to keep these experiences from taking a hold and controlling you?

3. Has anything good happened to you when you've relinquished control? Whether at work, home, or in a crisis?

I've wasted a lot of time trying to control things that were just simply too vast, too wide, and too big for me alone. I thought that if I could somehow bend the situation to my liking, that I would feel better. I thought I'd feel less like a victim to my circumstances. I thought I'd be happy if life went the way I wanted it to go. Some of the most amazing things I have in my life are because things went the opposite of what I planned.

Look at your own life. What do you have now that came after a deafening and soul crushing no? Take a minute to appreciate the way things have worked out, whether or not it was your plan.

Chapter 5

Throughout my struggles to carry my babies to term, a few people worried out loud that maybe my running was affecting my pregnancies. They were concerned I was doing myself and my baby harm by running. However, every medical professional I asked (and there were several) and every article I ever read in our journey to have another baby assured me time after time: running does not cause miscarriage. Running did not endanger our child.

I like to think I've got pretty thick skin; I kind of have to with sharing our life out loud. I blog about our family's life, I speak out about what has affected us, and I share my entire history in this book. But no words have stung quite as much as those that told me I was careless and selfish, that running killed my babies, or that I killed my babies. I take full responsibility for my life and that of my child. I have always been under excellent medical care during every step of my pregnancy. What if I told you that running didn't kill, but rather helped save, my babies?

I had run during each pregnancy, four different times, with the blessing of my doctor. When I was pregnant with my first son Travis, I did a local 5K where two teenage girls attempted to sprint by "the big pregnant lady" and couldn't catch me. I was pretty pleased with myself. Running with Travis was an adventure; long before I knew what other kind of adventures lay before me. Travis' life was saved by God and running; those two things in that order. Back then, I just thought it was the running that saved him. I couldn't see how that was actually connected to God too until much later.

When I was seven months pregnant with Travis, we had spent the day before my twenty-fifth birthday at a glistening beach along Lake Michigan. It was an idyllic summer day spent walking around local shops, taking in the picturesque lakeshore, kicking around in the waves, and sampling fudge and ice cream. We were driving home with quite a few bags in the seat behind me, one of them containing the new pajamas that would fit my very pregnant frame. I was really excited about those pajamas. We were going to go home, order pizza, and watch a movie. The perfect ending to a perfect day.

Off in the distance, I saw a gray car sitting at a stop sign of the intersecting road. It struck me as odd because there was no one coming; it was just sitting there. We approached the intersection with the gray car, a place we had passed a thousand times before. We had the right of way and were doing close to sixty miles per hour. The little gray car was still there at the stop sign. We were almost through the intersecting road when I saw the car's tires begin to move. I could see what was about to happen. I screamed "Stop!" at no one in particular and we slammed into the car without any time to even slow down.

The sound of metal hitting metal and brakes screeching filled the air. I must have closed my eyes. The next thing that registered was Tony yelling "Get out of the car! Get out of the car NOW!" I watched as he flung his door wide open and ran around outside of the car in the middle of the road without even looking for traffic. There was smoke pouring from under the hood. Before I could even get my seatbelt off, he was at my door, pulling me out of the car. I stepped out onto the dirt shoulder and saw the teenage couple from the other car, unscathed, not even a scratch on them standing there staring at us. The first thing I said was in a panicked fearful anger. "My baby!" I screamed. "My baby!" "What is wrong with you? What did you do to my baby?" They didn't answer. The girl sat down on the grass and started crying. I instantly felt bad for yelling at her and decided to just leave her be.

I turned away from them and felt a sharp stabbing pain in my stomach. I let out a short scream of pain. I could see people were running towards us now. Tony was holding me up around the waist when another sharp stabbing pain came. I let out another scream. A woman who had been in the car behind us was rapidly approaching us and asking if everyone was okay. "Everyone is fine, but I think I'm having contractions," I said as I held my stomach that felt like it was on fire. She instantly took charge, directed me to a spot under a huge oak tree with shade on that hot June day. "It's okay. I'm a registered nurse. I'm going to take care of you," she reassured me. Tears silently streamed down my face. I nodded at her. I wanted to ask her about my baby, a question she couldn't possibly know the answer to but the only thing that mattered right then. She just kept telling me it was going to be okay. I leaned against the back of the tree with her beside me, breathing deeply and in sync with her calm commands. I looked up at the beautiful blue sky above me, an otherwise picture perfect day. She stayed with me as promised, breathing with me, rubbing my back, asking all kinds of questions, and performing a few checks.

Sirens wailed in the distance as a red truck screeched to a halt right in front of us. The first responders had arrived. Police came, fire trucks came, and even more first responders came. Witnesses of the accident stayed to tell the police what they had seen happen and to check in on me before they left. The police wanted to talk to Tony but he was reluctant to leave my side. The nurse assured him that it would be okay and that she would stay with me as long as I needed. The first responder that had arrived to tend to me was an older man that talked to me through my ever silently streaming tears. He asked me what was wrong and I told him my stomach hurt. He started talking to me while we waited for an ambulance. He told me how brave I was and how strong of a person I must be. He told me how much better it was for the baby and me to remain calm and keep breathing slowly. I flinched again with a new stab of pain. Another contraction and a rapid rush of tears fell from my face without my permission. I kept breathing, just like the nurse had told me.

Just then, a woman I hadn't seen before came walking across the lawn. She walked by all of the chaos, debris, and people sitting on the lawn and those talking in the road. The woman continued to move in my direction. When she saw me, she stopped and dropped down to her knees right next to me. I was still crying silently. She told me she lived across the street, asked my name and told me hers; I wish I could remember what it was now. Then she asked me another question. "Do you believe in God?" I nodded my head yes slowly. I guess I believed in Him, in something up there, but that was about it. This was long before I had found church, so God was just this ungraspable idea to me still. "Would it be okay if I prayed for you?" she asked. I nodded again. She grabbed my hand and whispered her prayers quietly and quickly, over and over, rocking back and forth on her knees. I was a little uncomfortable with how intense she seemed but figured she was just trying to help so what could it hurt. She kept praying like that until we heard the ambulance coming and commands from the first responders to make some room.

Onto a stretcher I went, staring straight up into the air, wearing a neck brace that I didn't want once again. Tony was at my side now as they put me in the back of the ambulance. The EMT was very kind and caring. When I asked her about my baby, she could only tell me she was sorry that she couldn't tell me anything right then. I'd have to wait until I got to the hospital to know anything. More tears escaped the corners of my eyes. "What if he's already dead?" I asked, with despair rising in my heart. She gave me a sad smile and patted my hand. "Hang on honey, okay? Just hang on. You're doing real good." I choked back a sob and tears silently streamed down my face. I wondered what we were waiting for until I heard the girl's voice getting louder. She was in full hysterics and walking towards the back of the ambulance. *She was going with us?*

Apparently her boyfriend's finger was either broken or sprained, so they were going to the hospital...with us. A new EMT showed up behind her and closed the doors. It was surreal to be back there; her yelling and screaming unnerved me. Then I could make out what she was carrying on about. "My baby, my baby, my baby. What am I going to do?" she wailed. The EMT caring for me turned around. "Wait, are you pregnant too?" The boyfriend spoke up. "No. She's talking about her car." A level of annoyance rose up in me at the selfishness and ridiculousness being forced upon me. "Okay. Well. Just for clarity's sake, how about only the person pregnant with an actual baby talks about a baby right now?" the mind-reading EMT offered. The girl made no response but continued to cry loudly. I wanted to feel compassion for her but I was too irritated at that point. All of that fuss over a car, a completely replaceable car, as I lay there seven months pregnant with a stomach that felt engulfed in flames and worrying if my child was alive.

They rolled me into the hospital, into the care of a compassionate looking nurse. I was sent to the maternity floor. I lay in that room, staring up at the ceiling and waiting. The nurse pushed down on my very tender, delicate stomach with the hand-held Doppler to detect our baby's heartbeat. I loudly sucked in air at the pain it caused. What was wrong that it should hurt so much just to be touched? She moved the Doppler around and every second that passed without noise caused my heart to pound quicker and faster in a state of panic. I knew, by now, the sound of my baby's heartbeat should be filling the room. I could feel the wheels falling off, I was trying to steady my breathing but it was shallow and useless. Tears slipped out of the corner of my eyes quicker and quicker. *Stay calm. Stay calm. Just stay calm*, I commanded myself. My mouth was so dry it hurt to swallow.

The nurse moved the Doppler around some more until the distinctive *thump thump, thump thump* filled the air. It was steady and strong. It echoed in my ears and burrowed in my frightened heart. I gasped in a shocked relief and began crying harder than I could control. The nurse stopped. "Does it hurt when I push here?" I shook my head. It hurt when she pushed anywhere but that wasn't what was wrong.

I opened my mouth to speak but nothing came out. Thankfully, Tony spoke up. "I think she's relieved he's alive." I nodded my head in agreement. "Okay. Let's move on then." The nurse then got out the ultrasound machine. I held my breath as Tony held my hand tightly. We waited for what felt like forever while they performed the exam. Finally, she spoke up and told us there was nothing wrong. He was completely safe, unharmed, and untouched in there. More crying ensued and this time she didn't ask if it hurt. I hugged my stomach. He was okay in there.

They wanted to monitor me until the contractions completely stopped to make sure no complications arose. They praised me for remaining calm, controlling my breathing, and not going into a state of shock and panic that could have turned into full blown labor. It was about this time that I realized I had never eaten dinner. I was supposed to get pizza and I was hungry. They couldn't feed me, not yet the doctor said. I hadn't eaten since noon that day and it was well into the evening. The nurse was so apologetic and sympathetic; I believe she didn't necessarily agree with the ruling. I couldn't bring myself to complain as I believe she would have given me something if it were her choice. The later it got the more hungry I became. I was prone to hanger, that obnoxious state where hunger and anger coexist and feed off of each other in the absence of food, long before someone had coined the term hanger. While pregnant, that hangry state intensified.

Hours and hours passed and now that I knew my baby was okay, I was anxious to get home. I was uncomfortable in that bed, tired of being hooked up to things, and truly very hungry. It was well past midnight, now officially my twenty-fifth birthday, when my nurse and another entered the room. "I have a surprise for you," she said in a sing-songy voice. The surprise was behind her back. It was a ham and cheese sandwich with a toothpick that was supposed to be a candle. They sang Happy Birthday to me, gifted me with the glorious sandwich, and then told me they were gathering my paperwork so I could get out of there.

My baby was fine, my contractions had stopped, I had a sandwich in my hands, and I was going home. What more could a girl ask for on her birthday?

We were going sixty miles per hour when we slammed into that car at the last minute. I had a seat belt on, with very deep black and blue bruises across my arm and waist for weeks to prove it. At impact, I instinctively covered my face. My wrists were crisscrossed and in front of my face to avoid the windshield, I'm sure. When that air bag deployed, it hit my arms with such force, my elbows went into my stomach and my hands smashed into my face. I gave myself two black eyes, but that seatbelt kept us safe. I was okay. My baby was okay.

In the weeks that followed, I wondered how Travis and I had walked away from the accident unscathed. It didn't take long for my doctors to lend their thoughts. More than one doctor told me how lucky I was that the placenta didn't rupture and that the baby was unharmed. According to one of my doctors, the more someone exercises while pregnant, the more certain beneficial proteins are released within the placenta. As I ran regularly four days a week, I firmly believe my running contributed to a healthy amount of protein build-up in my body. Running had helped save that baby.

Not only was running a reprieve from long, stressful, and sometimes scary days; running was saving me. Running was offering me freedom and hope within its purposeful miles. That accident had shown me how lucky we all were to be alive. There was no guarantee for tomorrow. I had felt so young and powerful and untouchable before that accident. Life suddenly seemed way more fragile than I had ever believed it was. It could be wiped away in a matter of seconds. Beyond my experience with baby Travis in the accident, my other pregnancies offered evidence that running played a part in helping save those babies as well. It was all so connected, so intricately and delicately connected, on this thin thread of hope and possibility.

When I was pregnant for the second time, I enjoyed weekly long, slow runs. I was getting dressed and ready to go for one of those runs on a Saturday morning when it happened. Sharp, stabbing pains in my stomach accompanied by some very worrisome symptoms. That's when Tony first brought me to the emergency room. "Dr. Doom" had been on call. We had never met him before, but we decided to give him that nickname because of his stern face and the no nonsense way he delivered the news that our baby was dying and nothing he did or ever could do would change that. I don't know why, but I remember actually laughing after he left and telling Tony "And I had been expecting bad news."

Laughter in a time of serious fear and sorrow can strengthen a breaking heart. We laughed about Dr. Doom for a long time after that as Tony did his best impression of Dr. Doom delivering other terrible news to people. A friendlier doctor came in shortly after him, all bright eyes and blond hair. She compassionately held my hand and explained what was happening. She explained what they would try to do for me but told me that I needed to prepare myself to lose the baby. As much as I didn't want to believe either doctor, they were right. This new doctor had told me she was surprised that I hadn't miscarried already with such low progesterone numbers and had asked me a few questions. I told her I had been running and she smiled. She said regular exercise can increase progesterone levels. Sitting in that emergency room while the world was crashing down around me, she had given me something to hang onto and be proud of. I had more time with that baby because of my regular running routine. Once again, I sat in amazement as to what running had helped my body do. It had kept my second baby alive, just a bit longer, before I had to say goodbye.

I never had a chance to run with our third baby, the pregnancy was so short-lived, it was over as soon as it had begun. While I technically ran while I was pregnant, the baby was already gone at that time. I'm not sure that it officially counts, but I count it anyhow. That baby was with me, not by accident, not by mere circumstance, but by fate. That was my baby to take care of and love, regardless of how much time I was given. I was supposed to carry that baby with me while I ran and afterwards in my heart still.

These three very different pregnancies gave me one child I carry in my arms and two I would carry in my heart for the rest of my days.

After hearing the amazing news that baby number four was going to live and be okay, and that the sub chronic bleed was gone, I felt a resurgence of hope in my soul. I set out for my first official run of the pregnancy, slowly plodding down the road, pregnant enough to be noticeable and just about delirious with my newfound freedom. I was ready to throw my arms out wide and twirl in circles like I was starring in *The Sound of Music*. That first run back was the epitome of hope. I had come full circle from standing at the lake feeling abandoned, hopeless, and without God to a heart bursting with gratitude, surrounded by people who loved me, and thanking God for this life. I ran a few local 5Ks. I dressed up for Halloween as a speed bump in all black with yellow tape accentuating my huge stomach. I ran the Grand Rapids Half Marathon six months pregnant and relished every single slow and amazing step. My baby was okay. I was okay. I was running again. Everything was perfect. We had gotten over the hard part.

Now our amazing life was ready to begin.
I was so sure of it.

#Kathyfacts

When the world stopped making sense, running never did. Running always made sense to me. Running is many things to me, but during such a turbulent time in my life, it was an important coping skill.

1. When tragedy hits, do you find it hard to maintain your faith in God, the universe, or even yourself? Why or why not?

2. What sort of healthy coping skills do you have to fall back on? Faith? Running? Drawing? Therapy? Writing? Praying? Talking with friends? Shopping? Yoga? Meditating? Or something completely different?

I employed every skill I had when I was thrown into a situation I just couldn't understand. Unfortunately, some of those weren't healthy, like trying to shut down my emotions with food, but others like running were extremely healthy. Even if others don't necessarily understand why you NEED to do something you feel you need to, I believe you should keep going. You can try to explain, but some things feel pretty unexplainable, like loving the tortuous process of running for one-hundred miles at a time. If you don't have any healthy coping skills in your tool bag, start finding some. Look for activities that bring you comfort and peace even in the most trying of situations. You most likely already have an idea of what brings you hope; pursue it as often as needed.

Chapter 6

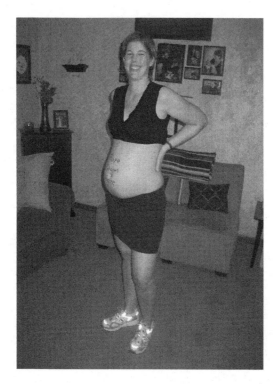

You know how some things seem like a made for TV movie? Things that seem too much of a "coincidence?" Dramatized for effect? Well brace yourself; because here comes some of that but I promise you it is all true.

When I was on bed rest while pregnant with Emmett, I spent my days alone on the couch. Tony was working and my mother-in-law watched Travis during the day for me. To fill my time, I watched a lot of television, read books, ate way more than I ever should have, and slept. It was tiring being on bed rest. I napped frequently during the day. How foreign that all seems now, that I would ever grow tired of taking naps and not having to do anything, but it was true. The point is I spent a lot of time doing nothing.

One long, boring afternoon while waiting for Tony and Travis to come home, I fell asleep yet again and I dreamt about our baby. I dreamt that we named him Emmett. The baby was a boy in my dream. We didn't even know the gender at that point yet. I had no reason to pick the name Emmett, and no attachment to it. We hadn't even talked about names at all. I was scared and trying to prepare myself for what would happen if this baby didn't make it. I was trying my hardest to stall normal progress. There was no talk of nursery color, strollers, or baby names. When Tony came home, I told him about my dream and that we named the baby Emmett. Tony liked the name a lot. He was insistent it was a good sign. He was so sure that the dream meant the baby was going to be okay. He saw it as a glimpse from God and reassurance of what was to come. I wasn't so sure, but agreed to name this baby Emmett if he lived and was a boy.

Many weeks later, I lay on the table and anxiously waited for the screen to turn towards me. I wanted to see my baby. I wanted to know my baby was still in there. I wanted to make sure my baby was still alive. Even though the sub chronic bleed had vanished, I was still very anxious and worried during each appointment. I was afraid it was a mistake somehow and they were going to deliver the bad news at any moment. The technician turned the screen to us and smiled. "It's a boy!" she exclaimed. Tears rolled down my cheeks. *It's a boy. It's Emmett.* I had a name to call the baby now. I looked at the fuzzy black screen and my tiny baby Emmett curled up in a ball. My heart swelled with love; it was Emmett.

I took a few pictures early in the pregnancy, even though I gained a massive amount of weight and was a bit horrified by my ever rounding body. I wanted to have pictures to show Emmett. I wanted to have pictures to show him I was proud of who I was and happy to have him there with me. I got into my favorite running clothes and had Tony write the words "Hope grows here" on my stomach. I pictured it coming out better than it did but that was okay. It was the sentiment that mattered. Hope really did grow there. I was hopeful just as much as I was afraid. The two would mix together regularly.

It is that picture of my round belly with Tony's sloppy handwriting in a grey washable marker that stops me every now and then. I look at that picture and I can almost feel the desperation. I can feel the worry and heartbreak over what I was so sure was going to be taken from me, and what I fervently hoped and prayed would be mine. I would be remiss if I were to say that it was all one or the other. I had extreme mood swings, like many pregnant women, but these mood swings came in the form of whether or not I would indeed have this child. I think back to how almost prophetic that picture is. *Hope grows here.* If only I had known then what I know now. It wouldn't have made anything different, nothing at all, but it was foretelling of the future. The word hope would become my personal mantra. I would latch onto that word in so many ways. *Hope grows here.* Hope. Grows. Here. What an underlying theme for our entire existence. Hope.

After I was taken off of bed rest, it seemed like it would be a smooth sailing for the rest of the pregnancy. I became someone who thought a little bit more like a new mom to be but I was still on edge. I kept saying "if the baby makes it" in regular conversation. I couldn't help it. "If he makes it, we will have to get family pictures of all of us. If he makes it, we should paint the room yellow, that way it's not so babyish and can still be used as an office if he doesn't." I saw it on people's faces, how it unnerved some of them the way I seemed so nonchalant about it. I had no more reason at that point to believe he wasn't going to live, I just couldn't stop myself from preparing for the worst. I thought I was saving myself from getting my hopes all the way up only to have them crushed. I was afraid I would face that devastation again.

I cautiously proceeded. I painted the room a safe yellow. I bought a used double stroller off of Craigslist because I didn't want to spend too much money on something I may never use. I dug out the maternity clothes I had hidden in the back of the closet after the first miscarriage. I wrote letters and notes to the baby that I wasn't sure would ever be. It seems melodramatic, to still be concerned about it after the doctor had said it was okay, but things were never quite so black and white to me. Things went wrong suddenly. There were no guarantees for tomorrow. Instead of savoring the pregnancy and the time, I anxiously dipped my toes in one at a time. Maybe it was really going to be okay.

We thought long and hard about a middle name. We put a lot of effort into it. We eventually landed on Josiah, which means "God saves." I loved the name. It sounded nice and it was oh so fitting. God saves. He had saved this baby so far. He gave me this little miracle so that I could fully see Him at work. I could finally see the big picture, it seemed. We waited anxiously for Emmett Josiah to be born.

While they prepped me for the C-section, I began crying. I was hot, nauseous, and very scared. *What if he wasn't okay in there?*

What if he wasn't alive after all? What if they were all wrong? The medication and nerves got to me and I was soon throwing up into a pan, while sobbing. Tony pulled my hair out of my face and kept whispering in my ear that it was going to be alright. I just wanted them to hurry up and get that baby out. I had to know. I had to know right then if it was all going to be okay. I had to know if I could stop saying "if." God, how I wanted to stop saying "if he makes it," and see my baby alive and well on the outside. I was convinced he would be so much safer as soon as he was out and in my arms. Everything was going to be alright if I could just hold him and see him. Sometimes I feel a little sick reliving this memory. I was so sure he was going to be just fine once he was born. I thought I could keep him safe on the outside. Once he had survived the pregnancy, we would be past the worst of it.

There was some trouble, until finally they were all exclaiming at what a big boy I had on my hands. I waited for what felt like forever until the sweet sound of a baby wailing echoed through the room. They laid him on my chest and I sobbed into his tiny little head. I must have mentioned the room was spinning, because they handed him to Tony. I couldn't see over the thin blue curtain that separated the doctors from me. That was the last thing I remember. I must have fallen asleep or passed out. I'm not sure which. I awoke about an hour later in a recovery room all by myself. There was no Tony and no Emmett. I yelled for a nurse and was quickly reassured everything was fine.

Tony returned with baby Emmett and life was perfect. He was perfect, even with his misshapen head. We asked the doctor about it the first day he was born. The doctor told us it was just the way I had carried him. Big baby and all – it would just take some time to pop back out. He was beautiful. His mere presence took my breath away and filled me with gratitude, but I was worried, as any new mother would be. Would people make fun of him? Was that how he would always look? Even as a newborn, we heard a few unsavory comments about his appearance, which were daggers to the heart of an emotional new mother who was ecstatic her child was alive and well. But it didn't matter. He was finally with us and the worst of it was over. Now we could get on with our life as a family of four, the way I believed we were meant to. I was so sure things were going to be perfectly fine from there on out. I thought it was only natural. I had put in my time. I had been through more than my fair share of terrible circumstances. The hard part was done. I would have never believed anyone if they had told me that I hadn't even seen the hard part yet.

I would have never believed that was the easy part compared to what was coming.

#Kathyfacts

So often, our fear can take on a life of its own. It can keep us from experiencing the full joy of the moment. I know personally, I missed out on a lot of the joy with Emmett's pregnancy because I was so afraid. I didn't want to be, but it was hard to stay in the moment and appreciate the life that was one day at a time.

1. What is one situation that has kept you from seeing the joy in life?

2. Can you look back now and see it a different way than when you were in it?

Finding joy and hope in the moment is an incredibly hard task at times. I think we all slip at one point or another in our lives, and realize we have let days, weeks, months, maybe even years, go by without enjoying them. When you look back on those days, it's easy to be overcome with regret. It's easy to see all of the things you should have, could have, or would have done differently.

Take a moment to acknowledge that you have done the best you could. If you are constantly beating yourself up over the past, I challenge you to let it go. If you see what you would do differently now, that means you have grown. See that growth as a positive, one of many in your journey. All of that time has not been a waste or in vain, because you have learned something and grown from it. Keep reminding yourself to look forward with the assuredness that things happen the way they happen. All you can do is keep moving forward.

Chapter 7

I'd like to paint a picture of the calm, cool collected person I have always been. Surely when I have lost my temper or fallen apart, I have always done it in the quiet reprieve of my own home or on a deserted old trail with no witnesses. Sadly that has not been the case.

The word angry wasn't strong enough. I was seething, red faced, and burning with pure unfiltered rage brought forth by fear that had no outlet. I wanted to scream at the top of my lungs. I wanted to smash something. I wanted to set fire to the entire world. It was, in hindsight, a bad time to lose my cool. In the middle of the mall, we got a phone call from the neurosurgeon's office. This was the first neurosurgeon we sought out seeking an official diagnosis for fourteen month old Emmett. Emmett had begun having seizures just after his first birthday. He seemed to only be getting worse. He had stumped a few doctors, so I decided to take matters into my own hands. My research had led me to believe Emmett had Craniosynostosis. I was positive I was right about that diagnosis, but of course, we needed a real doctor to confirm.

For many reasons, that was not the neurosurgeon we ended up with. That neurosurgeon's office wouldn't even look at Emmett's CT scan; give us an opinion, or any direction. They wouldn't listen to us. They told us Emmett was fine and we could come into the office in another six months to talk about the diagnosis if we wished. These were all the wrong things to say to a frightened mother waiting on this very important call.

Emmett wasn't fine. I already knew he wasn't. Why was I surrounded by people who couldn't tell me anything? How could I make my own diagnosis from Google but yet not have a single doctor tell me if I really was right? I only wanted someone to look at his records and tell me something. I knew six months was way longer than we should wait. We were already past the optimal age for this surgery, which is primarily done on children between six and twelve months of age for the best results. Thus proceeded one of the only times I have completely and thoroughly lost all composure out in public. Not just in front of my children or Tony, but everyone within a mile radius, and most of all the poor clerks working the perfume counter at Macy's department store.

While Tony held the phone in between us so we could both hear it, I couldn't control it for one second longer. I was like a pressure cooker. I was trying to be rational. I was trying to remain calm, but abruptly the lid just blew and all bets were off. I screeched in a loud hysterical voice "So we should just sit around and wait for it to get worse? For more seizures? For him to die? I know what's wrong! And you don't? What kind of doctor are you?!" Tony attempted to wrestle control of the phone from my hands but I was on fire. There was no stopping me. I started screaming, words I shouldn't have, words I would be aghast for my children to repeat. I screamed a string of terrible words punctuated by the desperate, hysterical, and ever increasing in pitch phrase "He's going to die if you do nothing!" I started crying and put my head in between my knees to keep from throwing up.

Tony pried the phone away from my death grip and I overheard his request to be on the cancelation list. I proceeded to sob with reckless abandon, choking on the sweet smell of perfume as the loud obnoxious techno music coming from the "trendy" makeup counter rang in my ears. What a surreal place to have a breakdown. I could feel the stares burning into my back as we left. I sobbed with my hands covering my eyes as I pushed Emmett's stroller out the side door. Tony carried squirmy, three-year-old Travis who kept asking "What's wrong with mommy?"

We shuffled out of there with many onlookers and people whispering loudly. I was embarrassed, sure, but more than anything I felt the very hope leave my soul. That was it. There was nothing.

There was no grand plan in the works connecting one terrible event to the next. There was no reason for any of this. There was no help coming. There was nothing. The small amount of hope I had amassed leeched out of my skin and dissipated into nothingness. I was heavy and empty at the same time.

Later that night, I went for a run in the hopes of clearing the rage out of my system. I ran hard; going faster than what was comfortable. I was tired and angry. I was afraid. I was beaten down and lost. I was being thrown up against one wall after another. There was no predictability to this storm. It raged on long after I had given up. It got stronger when I stood up to it and knocked me back down with such ferocity, I almost didn't see the point. I gave up. I turned my back on a God that I was sure had left me here to flail. I was so helpless to do anything but sit back and watch Emmett suffer. He was in pain. He was screaming, crying, holding his head, staying awake all night long, and having seizures. For months, I did not know how to help him. Finally, I believed I had found the answer but I just could not get anyone to help him.

We sought out our family doctor for referrals to every craniofacial plastic surgeon and pediatric neurosurgeon in the state of Michigan. Turns out, there aren't many. We held that small list in our hands and started calling. We heard of four, six, and even nine month waits. We were told one doctor wouldn't do this type of surgery on our son because of his advanced age. I was on the verge of losing my cool again, of screaming in frustration, and demanding someone help us when I noticed a change in Tony's demeanor. He was on the phone with C.S. Mott Children's Hospital, a University of Michigan Hospital. It was the very last hospital on our list. Apparently a person had called just five minutes prior to Tony and canceled their appointment. They had an opening in just two weeks. I started crying as I listened to him confirm the appointment and specifics. It was a grateful fear to be one step closer to an answer.

We were excited to have the appointment and finally move forward. Except then our insurance company wouldn't cooperate. They told us over and over, they would only cover a consultation at the University of Michigan, but they would not pay for a major surgery at this out of network hospital. After meeting with the team and feeling relief at their compassion, willingness to move Emmett to the front of the line in light of the circumstances, and obvious skill, we knew we were going to have the surgery there. We went ahead and scheduled the surgery that we had no clue how we would pay for. We knew he needed the surgery now and not later. The longer we waited, the greater the occurrence of additional surgeries would be. As children age, the bones in their skull begin to harden and toughen up. They are no longer soft and pliable to easily reshape. The surgery needed to happen now and a hundred-thousand dollar price tag couldn't dissuade us.

We called the insurance company nearly every day, trying to fight our way up higher in the chain of command. We made our case over and over to every agent we spoke to and pointed out the complications if left untreated. We used heartfelt pleas, told them how far behind he was in treatment already, and asked what they would want if it was their child. We finally went up as high as they'd let us and were told they'd meet about it. We called regularly, checking on a status, and pressing for an answer.

Two weeks before surgery, we still didn't have an answer. We were actually told to stop calling by a woman in charge, which only made me laugh. I was going to keep calling until I understood where we stand with that surgery. It got ugly near the end as we got closer to the surgery date. We threatened to go to a local news station and use the cutest baby pictures we had to win the public's approval and hopefully help pressure them into doing the right thing. It'd be this sweet baby boy that needed a life threatening surgery versus the cold, giant corporation that refused to allow it. I wasn't above playing my cards ruthlessly to get what Emmett needed. I hoped that if it came to that, we could win over the insurance company but there was so much red tape and policy, I just wasn't sure. I was afraid we were completely out of our league trying to play hardball with this company.

A certified letter came in the mail a week before surgery. It detailed Emmett's complete coverage for pre-operative testing, surgery, recovery, and all follow-up appointments. I was so proud; I framed the letter and cried. They agreed that we couldn't find the same standard of care near us in a timely manner. Our relentless battle with that giant corporation had been won. I could see things clicking into place. I could feel the plan coming to fruition.

I held onto the hope that this was the only way.

#Kathyfacts

Anger has been a powerful theme in my life. I've hidden behind it. I've used it to cover up my own pain. I've been embarrassed about it. I've lost control over it. Anger has called the shots in my life for much longer than it should have.

1. Have you ever lost control of your anger? What does that look like for you?

2. Do you have ways of calming yourself down once you are angry or do you just let it run its course until you are done?

3. Do you think your anger has negatively impacted those around you?

In dealing with anger, I have learned a couple of things about how to manage it. Coping skills really do help. When I'm feeling out of control and like I'm going to say something I shouldn't, I pop a sour candy. It produces a physical response, a distraction from the current situation. In case of extreme anger, I keep those super sour crybaby candies around. Another way I control my anger is by leaving the situation for a moment and focusing on something in front of me. I will stare at my hairbrush until it blurs in front of me. It's almost like a mini meditation. I run. Punch a pillow. Take long, deep breaths in through my nose and exhale even longer out through my mouth.

It may take some time to find something that works for you when your anger is about to boil over. Try a distraction technique the next time you get angry to see what could work for you and keep searching until you find one that does work for you.

Chapter 8

Fear. That was always the true source of my motivation. Fear of the unknown, fear of the future, fear of watching Emmett suffer, fear of watching Emmett die, and fear that my life would lose its meaning without him. Fear that this would render me useless in the eyes of the world. The word failure stamped upon my forehead because I couldn't do enough. There was no getting through to me, a frightened mother being pushed beyond her limit, trying to find and hold onto hope. The hope, the strength, the purpose, it ebbed and flowed with my ever changing mood. The one constant I had was fear. It was rooted deep and at the base of every other emotion that sprouted from it.

Emmett's first seizure at twelve months old was only the beginning of the change we were in for. Watching Emmett in pain twisted the knife deeper. Our house echoed with agonizing screams all through the night. There were periods of time where Emmett would lose the ability to even sit up on his own, screaming, crying, twisting, twitching, and hyperventilating in distress. He would hold his head and push on it like he was trying to drown something out. The pain. He couldn't speak a single word. We had no way of communicating with him. Nobody knew where it was coming from, what was wrong, or why it was happening.

It was during this time that I hit the rock bottom of hopelessness. I tried so hard to be strong, to be brave, and to believe this was all part of God's plan but when I'd watch him roll around on the floor in such obvious pain and misery it was too much to bear. *Why couldn't the doctors help him? Why wouldn't God just help him? What did he ever do to deserve this?* This cycle of pain and my helplessness to fix it became a daily struggle. Life went on around me, although I couldn't understand how. My life had become a constant battle against myself. I spent my time telling myself I could do this and telling myself I just had to figure it out.

Every time Emmett cried, I would dart out of bed to check on him. When he was too quiet, I would be out of bed checking on him. I was a woman obsessed. It's no wonder I developed insomnia. In the early quiet hours of day, I was awake. Perpetually awake and waiting. I was waiting for the other shoe to drop, waiting for the inevitable, and waiting for my life to make sense.

That was it for me. I took to the internet, fed up with a lack of answers. I started Googling everything seizure related I could. I was reading everything headache related I could find. I got a copy of Emmett's CT scan from his latest hospitalization after a seizure and looked up a few words from the radiologist's report. I was attached to my laptop. I brought it to the kitchen table; I carried it with me to switch loads of laundry. I brought it into bed and read late into the night. I sat for hours and hours out in the living room, looking and searching for something I felt was there but couldn't prove. Tony thought I had gone off the deep end but I just knew there was an answer somewhere. There was something wrong and no one could tell me what, so I was going to find out for myself.

I'm not sure that it was arrogance as much as it was just the fear that time was wasting and something terrible was happening while no one did anything. It drove me to my obsession. I didn't have a degree. I didn't know anything about the medical field. I didn't even know anyone who was sick, but I kept at it with a crazed intensity until one surreal night I landed on a page of side effects. It talked about intracranial pressure, seizures, headaches, lethargy, delays, and other things. It said children with different types of Craniosynostosis usually share a lot of similar facial characteristics. I started clicking on the different types: Coronal, Bi-coronal, Sagittal, until I saw a picture that made me gasp out loud. It was Emmett staring back at me.

Of course, it really wasn't a picture of Emmett but a picture of a baby who looked just like him. I screamed for Tony who was becoming increasingly used to my erratic behavior. I told him what I'd read. Tony had a lot more faith in the medical system than I did and assured me if it were something that serious, someone would have told us a long time ago. It's a birth defect after all, meaning he was born with it. Emmett was over a year old, someone would have had to notice.

I turned my screen towards him and covered up the bottom part of the face with my hand so all he could see was nose up. Tony's eyes widened. "Oh my God!" He took the laptop out of my hands. "Oh my God, it looks just like Emmett. Look at his eyes. Look at the forehead and the sides of his head. It looks just like him." I pointed at the ridiculously long words on my screen - Metopic Synostosis. "That's what it is called. It says surgery is the only way to fix it. We should call a surgeon." Tony stared at me, I could see the doubt on his face again, but I couldn't be angry. I knew it wasn't me that he doubted, but rather that our one-year-old baby would need to have some massive skull surgery.

I told everybody Emmett had Craniosynostosis. It is a blanket term that encapsulates all different types of the skull defect. More specifically, Emmett had Metopic Synostosis. I knew it. People thought I was a touch crazy, diagnosing him myself before any doctor or anyone else could agree with me. A friend had asked me about it and I told her that this was my own internet diagnosis. She reassured me it wasn't a big deal, because if I was wrong, I could always just say it was a suspected diagnosis that they ruled out. It was good of her to attempt to save my ego but I knew in my heart I wasn't wrong. I knew I wouldn't be taking anything back. I could feel it, the same way I could in the back of the ambulance after Emmett's first seizure. I could see a plan on the horizon. I could see the purpose behind a seizure and a CT scan. I could see the wheels moving and things starting to click into place.

We tried everything we could to get in to see the closest surgeons but it wasn't happening. The waiting lists just to be seen were out of control. A couple people assured me this was normal in the world of specialties but I refused to accept that. This was too important. It was his skull and his brain. We called around, trying to get into anywhere that would take us. I talked to a neurologist, a pediatrician, a family doctor, and anyone that I hoped could give us a quick yes or no and put our minds at ease, but no one was qualified to make that diagnosis. Finally, we made an appointment with a craniofacial team at a hospital about three hours away.

The night before Emmett's meeting with the craniofacial surgeon, we had driven to my sister-in-law Amy and her husband Darryl's house for an easier trip to get to the 8 am appointment. They lived very close to the hospital and I was afraid of being three hours away from the hospital the morning of the appointment. *What if the car broke down? What if we hit a deer? What if there was a huge accident on the highway and we got stuck for hours and missed our one big chance?* That wouldn't do. I had to be closer to the hospital.

That night, I tossed and turned on the couch with Emmett sleeping in a pack and play next to us. I was half asleep when I heard it. The telltale shriek before a seizure. I thought maybe I was dreaming or having a flashback at first until I heard the rattling. The pack and play was a few years old, it had been our older son Travis' when he was a baby. Sometime in that usage, one of the small metal bars underneath it had come undone. There was still an entire support underneath but that one piece in the corner didn't connect to anything anymore and just hung loosely.

When I could process what the sound of the metal bar shaking meant, I knew I wasn't dreaming. I yelled for Tony and we sprang into action, turning on the lights and getting out the phone to record the seizure. It seems insensitive, but there is absolutely nothing you can do for a person having a seizure, and taking a video can do a great deal of good for a neurologist. They can tell a lot from the movements and the nuances of the seizure. When it was done and Emmett collapsed down onto the thin cardboard-like pack and play mattress, I closed my eyes and prayed fervently. *Dear God, let him just breathe.* I didn't need to open my eyes to hear him screaming and crying in terror once again, and that terribly painful sound was music to my ears. It was life. He was okay.

Tony went upstairs to get his sister, Amy, who was once a PACU (post-anesthesia care unit) nurse, then a manager of an entire OR, and now something with even greater responsibility. She keeps climbing so that I no longer have a clue of her title, not that it would mean much to a layman like me. The important thing to note was that Amy had spent many, many years in the hospital taking care of people in a critical state. She knows things; a lot of things. Help was just a few stairs away.

Emmett continued to scream and cry, absolutely terrified at three something in the morning. He could not be comforted or calmed down when Amy came quickly padding down the stairs behind Tony. I held Emmett in my arms with tears streaming down my face. Her face was serious and I could tell by looking at her she had a plan. We took Emmett's temperature and pulse for the neurologist.

Amy then placed her hands on Emmett's back and began speaking quietly and quickly. She wasn't saying real words that I could make out. I didn't understand what she was doing because I had never in my life seen anyone do anything like that, but just as quickly as she had started speaking; Emmett had stopped wailing and screaming. I recalled an old movie I had seen once where someone had done something similar and it clicked. She was speaking in tongues. I didn't know anything about it except for the fact that when she started doing it, Emmett quieted right down and was almost instantly calm. I could feel the calm myself.

God was there in the basement that night. God had sent Amy for us. I continued to cry quietly and she continued to speak until Emmett fell deeply asleep on my shoulder. This is the postictal state, completely normal after a seizure. Every single muscle in the body has just been contracting for five minutes straight and it makes one extremely weak and tired. I was grateful for this deep sleep for him, rest for his weary body. I couldn't say anything but nod in appreciation to my loving sister-in-law, or as she would more accurately say sister-in-love. What a difference she had made that night for Emmett, for all of us. Hope. Love. Faith. It emulated from her until we were wrapped in its warm embrace too.

Morning couldn't come quick enough. *Was I really right?* I felt so sure, but I was no doctor. If a doctor in the emergency room told us nothing was wrong with our son, who was I to contradict him? *What if they laughed me out of there?* I was this random woman, bringing them a printout of a diagnosis I found on the internet late one night. *What if they couldn't do anything about it? What if it was too late already?* A thousands questions swirled around in my mind. I sighed and turned over, settling in for the long night ahead of me.

The next morning, we were ushered into a small room where I filled out mountains of paperwork and answered a slew of questions. I clung to the Styrofoam coffee cup from the hospital food court. A nurse examined Emmett, took measurements of his head, looked him over, and left the room to confer with the team. We waited on pins and needles. I kept waiting for these elusive surgeons to show up, but they didn't. After about twenty minutes, the nurse entered the room and simply said "Come with me." I followed her, with Tony at my side pushing Emmett in his stroller. She led us into a huge conference room with boards at the front and a row of computers at the side. At the front of the room sat the neurosurgeon and craniofacial plastic surgeon, along with their team of four or five others behind them.

We were greeted warmly and the craniofacial surgeon got right into it. He started telling us what Craniosynostosis was and what it does. I nodded my head politely even though he wasn't telling me absolutely anything I already didn't know, or rather suspect. He was even dumbing it down for me by not calling it out by its specific name. I knew all about the Metopic suture already. I even knew why it was called Craniosynostosis – Cranio – cranium, syn – together, ostosis – relating to the bones. I already knew what Trigoncephaly referred to, the triangular shaped forehead caused by the closed Metopic suture, and the varying degrees of severity. I knew that there was a noticeable ridge running down from the top of his head to his nose. I knew his eyes were too close together. Judging from the pictures I looked up, I also believed I knew that Emmett's case was severe. Still, I waited for any kind of confirmation.

Finally, the surgeon motioned to Emmett's head. "What your son has is a severe case of Metopic Synostosis. I would like to schedule him for surgery as soon as possible as he's already past the average operating age for this procedure. I'd like him to see a neurologist about the seizures, a neuropsychologist, and do a full work up before we proceed." It was silent for a few moments before I exhaled deep and long; then I started to cry. Pure, absolute relief washed over me. *Finally. Oh thank God. Someone was going to help him. I was right. Oh thank God.*

The neurosurgeon held up her hand, assumedly for her colleague to stop talking. She reassuringly patted my hand and started speaking softly "I know it's scary and I know it seems like" "No!" I blurted out, interrupting her. "It's not that. It's..." I struggled to keep my voice even, to not turn hysterical. "It's that... It's because.... It's just....I'm relieved. You can help him now. I was right." I started to laugh through my tears, earning myself a few appreciative chuckles and smiles from the room. Even as I listened to the specifics and the unique, additional risks to him for this surgery due to his history of seizures, I felt like a weight had been lifted. I smiled at them through my tears and felt hopeful. Just like that, I could see another piece of the puzzle sliding into place. I could see God backstage pulling all of the strings.

Emmett was officially diagnosed with Craniosynostosis at fourteen months old. It had gone undiagnosed his entire life. He had been born with this birth defect of the skull. It's about to get a bit technical, so brace yourself. Craniosynostosis is the premature fusion of a suture in an infant's skull. The sutures in a skull are a kind of fibrous joint. The bones of the skull are held together by these joints/sutures. In infants, these sutures are open, meaning they have a bit of movement to them. When the suture is open, they are elastic and can move and expand with a growing skull and expanding brain. When one of those sutures is closed, the skull cannot expand in that direction as it planned. To the credit of the human body and all of the amazing things it can do, the skull does not just stop growing because of that blocked off suture. The skull instead compensates. It will push out in another direction, however wrong that may be; in any way it can to find the space it longs for. It will continue to grow that way. As the skull shifts its growing patterns, many of the facial features are affected, meaning there can be vision problems, dental problems, and possible airway obstructions because of the facial deformities. Left untreated, the intracranial pressure can cause other serious symptoms such as seizures, blindness, and brain damage.

For whatever reason, the Metopic suture in Emmett's skull closed in utero. It wasn't supposed to close for many more months. Typically, around nine months old, the suture will close on most babies. As Emmett grew, his skull grew triangularly; the skull desperate to make room for his growing brain. As time went on, the severity of his skull shape worsened and his brain began to run out of room. Intracranial pressure began to build up and the symptoms started to show. In a great many number of ways; the serendipitous seizure that would start everything in motion was able to alert us to a very urgent diagnosis. Life would never be the same again.

Because of the late diagnosis, it was important that we acted quickly. Our team told us the optimal age for Emmett's surgery would have been around six months and we were pushing fifteen months, on the very outer limits of when they believed they could do the surgery successfully. Emmett became a priority case. We went to the front of the line, bumping others out of long standing appointments and taking someone else's surgery date. They moved with haste. The older he was, the harder the surgery would be on him they told us. There would be a longer surgery, a harder recovery, more facial swelling, and the clincher: a much higher chance of additional surgeries. My heart sunk. For so many children, this surgery is a one and done kind of experience. But because we were so late, he would most likely be facing more than one surgery. It's strange how heartbreak and anger can coexist together in a deep and tumultuous state.

And even hope and desperation
can entwine themselves.

#Kathyfacts

I'm a strong believer in gut feelings. When I know something, sometimes I just know. Even if it doesn't make sense or seems completely crazy to those around me, I have to follow my intuition.

1. Do you believe in gut feelings or your natural instinct?

2. Have you ever followed your instincts about something and been right? Wrong?

3. Have you ever been so sure about something that you didn't need or even care to hear anyone else's opinions about it? How did that work out for you?

When I am sure about something, I am hard to rationalize with. I won't hear it. I won't believe it. I'm sure I can see so clearly what others can't. It's a fine line to walk between knowing you are right about something and blowing off those around you when you don't agree with them. I believe having those tough but careful conversations have made a difference. I also believe we all need a few key people in our life that we trust to be our sounding board and voice of reason when we need to hear the hard stuff.

I encourage you to have a conversation about your differing opinions in a certain situation. It's hard to understand each other when we aren't listening to each other. Follow your instincts; just don't forget about those that love you, watching from the sidelines.

Chapter 9

I was curled up on the bathroom floor, screaming at no one in particular, pieces of the broken vase that had shattered against the wall scattered all over the floor. My hands were still covered in blood. I stared at myself in the mirror so long my reflection started to blur. What I saw didn't make sense. I couldn't reconcile this strange image with who I knew myself to once be. My hair was tangled and messy, my face sickly pale and deep dark circles lined my dull green eyes; eyes that once upon a time sparkled with life and hope. I lay on the cool bathroom floor and a flood of memories assaulted my senses. *Was this the first time I had been here? No. Of course it wasn't.*

There I was, two and a half years after that fateful and awful day when I had lost baby number two. That was the baby that would eventually lead me to church. To God. To hope. To healing. I was lying on the bathroom floor after an extraordinary bout of rage. I was defeated. Insomnia had ravaged every part of me. I wore the fear, anxiety, pain, and exhaustion all over my face plain as day. I couldn't hide it even if I wanted to. It was always there, right at the surface, just barely contained. I cursed a God that wouldn't listen. Desperate pleas, cries, screams, and prayers all went unanswered. I didn't understand why. I couldn't understand what I had done to deserve this. It seemed like I was being punished over and over at every turn in my life. *Would there ever be a way out? Would it ever get easier?*

It was worse this time, because now there was God to believe in and to look to for answers. He was right there. He was just ignoring me, it seemed. He refused to intervene and that filled me with uncontrollable anger. *Why wouldn't He heal Emmett? He gave me this little boy, this miracle that wasn't even supposed to survive the pregnancy, and now He was going to do what? Take him away?* I begged God to take me instead, to strike me down dead right that instant, and spare my son. I alternated between drowning in a sea of helplessness and burning with anger from the inside out. I begged God to heal his brain, heal his skull, and make everything okay. But I couldn't bargain with God. I just wanted Emmett to live a long, healthy life and I was ready to die in his place without a second thought. I refused to believe there was nothing I could do.

All I wanted was to know that he was going to be okay, but none of his doctors could give me that hope to hang onto. There was only the great unknown; a giant question mark regarding the life of my baby boy.

Desperation consumed me. It raked me over the hot coals of Hell and left me there to rot. It took all hope, the possibility I felt in this life, and my faith away from me. I lost myself and everything I ever knew about myself watching him suffer. There was nothing left in its place but a desperate, scared little girl pretending to be a grown up. I was gone and I didn't think I would ever be okay again.

I remember those first few shell-shocked days after Emmett's diagnosis of Craniosynostosis, knowing what that surgery would be like and do to him. I had been stumbling through my days trying to pretend like I was still a functioning member of the human race. I was trying to pretend like surgery was such a long ways off that it wasn't even really going to happen. I was pretending like I had it all together, that I was holding up just fine, and like I wasn't just this miserable person slapping on a smile for the world. I was a fantastic pretender. I fooled everyone: family, friends, coworkers, running partners, everyone. The only one I couldn't fool was Tony, who saw it all unfold. Even then, I was only okay with letting my rage show. I locked up everything else safe and sound and threw away the key. If I pretended it didn't matter, maybe it really wouldn't. If I could just push through this and try to survive this, then maybe it would all be better after that. Oh the things I could convince myself I could do, like change the outcome of the future, single handedly heal Emmett if I spent enough time trying to find the answers, and more.

I thought I knew about suffering. I thought I knew what it was to feel desperate and afraid of the future. I guess, to a degree, I did. However, this was a new and torturous piece of the puzzle, watching Emmett suffer. I never had experienced such deep pain in my life. I never knew heartache could travel to the very depths of my soul. It hurt in my bones to watch him having a seizure. It burned through every layer of skin I had to see his broken body in a hospital bed.

In the overwhelming unknown, there were too many things to focus on. I had no direction anymore. I was an obsessive planner and a control freak confronted by the ever changing, never predictable life with a child with medical needs. The boy who lived. Just like in *Harry Potter*. He was here and he was mine and I desperately needed him to live. When everything I had pretended to be and feel started to slip from my grasp, I panicked. I had to get a hold of myself. I couldn't let anyone know the truth. I wasn't willing to share my grief with anyone. I wasn't willing to confront my fears in the real world. I hid it as best I could because I didn't want to have those conversations. I didn't want it to be real. I just wanted it to go back to the way things had been. I wanted everything to be okay again. I spun my wheels in place trying to figure out how to go back and what I should do next. I racked my brain for a solution. I spent weeks coming up with a plan of attack. *How could I still be okay? How could I fix this?* Clearly, I had been in denial for a large chunk of that time. When the initial shock wore off, I realized there was no fixing Emmett's diagnosis. It was not a problem I could solve. I fell apart. The ceiling crumbled in on me. I couldn't pretend for one more second. I couldn't force one more smile.

I lost all hope.

#Kathyfacts

When Emmett's diagnosis first hit, I was shaken to my very core but that's not what I allowed to show. I pretended like it was fine. I pretended like I was holding onto my faith and praying. I pretended like I believed it really would all be okay. I put on a big, sweeping production to show the world I was someone I was not. I was confident, in control, hopeful, and had an unwavering faith. More accurately, I was a liar.

1. Why do you think we pretend like everything is fine when it clearly isn't? What is to be gained or lost with this strategy?

2. Fear can be an immobilizing feeling or a motivating feeling. Do you tend to be frozen in place or moved to do something in deep fear?

3. What is one thing that scares you that you could talk about? Do you think it would help?

Write a list of the people who love you who you could talk to if everything suddenly wasn't okay. Thinking clearly is hard in crisis mode, a list helps. Remind yourself that fear is okay to talk about. I believe confronting the things that terrify us can actually help. Running from it, pretending it isn't happening, that's how we get stuck. That's where the fear starts to own us. When we own the fear, that's how we become free. You can face the fear head on and then push right past it.

Chapter 10

I didn't always want to run. There was a time when I hated it and when I wanted to stop running altogether. I know what you're sarcastically thinking, "Oh scandalous." I'm a grown adult. If I didn't want to do something like run for hours, I could have just stopped. Except I couldn't. I was going to be pacing for the Fifth Third River Bank Run 25K (fifteen and a half miles) for the first time ever a month after Emmett was diagnosed with Craniosynostosis. It was a terrible time for me. We were still in the midst of shock and trying to absorb what was going to happen.

After Emmett was diagnosed, I kind of went numb. Everything felt fake and unreal. It was like I was dreaming. I wasn't quite sure if it was really happening or not. I was swimming in a hazy world of strange words, strange people, and strange machines. It was my life but it felt like someone else's.

I don't really like to talk about myself much, which seems laughable as I write this book, but I mean it. I am fine writing about life and events. I am happy to dissect the who, what, where, when, and how for others. When it comes to writing personally about me and about who I am, it's about as much fun as going to the dentist. I'm better at keeping secrets and pretending than I am with truth telling. Each page of this book has been a radical experience of both discomfort and growth. So let's go to the dentist, shall we?

To understand why I couldn't just stop running, you have to understand me. I am obnoxiously driven. If I say I am going to do something, I will. If I agree just to myself to do something, I will. I hold myself to impossibly high standards that I would never in a million years expect from others. From myself, I demanded perfection or as close to perfection as I could get. It had been a problem for many years, but yet I couldn't stop. I knew I could do better and be better. If there was room for improvement, it was a waste not to seek it out.

I was a self-seeking perfectionist that had been thrown into chaos, a world of sleepless nights, doctor appointments, and spending too much time on the road going back and forth between hospital and home. Add to this one local race that I'd already agreed to pace and you have the perfect equation for me to continue on despite circumstances.

I had really wanted to pace that race before all of this. I wanted to encourage other runners, help them get to the finish line in the time they wanted, and be a source of support. I was also trying to get my foot in the door and show the race committee how responsible and enthusiastic I was. For the previous five years, I had attempted to be a part of the Fifth Third River Bank Run Road Warrior Program. I'd applied every single year but could not make the cut. The Road Warriors were a group of ambassadors for the race. They got to represent the race, wear cool stuff, write blogs, raise money for charity, meet local running heroes, and just be out there doing something that made a difference, and how I longed to make a difference even then. Even before everything with Emmett, I felt like I was missing something and that things weren't quite right yet. I really wanted to be a part of the Road Warrior team. I didn't want them to see me as flaky, so I decided I had to pace for this race still. Ever pragmatic, ever able to see things in the long term, I decided to still pace the race.

I kept running and training for that race begrudgingly and hating every single step. It didn't make me feel any better. I was exhausted and it felt dumb. I wanted to quit so badly. I debated it so many times but something inside of me told me to keep going. I don't let people down. I don't give up when it gets hard. I certainly don't quit.

I finally could see running from other people's perspective. *Who thinks this is fun? My legs hurt. It's hot out. I'm tired. I want to go sit down and watch a movie.* It was such a strange feeling with this stranger living in my head. I would run past places that used to make my heart swell and just stare at them blankly. I would run through the trails that used to feel like home and I only wanted out of the stupid forest with all its stupid trees and stupid leaves.

That's when I realized what the problem was. I had run while I was pregnant with Emmett. After I was released from bed rest, we ran all the time together. We ran a half marathon when I was six months pregnant. I continued to run and train for a marathon after he was a newborn. I even nursed him at the side of the road during a race. They were tied together. Running and Emmett. I couldn't untangle them no matter how hard I tried. If Emmett suffers, I suffer, and running suffers. I can't enjoy something that reminds me of him so much when he is suffering.

I wasn't sure how I was going to run for fifteen and a half miles surrounded by thousands of people and look happy about it. I considered dropping out yet again. I had that email drafted but just couldn't send it. No one would blame me. I had every reason, every excuse, and every valid, legitimate argument about why I couldn't or shouldn't do it. I just couldn't bring myself to hit send on that email. I deleted it instead. It was just one race. I could make it for just a couple more weeks. I could fake it for just a little bit longer, and then after the Fifth Third River Bank Run, I was never going to run again. I had it all figured out.

It hit me like a ton of bricks. We scheduled the surgery date for Emmett: June 20, 2012. My skin was on fire. My head swirled out of focus. My stomach felt like it had acid in it. I laced up my shoes with shaking hands. It was all wrong. I could feel it. Everything was wrong. Everything was different. I wasn't numb anymore, although I found myself almost wishing I was. Maybe that would have been better than the turmoil I felt.

I stepped outside and onto the road and immediately started running. There was something inside of me. Something deep down in my stomach that was just wrecking me. I had to get it out. I ran faster. I ran until my legs hurt and my lungs burned. In the middle of that trail, the one that used to feel like home, I felt a glimpse of it again. It was the old familiar feeling that I belonged there. It produced a choking sound from the back of my throat. It was like home, except it wasn't. It was darker there than I remembered; my mind tampering with the entire world before me. It was scarier there than I remembered. *My baby boy.* My breath caught. I could feel it, invading my head and my heart mixing with the blood within me. It was a part of me. I screamed loud and long. It was a scream of pure frustration and despair. I screamed again and then I was crying. I was down in the dirt on my knees, my head resting face down on the dusty trail as tears streaked clean pathways down my face.

I screamed like a woman on the edge of all hope and desperation. I prayed to keep that feeling. I prayed to not go back. I didn't want to be numb anymore. I didn't want to disappear from this world. I wanted to be a real person again. I prayed for Emmett, for my baby boy to live. I screamed and cried down there in the dirt. I could almost see the darkness that had possessed me dissipate into the air. I stood back up and ran even harder. I was on the other side. I had gone through the door. I had broken through the wall. I felt to a very small degree, like myself again. I surely didn't have it all together, but I was *really* running and that was the first step to living again.

Running had always taken me places. Running had always brought me where I wanted to go. Running was what bridged the gap from the old me to the new me. Running helped me settle into a life with a life threatening diagnosis for my child. Running helped me make my peace, to a degree. I could feel it, the life surging up from the road itself. It was illuminating me, healing me, and putting me back together. Shortly after that day, I found myself wanting to run again. I felt hopeful when I returned from the run and I knew that was what I needed to do next. That was the plan. Take the pain and run with it.

These were my actions and my decisions, but I will forever be grateful for the fact that I was pacing for the Fifth Third River Bank Run that year. Had I not broken through while running, I may have just spiraled even further out of control. Because of that race, I went on. I went through the motions until it felt real again. I'm not sure I could have done that on my own without anything that I felt bound by responsibility to do. I paced that race with a bit of real happiness in my soul. Fear, anguish, uncertainty, hope, and happiness coexisted in my heart. I wore a sign on my back about Emmett and Craniosynostosis and was able to tell so many people about it, including a midwife.

Two years after the race, I was named one of ten Road Warriors for the Fifth Third River Bank Run. I know it had nothing to do with me pacing that race and much more to do with what I could bring to the table, but still I felt validated in my efforts. I wanted to share the way my spirit soared when I ran and I finally landed on that team after seven years of trying. I waited seven years to make this little dream a possibility. I realized that my persistence and borderline obsession of getting what I want does not necessarily hinder me but can help me. I make things happen. I refuse to go away disheartened and unnoticed. Not until I've accomplished what I want accomplished.

There will always be a strong bond between running, my son, and my forward momentum in this life because of that race. Continuing running through the pain was the best thing for me. I wanted to give up and because of that race I didn't.

In continuing on despite my lack of drive, I found a renewed purpose and hope in those miles.

#Kathyfacts

Occasionally, we set goals for ourselves or make promises that we end up regretting later. Life gets in the way and can make us feel resentful and burnt out by these responsibilities that we once agreed to carry long ago.

1. Have you ever wanted to quit something after you made a commitment to do it?

2. Did you quit or did you go ahead and do it anyhow?

3. Why do you think you quit or completed it? What was your driving force?

It's easy to say we are going to do things. It's much harder to follow through and actually do them, especially when the will to do them leaves us. If you've quit something in the past, give yourself some grace. Quitting is not just a waste. Quitting does not mean you stop trying. You can keep trying, again and again and again. Progress is one step at a time.

If you are contemplating quitting or giving up on something, ask yourself some hard questions. Is it worth it to you? Will you regret quitting more than the struggle you are in now? What is the struggle doing to you? Contemplate your place in a tough situation you are in. Not everything is hopeless and not everything can be fixed. You need to take stock of the situation and figure out whether you want and need to invest more time into it or whether it's time to take a step back for now. You already know the answer in your heart. You just have to be brave enough to follow it.

Chapter 11

One afternoon, we were in the car driving home from some pre-operative testing at C.S. Mott Children's Hospital. We still had about an hour and a half to go before we arrived home. Emmett was in the back seat sound asleep and the car was filled with silence. It was less than one month until surgery number one. Emmett had just one more pre-operative appointment until surgery. That day, they had said the surgery would be an estimated seven to eight hours, with the possibility of it running longer. I stared out the window as the world danced past me. *Seven to eight hours they would have my baby boy. What was I going to do for that long? Sitting in the waiting room, games, movies, none of that was acceptable. He could die. He could seize on that operating room table and never, ever come back to me.* I felt sick just thinking about it. I couldn't just sit calmly in a waiting room. I closed my eyes and tried to envision Emmett being pushed away from me down the long white hallway. I tried to feel what I would feel at that moment. The dread I felt in my stomach was real. I had to do something I wanted to do, that was the only way. *What on earth would I be able to do at the hospital for eight hours?*

I looked down at my bright pink running shoes. It was so obvious I couldn't believe I hadn't thought of it before. "I could run!" I abruptly said. Tony nodded his head. "Sure. It's going to be late by the time we get back, but you can go for a run if you want." "No, no, no," I said. "During the surgery, I could run until Emmett is out." I let the words hang in the air. No one said anything. I waited and worried about what he'd think. If he thought I was going to hurt myself or that it wasn't a good idea. "Do you WANT to run for that long?" he asked me slowly. "Yes!" I shot back. "It's the only thing I can do." We talked through the details the rest of the way home and the more we talked, the more excited I became. The ideas were coming fast and furious.

I dubbed myself Team Emmett. I decided to run on the treadmill in the hospital's gym. I would make a Facebook event and our friends and family could run or walk with me virtually on the same day. I could get the word out about Craniosynostosis, run for Emmett, and have something to do to distract me in the process. It was perfect. A month wasn't exactly ideal training conditions for the longest run of my life, but it didn't matter to me. It wasn't about time, talent, or training. It was about the art of surviving.

When I got home, I jumped head first into training. Previously, the longest I had ever run was a marathon, twenty-six point two miles. The slowest one of those was four hours and thirty-two minutes, almost half as long as I would be attempting to go. This was before I had ever even heard the word ultrarunner. I didn't even realize there was such a thing as an ultramarathon. I just loosely based everything on a marathon training plan I had at home and ran for a certain number of hours each time. Two weeks before surgery, I did a five hour run. It was hard because I wasn't fully trained for it and it was way more than I was used to doing. With my newfound title as Team Emmett, I had a fire lit under my feet and a new purpose. I kept running up and down that hot, dusty trail for five hours. I was weak. I was tired. I cried. When I wanted to give up, I channeled all the fear I felt for Emmett and for what would happen. I used it as fuel to keep going.

The night before surgery, we were staying at Amy and Darryl's house. I was on the couch in the basement staring up at the ceiling. I should have been sleeping but I just couldn't. I looked at my phone. 1 am. Sigh. 1:36. 1:52. 2:14. 2:47. On and on it went. I shut my eyes, sure that I might fall asleep for a minute or two, but I didn't. Every time I made the mistake of looking at the time, it had barely moved. I was sure morning was never going to get there. I just wanted to get it over with until 6 am finally hit, and then I wasn't ready. I didn't want to do it anymore. *No, no, no. Just another hour.*

I picked up my sweet little boy who didn't have a clue what was about to happen. *I could leave. I could. We could just get in the car and drive south instead. Go to Florida. Disney World. We had two weeks off.* My mind swirled with ideas and reasons why I should just change my mind and not show up but I couldn't do it. I knew it had to be done. We drove to the hospital in silence. I questioned every decision I had ever made leading up to that early morning drive. All the ways it could have been different, all the ways it should have been different. All the ways we were failed by the medical system all that time, and all the things that could go wrong, so very wrong. I stared out the window and saw a young woman running, charging up a hill. She looked determined, focused, and even a bit angry. I understood her. I understood her anger just looking at her. I flipped down the visor mirror and looked at myself. I looked tired, scared, and a bit angry myself. I sighed loudly and dramatically. *How on earth was I ever going to do this?*

I stood in the pre-operative room nervously pacing back and forth five steps the cramped room allowed me. The curtain was pulled back and I could see everyone coming and going in the hallways. Emmett had already been given a dose of medication to calm him down and was wearing the ever so familiar tired little tiger gown. Then they were there. Two women and one man all dressed in blue scrubs, caps on, and paper on their shoes. They were promising me they'd take good care of Emmett. I kissed him goodbye and felt the desperation surge. I struggled to keep from picking him up. I knew if I did, they'd have to pry him out of my hands. I wouldn't let him go any other way. The clang of the hospital bed being shifted and unlocked for transport made me jump. *No. Not yet.* I panicked. I took a step back and watched them. They started to push him away and I stared after them. Emmett was gibbering happily as I watched them push him out of sight. It felt like I had gotten the wind knocked out of me. I was gasping for air that wasn't there. I couldn't breathe. I had to get out of there. I bolted out of the room and towards the waiting room. I tried to breathe and act like a normal person, but I couldn't. I was crying, my eyes were shifty, and I wrung my hands together as I ran down the hallway.

I looked at the tiny little room that would be my companion for the next eight hours. There were two treadmills, a bike, and an elliptical. There was a small TV in the corner. There were no windows but a half glass partition where I could see out into a windowless hallway. It felt claustrophobic and like the worst idea I had ever had in my life. Regardless, I opened the door and stared down the treadmill. We were going to be good friends. I was going to give it a run for its money. I stood next to the treadmill, sizing it up, with a hardened resolve. It was almost time to start.

All I could hope was that
Emmett would live.

#Kathyfacts

We all have stress in our lives. Some situations are more stressful than others, but sometimes we aren't very good at dealing with these stressors no matter how big or small. I will be the first to admit, I had no idea where to go with my stress, anxiety, and panic. They jumbled up my mind and left me wide eyed and wired.

1. What do you do when you are feeling stressed?

2. What type of stressful situation do you most often find yourself in?

3. Do your own expectations of yourself add to your stress?

Sometimes I forget that whatever is happening is not the end of the world. There are times, like pre-surgery, that it really does feel like the end of the world. But then there are times in doctor's offices or when receiving a mailbox full of hospital bills can send me over my very steep edge. My panic threshold can be incredibly low at times. Sometimes, I can't differentiate between life threatening danger and imposed responsibilities.

In those times, I can see I need to start taking care of myself better. I've allowed myself to be filled to the very edge of my cup and just one drop causes everything to spill over onto the floor. I started setting time aside each day to do something I want to do. Read, color, or journal. Twenty minutes can make a huge difference in bringing my panic threshold back down. Start scheduling some time each day for you. Find something that you enjoy, that is fun, and relaxing. Then, schedule it into your day as you would anything else in your life. You are worth the investment of time.

Chapter 12

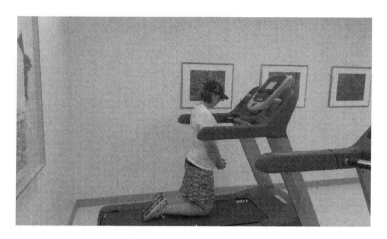

The sounds of the wheels unlocking underneath Emmett's hospital bed ripped through me. I felt desperate. The world was moving in slow motion. I couldn't make my arms and legs move like I wanted them to. I watched him being pushed down the long hallway by a team in blue scrubs and surgical gowns. I stared after them. *No. No. No. They can't have him.* I wanted to run after them, to get to them before they got to the double doors. The nurse turned us away, gently steering me into the other direction but I didn't want to go. I remained unmoving staring after him until he disappeared into the great unknown. My baby boy was in some scary sterile room all alone. Tears rushed down my face as I started running down the hallway. I had to get out of there.

I tried to think of anything but the impending skull surgery but it was all I could think about. As I rapidly approached the elevator and tried to talk myself into focusing on the run ahead, my mind tormented me. They were going to use a scalpel and cut the delicate skin of Emmett's head in a zigzag pattern from ear to ear. They were going to peel his face off. His face. Honestly. They were going to need to peel it down past his cheekbones. They were going to get out a saw and start cutting his skull apart. Then they were going to remove those pieces. They were going to take his skull off. They would need to reshape the bones, shave them down, make them fit, and put the masterpiece that was his new skull back on his head. They were going to use plates and screws to hold it all together.

They'd pull his face back on and stitch it back together on his battered, bruised, and bleeding head. I shook the images from my head. I couldn't go down that road.

It was June 20, 2012, the day of Emmett's very first major skull surgery. An estimated seven to eight hour procedure with no guarantees. I had vowed to run every second he was in surgery. I had to do something. It was a show of solidarity and a way for me to hold onto hope during the long wait.

I willed myself to step onto that treadmill. My feet wouldn't move on their own. I was frozen in fear. I felt the panic rising in my chest. My heart started to pound faster, my breathing picked up, and my hands balled up into fists without my own knowledge. I stood next to the treadmill and stared at it. I didn't want to do this anymore. I didn't know if I could even do this anymore. I couldn't focus. *What if something happened? What if he had a seizure while he was in there? What if they accidentally hit his brain? What if he was already dead? Oh my God, what if he's already dead? Would I feel it if he died, like a mother's intuition and just know? What if it didn't help? What if we have subjected him to this for no reason?*

Every unreasonable bone in my body screamed at me to go get my son and take him far away from that place. I took in a breath so deep it hurt, and instead of pressing the start button, I did the only thing I could think of. I dropped to my knees and prayed right there on the very hard and uncomfortable treadmill belt, in the middle of the hospital. Tony snapped a picture and Emmett's Endurance Event was officially underway. After a moment, I stood back up and pressed the scary green start button. Instead of freezing in place like I was afraid they would, my feet started to move with the belt. Fear moved them. Instinct moved them. I moved them. God moved them.

Our pastor and friend at the church we attend, Scott, drove three hours to be with us at the hospital. Pastor Scott is a very dedicated marathoner and he ran on the treadmill next to me on and off for most of the wait. He prayed with us. He sat with us. He encouraged us. He was there with us unflinchingly throughout it.

Hour 1: Running is known for being a reprieve from the hustle and bustle of this life. Running provides the opportunity to think, take in the sights and sounds around you, figure out life, focus on a goal, or just listen to music. Many runners will tell you they do their best thinking and problem solving in the middle of a run. It's just you inside your own head. Normally that wouldn't be a problem, but on a day like that day, it was the very last place I wanted to be. My thoughts were louder than any music I could listen to, they crept up and burrowed through my mind with a morbid toxicity. I willed myself to stop thinking, to do anything else but think about my sweet boy in that operating room cut open to pieces. I focused on my feet. My footsteps were soothing to my overly anxious mind. I breathed with each footfall, trying to calm myself into a quiet rhythm. Left, right, left, right, left, right. It brought peace and a sense of stability to my frazzled nerves. In my mind, a mantra formed. "I can do this. I can do this if I try. I have to try. If I try I can do this."

Hour 2: I was already tired of running. I could not believe it had only been two hours. My eyes kept flitting back to the clock on the treadmill. That was ALL? That couldn't be right. You know when you think "that seemed like a good idea at the time?" but then you start feeling regret for what you had agreed to. That was one of those times. I began to question myself for attempting something so dauntless in the wake of such difficult circumstances. Sure, let's train for an ultramarathon run while battling chronic insomnia with a newly diagnosed son! What was I thinking? A clear thought interrupted my self-pitying inner monologue. *It's for Emmett.* Of course it was.

God was there in every detail. I could see it in the tiny room and the way the emergency stop cord made a cross across the front of the treadmill. I saw it in the movie on TV, *Finding Nemo*, which incidentally would two years later, become Emmett's favorite movie and character without any prompting from us. I stopped in my tracks and cried when I saw Emmett watching *Finding Nemo* on TV for the first time. It struck a nerve so raw and deep, I just couldn't control it. I saw it in the caring faces of the nurses that stared in at me from the glass partition that separated us. I saw it in their nods of approval and their occasional thumbs up when they walked past. I saw the sympathy in their eyes, the look that said they understood more than any words could ever say.

Hour 3: The monotony of my footsteps began to threaten my sanity. It was no longer soothing. My footsteps echoed loudly in my ears, to the point where I considered plugging my ears to drown out the noise. In my head, I was a thousand miles away: far away from that treadmill, that hospital, and that new life. In my head, I ran away from all of it. In reality though, there I was running through the thick of it. I was going nowhere on a treadmill on the tenth floor of a hospital, running with no destination in sight, while my son had his entire skull broken apart. I was waiting for a call to hear he was okay, waiting for it to be over with, waiting to see him, and waiting in an agonizing state of the unknown. Always waiting. I was running hard, pouring out my heart, body, and soul onto that treadmill. I was holding back tears and fighting for it with every ounce of strength I had. My legs moved in steady fashion, the hum of the treadmill, the sound of my feet hitting that belt created the atmosphere of discipline; I was there but really, I was not. I didn't know how many hours it had been. I was a shell shocked woman, a terrified mother, an exhausted insomniac running as if her life depended on it. I was the face of the waiting room, encompassing every human emotion possible, set hard in a mask of determination. I just had to keep going. I just HAD to keep going.

Hour 4: I couldn't bring myself to think about being halfway there. I couldn't bring myself to do anything but lift my feet, one after the other, over and over. Tony came to the rescue and started reading to me and showing me pictures from Facebook. Somewhere in the middle of our crisis, unbeknownst to me, the most amazing thing happened. The running community and strangers from all over the world united with us. I had created an event on Facebook for friends and family to virtually join me, but it turned into something so much bigger than I could have ever imagined. I saw endless pictures of people running, biking, walking, golfing, gardening, swimming, doing Zumba, CrossFit, lifting weights, band practices, meetings, and more. All of these were people holding up a picture of Emmett or had Emmett's picture pinned to their shirt. Hundreds of messages, prayers, and emails flooded in, an overwhelming response. Over a thousand people from forty-five states and thirteen countries participated.

It's hard to explain even now how much strength that gave me to keep going. I cried, laughed, and was rendered speechless by the response. I wasn't alone in that tiny windowless room, over a thousand people were right there with me. People think they can't make a difference in this world and that they are only one, but to families like ours, going through that, every single one made a difference. Every single person who knew my son's name made a difference. It solidified his life, his pain, his journey, and my cause.

They made that difference. And so I kept going even when I wanted to quit.

Hour 5: My poor packing came back to haunt me. In my overly anxious state, I forgot to pack my running socks. I only had a regular pair of everyday socks with seams. If you are a non-runner, this doesn't seem like a big deal. If you are a runner and especially a distance runner, you will know what a terrible, critical error I had made. My feet were blistering in three spots. Add to this that one of my toes was practically numb, my knee was throbbing, and my stomach was upset. I started to swerve a bit on the treadmill, trailing off to the right a little too far and then overcorrecting back to the left a little too far. It was like watching someone else run. I was in this exhaustive daze that made it hard to process any thoughts more complicated than more water and more food. I felt like I was connected to Emmett and his surgery on a much deeper level. As long as the treadmill belt kept turning, as long as my feet kept shuffling across that belt, I knew everything was going to be okay. I couldn't stop before his surgery was done. I just felt like I was somehow personally responsible for contributing to his well-being in any way possible.

Now, I've never been a superstitious person. I don't really believe in coincidences or luck. I believe in God. Either way, I felt it in my heart of hearts that I must keep going for Emmett. As long as I kept running, I was letting him know that I would not give up, so he couldn't give up either. The human mind can be a fragile object. Most of us know this; some of us may have even experienced it. My mind was a fragile object that day. This is what my mind told me, this is what my heart agreed with, and this is what my legs had to pay for: I could not give up or give in no matter what happened or how I felt.

Hour 6: This was the hour that almost broke me. I had never run that long in my life. I was physically exhausted, depleted, running on empty, and desperate to stop. Everything hurt: my legs, my feet, my head, and my heart. I had started crying. I was scared. I was tired. I just wanted to stop. Stopping seemed like the only answer but I couldn't stop. I had to keep going.

There comes a point in every race or run when your heart must carry you because your legs can't do it anymore. It's sheer willpower. It's mental. It's what you tell yourself must be done. I had to force my legs to keep going.

I'd like to tell you I had a second wind, that someone's words shot through my heart and exhaustion and gave me renewed strength to start running even faster and stronger than I could have imagined, but I have no such story. When I didn't know what else to do and when I was sure I had gotten in over my head, I did the only thing that made sense: pray. I prayed for just enough. Just enough energy to keep going, just enough clarity to remember why I couldn't give up, just enough strength to not crumple onto the floor and start sobbing. Over and over I prayed for just enough, and just enough is what I got.

I will never be fast enough to be considered an elite athlete. In reality, I am far from elite. I am slightly overweight and, although I run a lot of miles, I am comfortably a middle of the pack runner. I am quite average; I have no qualms about that. All these facts aside, I felt like an elite athlete at that time. I was all heart, all soul, all passion, and bearing what I thought was once unbearable. Never in my life had I felt so very weak and yet so very full of power. I certainly didn't look powerful. I wasn't running any stronger or feeling any better, but I was doing it. I was hunched over and shuffling my feet loudly across that treadmill belt. The simple fact that I was still moving was about as powerful a statement as I could make.

Hour 7: We did not ring in this hour with a picture and a Facebook update as we had every single hour before. I could not force myself to smile at the camera and I did not want a picture of me scowling. If you ask Tony, he will swear my eyes were glowing red and I growled at him when he brought the camera over, but I'm pretty sure I just said "No picture." Guess we will never know for sure. Here is where I can tell you that someone's words shot straight through my heart and the exhaustion. My dear friend, Azsure, made a podcast for me to listen to during my long run. It was ten minutes long and I was given explicit directions to listen to it when I was at my wit's end. This was it. There were no wits left. As I listened, I cried and laughed and laughed and cried over and over in a barely comprehensible fashion. No doubt at this point, my pit crew was sure I had lost my mind.

I had run with Azsure for her very first marathon, just seven months after Emmett was born. Somewhere around mile twenty of the race, I started to feel a bit sick and ended up throwing up by the side of the road. Azsure was on a mission without an ounce of quit in her and insistent I could keep going. I stumbled slowly and pitifully beside her gazelle-like strides for longer than I felt I could. I was lamenting my state of being and giving her the "Go on without me," speech when Azsure suddenly stopped me. "See that guy up ahead, in the blue shirt? We're going to pass him first." *Sigh. I'm feeling sick and want to slow down but first we have to speed up to pass a guy in front of us? Okay Azsure.* I sped up with her and eventually we passed him. *Okay. Thank God that was done.* Azsure interjected once again. "See that girl up there, in the gray shirt? We're going to pass her." My thoughts turned slightly murderous towards my dear friend, but I followed her commands. For the remainder of the race, we chased down and passed many people in front of us. It was only because of Azsure and "that guy in the blue shirt up ahead" that I kept going when I desperately wanted to quit.

The podcast brought to life Azsure's presence, running beside me and pushing me through what I thought I couldn't do. I listened to that podcast three times in a row, following her commands and trying to pass the imaginary guy in the blue shirt. I was crying at the emotion in her voice when the call came, twenty-six glorious minutes later. Emmett was out of surgery and in recovery. He had lived and I could breathe again.

Seven hours and twenty-six minutes after I first stepped onto that treadmill, a different person stepped off it. A person who knew there were no such things as boundaries and limits. Someone who felt pain deeper and love stronger than ever before. Someone who truly believed anything was possible. I set out towards the recovery room. I had to steady myself and keep from running as hard as I could and kicking those double doors down to get to Emmett. Even amongst the fear of the unknown, the exhaustion and desperation, I could feel it clear as day as I smiled through the pain. It was my old friend hope, telling me that I could do this, that I was stronger and braver than I thought, and that I was more capable than I'd ever given myself credit for. It was patting me on the back for a job well done.

That hope was telling me to brace myself for what was yet to come.

#Kathyfacts

Desperation has set heavy in my stomach many times in my life. It worked its way into my heart. So many unknowns and so many different outcomes lay ahead of me. Even though I was terrified and overwhelmed by desperation, I chose to do something. In this case, I ran on a treadmill. I ran through the desperate aching fear that was everywhere.

1. What do you do in the face of the unknown? When you can't do anything to change the outcome, how do you find your peace?

2. Do you try to focus on the positive or do you let the negative thoughts run on a never ending loop in your head?

When you are stuck in despair, in a situation completely out of your control, it's hard to stop the thoughts in your head. The next time you find yourself thinking negatively about something you can't change, refocus. Push the thought out of your head. Actively attempt to think about something else. Don't get frustrated if it happens again, just keep trying.

One thing that has greatly helped me is "Five, four, three, two, one," a technique I learned in therapy. First, listen for five sounds. Notice five sights around you. Feel five textures or sensations. Next, listen for four different sounds. Notice four different sights around you. Feel four different textures or sensations. Continue on with three, two, and finally one. Whether that helps or not, when the negative has invaded your mind, you need to find a way to distract yourself sometimes. Keep trying different things until you find what works for you.

Chapter 13

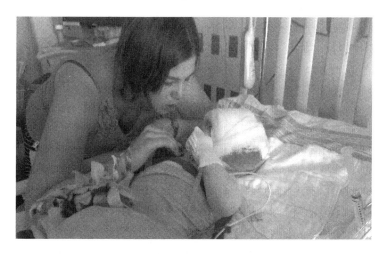

I stood over Emmett's bed and wept into his chest. I was holding his head in my hands, gently stroking the bandages that covered his broken skull. I looked down to see my hands stained blood red. It always comes back to that doesn't it? I remember almost laughing in the way only an overly stressed person can laugh about something like that. This is the thing my nightmares are made of. This is the thing that can unnerve me like nothing else in this entire world. The worst days of my life, the most desperate circumstances I have ever known, have smeared my hands with blood. It is tangible proof of my breaking heart: red. Always a deep, dark red.

The machines beeped with unnerving consistency. The same thing, over and over. *When was he going to wake up? Was he going to be okay? When would we know if everything went according to plan?* I watched his little body tremble and twitch. Every time, I braced myself, sure that he was going to start seizing. I piled another blanket on and returned to his bedside. Time stood still. I stood still. I silently prayed. Desperate prayers to a God that I knew I had doubted. I had cursed, screamed, raged, and hated the same God I was now begging for mercy.

In that bed, in that ICU, laid everything I am made of, everything I have fought for, half of my very heart. He just had to be okay. If it weren't for that first seizure, we wouldn't have even known about this birth defect. *It had to happen that way.* I remember repeating it over and over in my head, like a mantra. A scene from the movie

Signs flashed through my head. It was Mel Gibson's character rocking his unresponsive child on the ground in desperation, saying over and over "That's why he had asthma. It can't be luck. His lungs were closed. His lungs were closed. No poison got in." I looked back at Emmett. *That's why he had the seizures. There was a reason for it. It had to happen that way. It led us here.* If I said it enough, I could have almost made myself believe it. *It had to happen that way. It had to happen that way. It had to happen that way.* If I could believe it, maybe God would too.

I remember the day that I thought I saw Emmett die, the day he stopped breathing. It was a terrible, cold March day when I found him unconscious, foaming at the mouth, and seizing wildly in his crib. It was just days after his first birthday party. His cute blue party hat proclaiming "I am one" still hung from the diaper stacker. I stood there in shock, watching the rhythmic convulsions in horror. I screamed for Tony as I ran for the phone to call 911. I was on the phone with the 911 operator when the seizure stopped and Emmett collapsed face down in his crib. I waited but his chest didn't rise.

I felt the room tilt up at me, I was afraid I was going to pass out. Tony scooped him up out of bed as I stood there motionless with three-year-old Travis wrapped around my leg. He was an unresponsive ragdoll in Tony's arms. The 911 operator's voice was ringing in my ear "Is your son still seizing ma'am? Are you still with me? Ma'am?" My knees went weak and I felt a hot, white blinding pain rising in my chest. "Can you hear me? Is your son still seizing? Is he breathing? Ma'am? I need you to answer me." I was going to be sick, I was sure of it. *Breathe Emmett.* I willed his chest to rise. Tony's face was right next to Emmett's face. *No. No. No. This isn't real. This can't be happening. Breathe Emmett. Breathe baby. Breathe Emmett. Oh my God, please breathe,* I pleaded silently. I tried to steady myself and force myself to keep my stomach contents down. *Breathe Emmett.* Tony put his face back next to Emmett's face. I couldn't figure out what he was doing. The 911 operator's voice rang in my ears. Tony started yelling something at me, saying the same thing over and over. I couldn't understand him. I could only hear the sound of blood thrumming through my ears. The entire world was muffled. Tony yelled again. I stood silent. My voice wouldn't work.

It was then that the most beautiful and terrifying thing happened. Emmett screamed. It was unlike any scream we had ever heard before. A blood curdling scream that both unnerved me and grounded me. "It's okay. He's breathing again." That's what Tony had been trying to tell me. He was alive but he was emulating sheer terror. I could feel it. Just like that I could speak again. It snapped me out of my inaction.

As I sat in the back of the ambulance a short time later watching Emmett strapped in with the too big oxygen mask covering his small face, I felt a cold, hard rock of fear sitting in my stomach. *This is not it. This is not all there is. There is something big coming.* I wanted to waive that feeling off and tell myself I was just being paranoid, but I couldn't. A seizure was not just a seizure. Something was wrong. I could feel it deep in my bones. I could see it when I looked at my son and started making all those connections that had been there all along but I hadn't been able to see beforehand. As we made our way to the hospital, I knew I was right. I couldn't explain it. I couldn't prove it. I could only feel it. Call it mother's intuition. Call it a gut feeling. Call it God himself. I knew I was right. I had never, ever wanted to be wrong about something as much as I did about that. I hoped I was wrong. I hoped even for the wrong things, but I knew I wasn't wrong.

Three months after that first seizure, there I was in the ICU of a children's hospital. I looked at the tiny fragile body lying before me. A cacophony of sounds surrounded me. Sounds and sights that I never imagined hearing or seeing. It hurt to look at him. I had been prepared, researched this massive and terrifying surgery well. I had seen numerous, very graphic photos of other children post-surgery, but none of that could prepare me for what it felt like to see MY baby post-surgery. I felt it deep in my stomach, a stabbing sensation full of pain and fear, tinged with hopelessness. I couldn't turn my eyes away from the deep, red blood that stained the pristine white bandages. The blood was a never-ending well of horror. Seeping out onto everything and mixing with my tears. His eyes were swollen shut. He was pale, limp, and barely conscious. It took my breath away. I stood and stared at him until my feet started to ache from standing in place on the hard floor. On the second day, I pulled the green chair as close as I could get to the bed without running into the massive pole and wires that was cozied up next to him and there I stayed. I held vigil at his bedside, refusing to move.

I held vigil and people showed up for us. My friend Jacci got in the car on a whim with her son and drove the three hours to come see us. She brought my favorite indulgences, Diet 7-Up, chocolate, and *Runner's World* magazine, along with her caring heart. Her friendly face steadied me. We stood over Emmett's bed together as she anointed him with oil and spoke beautiful prayers of healing, comfort, and grace.

Two other friends, Pam and Scott also made the long trip to see us. They had gotten a babysitter for their two young children and came to the hospital on a Saturday, prime time weekend space and a day they were both off of work. We celebrated together as Emmett ate three bites of applesauce. It was the first thing he had eaten in days since the surgery itself. They were just as ecstatic about it as we were.

My mother-in-law was staying at Amy and Darryl's house with Travis, so they could be close to the hospital and easily see us. Our nieces Sydni and Stacie watched over Travis, keeping him busy having fun while we were apart. I could give my full attention to what was happening in front of me because I knew my family was taking great care of one another. One of our days in the hospital, the whole family showed up along with Amy's sweet mother-in-law Carol, who is also a family friend and a reverend. We stood over Emmett's bedside together while she prayed beautifully, fervently, and with passion while she anointed Emmett with oil. I felt God there with us, watching over our entire family. I felt His hand in taking care of us, by sending our loved ones to us in a time of great need and great pain.

There are so many other words I could use to describe the pain of seeing your child's broken skull. There are so many ways I could tell you about the blood that pooled at the base of his head over and over again. I could tell you about the drains behind his ears that spurted blood when he cried and how I screamed the first time it happened. I could tell you about the way he held his monkey in his tiny little fist, covered and taped up with wires and lines, and tried without success to suck his thumb for comfort. I could tell you how I cried at even this lack of comfort measure for him. I could tell you all about it, but it's too much. There aren't the right words. It's pure heartbreak. Its utter helplessness and hopelessness wrapped up in one dark package that buries you underneath it. It's the thing nightmares are made of.

It tested my faith, my strength, and my hope.

#Kathyfacts

Watching Emmett suffer made me feel completely powerless. I wasn't sure what to do, how to help, or if I could even help. I no longer felt like an adult or someone in charge or their own life. I felt small and afraid. I felt anxious and on edge.

1. Have you ever watched someone you've been powerless to help?

2. Have you absorbed their pain and anguish as your own? Or were you able to distance yourself from it?

3. What can you do to help someone who doesn't seem like they want help? Anything?

When I was in the deepest of my turmoil, I isolated myself. I didn't want to see people, ask for help, or talk about it. I felt exposed and fragile. The people who made the most difference were the ones who showed up anyhow. They loved me through it with patience and small acts of kindness. When I couldn't bring myself to even admit how greatly I was struggling and how I felt, they showed up for me. I think sometimes we can forget how even a small act can go a long way.

Perform an act of kindness for someone you know is struggling. Even if they can't acknowledge it right now, it will have an impact on them and you as well. An act of love can have a huge impact on the receiver when they are struggling. It can make them feel less alone, less scared, and less of an outsider.

Chapter 14

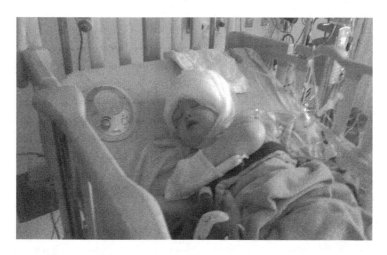

It must have been the third day we were in the ICU with Emmett after the first surgery. I had switched shifts with Tony, leaving the simple comforts of the Ronald McDonald House for the old steadfast green chair and allowing him a turn to rest. I stood over Emmett trying to soothingly rub his chest. He seemed restless, so I began my usual "It's okay baby, it's okay. I'm right here. You're okay. Mommy is right here." He must have been awake, because at the sound of my voice, he began stirring even more. Both eyes were completely swollen shut so he couldn't see anything, but he abruptly attempted to try and lift his head up off the bed for the very first time. His severely swollen head and all the extra weight proved to be too much for his small, weak body. He proceeded to tumble forward head first and land on his face. I had quickly shoved my arm over his chest in an attempt to keep him from falling, but it was no use. He lay bunched up on his face, with his IV and wires a tangled mess. He didn't even scream or cry or thrash in frustration. He was just lying there, unable to even protest to the pain or position he'd found himself in. I laid him back upright in bed, with his sore swollen head on a soft pillow after the nurses helped me untangle all of his lines. When everything was quiet again, my heart was still pounding. I couldn't shake the sick feeling in my stomach as I saw him scrunched up face first and not even crying, screaming or attempting to move.

He was an unresponsive rag doll, once again. I looked back at him and saw a single tear rolling down his cheek from his left eye.

A rational mind probably would have made a connection between a swollen head and both eyes swollen shut to tear ducts reacting appropriately. Clearly, this was a symptom but when your child is lying in a hospital bed in the ICU, connected to lines, wires, and machines with a broken skull, rational doesn't really have a place.

I wanted to call Tony, but I also wanted to let him sleep. I felt the hysteria rising quickly. *He's in pain. He's crying. He can't tell me, but he's suffering.* My hands began to shake as I started to pace around his bed. *He's in pain. He's crying. He can't tell me, but he's suffering. He's in pain. He's in pain. He's in pain.* It swirled violently around in my head. I looked at him again. I saw the trail the lone tear left behind and became unglued. I called the only person I was sure would understand without any explanation; the only person that I knew who had watched from a similar place with her own son, Pam. They were different reasons and different stories but the same connection. She had been there before.

I met Pam at church. We bonded over our love of running, laughter, and God. We became fast friends. She's a no nonsense kind of friend. A bold and blunt but loving and caring person. She's the one to seek for an honest opinion, whether it's asking if a dress looks too tight or what she thinks of a story I wrote, she can be counted on to tell the truth and nothing but the truth. Because of this, she can speak logical sense into many different situations.

The phone rang just once before Pam answered. She didn't even bother saying hello. I was calling from the ICU; she knew it wasn't just for a friendly chat. "What's going on?" she asked. At the sound of her voice, I dissolved into sobs. I couldn't get my words out. I was trying to explain what happened, but it was impossible to do so with clarity in the middle of my breakdown. Turns out, I had scared her quite a bit. When someone calls you sobbing from the ICU after a massive surgery, a mind can tend to go to some pretty dark places. Once I had calmed down, I told her what happened. I told her about Emmett falling face first, lying there limp and unresponsive, and the single tear running down his face. My voice broke as I ended my story "He is in so much pain." It was silent for a few moments. Then she said something back to me that to this day whenever I think of it, it makes me laugh. Truly laugh, out loud. It is something so true and observant that it cut through everything else I was feeling. It allowed me to see clearly once again.

After I had ended my frantic and heartbreaking story, she responded. In a kind and caring voice, she said "Emmett's never really been the type to suffer in silence, Kat." It took me a minute for the words to sink in. Then I started crying even harder because I was laughing so hard. She was right. She was so very right. Part of losing my mind had come at the endless cries and screams all through the night. If Emmett was in intense pain or didn't like what was happening, you and all your neighbors would know it. Sitting next to Emmett with his broken skull in the middle of that ICU, I laughed so hard I actually snorted and then cried tears of relief. After we talked about it, rational heads prevailed and I realized with her help, that it probably was from the swelling. We didn't have a big, long, deep conversation. Just the kind of conversation that grounds you. Before she hung up the phone, she gave me one last bit of hope. "It's going to be okay Kathy. You're okay and Emmett's okay. It will all be okay." Just like that, all the hysteria and pure madness I felt building was gone.

Hope had come pouring out through the phone and slipped into my heart.

#Kathyfacts

Someone that can speak honestly and openly to you about you is a gift. So often, we are surrounded by polite, superficial small talk. Even when things are going wrong, we can focus on the details of the event, but not the feelings it brings up in us.

1.   Do you have a person who can be completely honest with you, in a gentle and loving way?

2.   Has anyone ever offered you the right words at the right time? If so, why do you think those words made such a difference?

We were not made to do life alone. We were not made to keep everything to ourselves. We need a tribe. We need people. Friends. Family. Support. Love. These things make a difference in everyday life and even more in a crisis.

Sometimes people back away from those in a crisis for fear of saying the "wrong" thing. I think as long as it's coming from a place of genuine concern, it will be right. If you are struggling, tell someone. If you see a friend struggling, talk to him or her. Give that gift of friendship or be a friend to yourself even. Don't shy away from the pain. Lean into it. It will strengthen the bonds of your relationship when you are present in someone else's pain. It can be a comfort to both parties. Ask the hard questions. Listen to the heartbreaking answers. Continue to be present. That's how you make a difference in someone's life.

Chapter 15

Two weeks after Emmett's first surgery was our small hometown 5K on the Fourth of July. Many years prior, it was the very first race I had ever run. It was also the race I had run while seven months pregnant with Travis. It was the race I had first placed in my age group, full of pride at how far I had come. There was no question I was going to run the race.

It would only be the third time I had written Team Emmett in big, black marker on the back of my legs. The first time was while I was pacing the Fifth Third River Bank Run and the second time was during his actual surgery.

My mind flashed back to the Fifth Third River Bank Run that had taken place just a month before Emmett's first surgery. It had been early May and I was in a sea of runners, focused on the road ahead. Just a few more miles. I sighed. I was tired of it. *Why did I even agree to do this?* A small dainty looking redhead with a face full of freckles saddled up next to me. Her shirt was bright yellow, like the color of sunshine. She was running close on my left when I noticed her looking at me. I smiled and nodded my head, "Less than four to go – how are you doing?" I asked trying to force the friendliness out. I was pacing for the Fifth Third River Bank Run 25K race. That meant I was running the same exact speed mile after mile and encouraging and supporting those around me. I wasn't sure I was doing that great of a job. My time was exactly on pace, down to the second, but I wasn't feeling very chatty. I wasn't feeling like small talk or encouraging anyone. I had gone to a bad place in my head the last few miles and was now in a bad mood.

She was breathing a little harder than she should have been for the length of time we had to go still. "It's good. It's good so far!" she said, in between short jagged breaths. "I'm just glad I caught you guys finally!" I smiled again, this time more genuinely. She had been trying hard to catch up. She pointed to the back of my legs. "What's that for?" I stared at her for a minute. She was the very first person to ask. My head swam with questions. *What should I say? Was she just asking in polite curiosity or did she want to know the story? Crap. I should have rehearsed a concise little blurb or had some idea of what I wanted to say. What if I started crying? They would never let me pace again if I started freaking everyone out.* The silence stretched out and I thought for a few seconds. Team Emmett, in big bold, permanent marker on the back of my legs. *What's that for? What's that mean?* I took a deep breath in and exhaled my heart and soul with the words.

Over the last four years of Emmett's diagnosis, I have marked up my legs, my arms, my shirt, my race bib, and all sorts of other things with those two short words: Team Emmett. Two words that carry an immense amount of weight with them. *What's that for? What's that mean?*

It's for Emmett. It's so that one day, he will look back and hopefully see that I have tried in every way I could to be there for him. It was to show that even when I ran by myself, I always had him there. I carry him with me wherever I go.

It's because I want someone else to not feel so alone. There are other parents out there like me, and whether their child has the same diagnosis as Emmett or not doesn't matter. What matters is that one day; I'm going to come across some shell shocked parent navigating the murky waters of a new diagnosis. I want them to know they are not alone. I want them to know that it will be okay. I want to give them hope as a seasoned veteran in this life.

It's for all the other families out there that have fallen through the cracks like we have. It's for others that have been failed by the medical professionals numerous times. It's so no one else has to make their own diagnosis through a Google search. It's so people know what Craniosynostosis is and how to identify it. It's so that other people can hear about it and maybe one day see something a doctor may not.

It's for Travis, the unsung hero of our family. The one I worry will grow up not knowing how important he is too, because Emmett's medical needs continue to come first and conflict with other things. It's so that maybe he knows we are a team, all of us together. It's so that he can see we couldn't have gotten this far without each other.

It's for me. It's an outward expression of a fire that burns on the inside. It's the reason I can keep going. It's the boost when I feel like quitting. It's the hope that I can make a difference. It's more than just words, it's my life.

I've gotten good at giving a short, concise summary of what it's for by now. I can explain what it means and why I do it, but it still cannot unravel the depth of those words. When people ask "What's that for?" I say this: It's for my son Emmett. He had his entire skull broken apart and put back together when he was fifteen months old due to a birth defect of the skull called Craniosynostosis. I actually diagnosed him myself when he was fourteen months old because all the doctors missed it. Because of his late diagnosis, he had additional surgeries and other complications that probably wouldn't have happened if it had been caught it sooner. I write it to raise awareness of Craniosynostosis, to tell other people about it so they can recognize it, and in honor of my son, and his struggle. It helps remind me to keep going when it hurts because he keeps going when it hurts.

I smiled at the thought while walking to the start line of the Fourth of July race, remembering all the reasons why the words Team Emmett meant so much to me. I still felt a little weird about writing it on my legs though. I worried people would think I was just doing it for attention or to brag. Team Emmett wasn't really a thing and I wasn't sure about trying to make it a thing. I was second guessing myself over something so ridiculous when I saw a few of my friends who were running the race. A small group, all with Team Emmett on the back of their legs: Azsure, Andrew, Jacci, Pam, Scott, and even little Caitlyn. My love and appreciation for these wonderful friends soared. I was not alone out there. Not figuratively. Not literally. Not at all. They were there. Declaring to the world they were with me. Declaring to the world that they were on my team. On

Emmett's team. I had to look away to keep the tears from spilling over.

That was the first time I really felt like I was a part of something bigger. Not just because a few of my friends wrote the same thing on the back of their legs, but because maybe I could really make it something. I felt a passion surge up within me, with a need to change the world and have my voice heard. I had the ability and the will to really do something with this if I wanted to. It was about making a change. A change that came from our experiences, and maybe that change could make a difference for someone else.

Through numerous races over the years, I have kept up Team Emmett. I have found hope in this experience. It's the reason I run seven hours and twenty-six minutes on the anniversary of Emmett's surgery. It's the reason I write it on the back of my legs. It's the reason that in nearly everything I write I can work in the word Craniosynostosis. It's the reason for everything. I've told more people than I can even count about Emmett. I have hugged people mid run. I have seen people shed tears as they nodded with understanding and told me about their own child. I have heard people yell "Come on Team Emmett!" when I was slowly shuffling, teeth gritted, head down, and feeling like I couldn't go on. I have thought time and time again about what Emmett has had to endure and what Travis has had to endure. I have cried tears of empathy for both of them. I have felt sorrow at the struggle. I have found purpose in the pain. I have found the willingness to dig deep and keep running. I have done what I have done because it brings me hope, but I don't want that to be all. I want this hope to be bigger than me. I want others to see it too. I want others to feel that hope in their own lives.

I believe that there is someone out there in this world that I need to talk to. I can feel it. There has to be a purpose and a plan. I want to be part of that plan. It's possible I may never know. I may have fulfilled my purpose years ago without ever even realizing it but I have to keep going. I have to keep trying. As long as I feel this is the right thing to do, I will keep at it for myself and for that one person out there that is searching for hope.

Together, we are Team Emmett.

#Kathyfacts

I found purpose in running for Emmett. It was a way to redirect all of the things I wished I could do and change for him, into a separate area where I could do something. I could run. I run for Emmett because I have to do something. Being powerless isn't a comfortable place for me to be. By running, I am doing something I love for someone I love and spreading the word about something important to me.

1. Is there anything that you do that is not only for you, but someone else?

2. How does it make you feel to do something for someone else?

3. If you don't have something that you do in honor of someone or something bigger than you, do you think it makes a difference?

A great deal of drive and determination can be found when the focus is no longer on you but someone or something else. When there is a cause or a purpose, passion flows deeper and perseverance can be tapped into even when it gets tough. Look around for ways that you can do something for someone else. Find a way to attach a purpose and drive into an area of your life. When you do, it can renew your motivation and strength in this life. When you are doing something that is a part of a bigger picture, it can light you up if you let it.

Chapter 16

I've said it before. I don't believe in coincidences. I don't believe at all. I believe in signs. I believe in glimpses. I believe in a nod in the right direction. There have been too many instances of things that didn't make sense at the time that worked out through a series of events that almost never were. There have been too many impossible things that have been made possible. I believe these are more than coincidences.

~ I dreamt we would name our baby Emmett, before we even knew if he was a boy or girl. I choose his middle name because it meant God saves, because I thought God was saving him during that treacherous pregnancy. It turns out that middle name was prophetic. God saved Emmett time and time again.

~ I watched *Finding Nemo* with tears streaming down my face, running and exhausted, in the hospital while they broke apart Emmett's entire skull during his first surgery. Two years later, it would become Emmett's favorite movie with no prompting from us.

~ A Gavin Rossdale song would stop me in my tracks and cause me to scream out loud and then cry. The front man for my favorite band growing up, Bush, that I have followed for years and years, sang the words to a new song that were my words. "The only way out is through." Those were words that I had just written a few weeks prior in regards to Emmett's fourth surgery.

~The timing of Emmett. The way it had to work out that way. The other two babies that I wanted to save so badly that couldn't have coexisted if Emmett did. The timelines overlapped. It was fate, Emmett living.

~ Fellow Flowers. A running community and beloved company that celebrates all the reasons why women run. The picture and words they posted to my Facebook page during Emmett's first surgery rooted themselves in my heart. I couldn't forget it. How much time would pass by before I made the connection that the women in that picture were the same women who grew the company? Who would have believed the stars would perfectly align for some very busy business women raising families and doing life to be able to come to my neck of the woods? I was able to meet these women who spoke such life and encouragement to me years ago when I was running on that treadmill in the hospital. I met them face to face and ran side by side with them as I once again stuck to the treadmill for Emmett's third annual Endurance Event, where I ran seven hours and twenty-six minutes on a treadmill inside a running store.

~ The woman who overheard me crying in the party aisle at Target who just happened to have a son with a different, but equally devastating diagnosis. The way she held me tightly without a care of what the world around us thought. The way she whispered in my ear that it was going to be okay over and over.

The way she understood everything I couldn't bring myself to say and the way I felt the love pouring out of her soul and filling mine.

There have been so many signs that I am traveling down the right path. I can see that I am running in the right direction, even when it feels wrong at times. Sometimes it's so reassuring that I can sigh a breath of relief. I can smile even through tears knowing all along, but now actually feeling, I'm not doing this alone.

Just a few weeks after Emmett's first surgery, we were in a big grocery store to pick up a few things. I noticed an older couple behind us, just staring. Emmett's head was completely shaved, his entire face and forehead were so swollen his skin still looked shiny. The gnarly looking zigzag scar on his head was still a tender red with two angry looking spots next to his ears, where the drains were with faint lines of blood halfway down his neck. His eyes were no longer swollen shut, but they weren't fully open either. Light purple eyelids puffed out exaggeratedly above his eyes. We were no lie or exaggeration, show stoppers when we went out. People would stop and stare. People would look away embarrassed when I caught their eyes. People whispered. People gave us looks of sympathy and smiled sadly at us. A couple of rude teenagers even pointed and laughed. It was just the reality of the situation.

I had been minding my own business, pushing the cart with Emmett in it, when I noticed the couple pushing their cart in our direction. They had been staring wide eyed at us for a while, and now they seemed to be following me down the fluorescent lit aisle. I stopped, looking closer at the cheap flip flops on an end cap. I pretended to look the flip flops over while I noticed from the corner of my eye, the couple had stopped too. They were staring uncomfortably. I could feel them burning a hole through my back. I turned around and got a good look at the woman, maybe in her fifties. Something in her eyes was off, an overwhelming sadness reflected in them.

She started walking toward us with what I assumed was her husband following behind her, looking less sure. I smiled and she nodded towards Emmett and spoke up. "My daughter had the same exact scar. I've never seen anyone else with it before." I gave a twenty second spiel about Emmett's scar. She reached out her hand to touch Emmett's head and just held it there without saying a word.

Then she very gently placed her hand on the back of Emmett's head behind his scar. This random stranger was touching my baby, but something about her made me feel at ease. I was sad for her and her sad eyes. Her eyes were closed as she spoke the words quietly. "My daughter had a brain tumor. She died two days ago. She wasn't even thirty." The words hung in the air as we stood there together. That wasn't at all where I thought the conversation was going. I managed an "I'm so sorry," as we stood in the bright light, inches away from one another, while she seemed to expose her heart. It felt surreal. She looked down at her feet and now, I was the one staring. *Do I hug her? Should I hug her?* I felt the overwhelming urge to but I hesitated, unsure of what her reaction would be.

She looked back up at Emmett's head and seemed to study the scar when I noticed the tears running down her face. I gave what I hoped was a comforting smile. She mumbled something about keeping us in her prayers and quickly walked away. I stood there dumbfounded. All the things I could have said but maybe all the things I didn't need to say. She'd never seen anyone else with that scar. Of all the places we needed to be, of all the places she could have been, we would meet each other in front of the flip flops. I thought of her on and off for a long time. I regretted the fact that I didn't hug her. I wondered how she was; wishing I could have written down her name at least, and thinking of all the ways I might have done better in that situation. I didn't know if it was enough, but it was all I could manage. I have often wondered if she felt it was a mere coincidence or perhaps something much more divine. A small parting gift. A glimpse of hope.

Her daughter and my son, tied to one another for a brief moment through our love and heartache.

#Kathyfacts

I believe the right things happen at the right time for a reason. It seems like the universe is giving you a little gift by connecting the seemingly unconnected dots for you. It's in those times that I believe it's more than just a coincidence. I believe it is fate. God even.

1. Do you believe in fate? Or do you see things as a coincidence? Why?

2. Has there ever been something in your life that has seemed like more than just a coincidence? What was it?

3. Do you look for these signs in your life as evidence you are on the right path?

I believe if it wasn't where I was supposed to be, all of the pieces wouldn't be clicking into place. Sometimes that's a hard fact to accept because the pieces clicking into place aren't exactly the ones I would have chosen. Nonetheless, I accept them as my place in this life. I can see the good even in what I once thought was bad. When you take the time to look for the small signs around you, it can open up your eyes to all the amazing things that are happening.

Look around for a sign that you are in the right place and doing the right things in this life. Even in the everyday, small, commonplace events, you can see signs and nudges in the right direction if your eyes are open to them. Try to keep your eyes and mind open to what is around you.

Chapter 17

I was just fifteen years old when I remember clearly thinking I was going to die. I was flying through the air with reckless abandon. You know how in the movies when something terrible is about to happen they show everything in slow motion? That happens in real life too. Seconds turn into incredibly long minutes as a thousand thoughts run through your head. I was flying in slow motion as my hands desperately searched for something to hang onto, some sort of way to slow the momentum of my body. But it was no use. I stared ahead at what would inevitably kill me: the windshield of the car. A frenzy of thoughts assaulted me: *Will I go all the way through the windshield? Will my body hit that tree we are heading for? What does dying feel like? Will it hurt?* I hoped I wouldn't die slowly and painfully. I looked down and saw the face of the driver of the vehicle below me. I was a mere passenger in the car with no control whatsoever.

In that moment, I closed my eyes. I waited for it. I invited it in even. *Breathe in, breathe out. So long world. Surely dying had to be easier than these agonizing seconds of waiting to die.* The blackness surrounded me and I waited for the end, but it didn't come. I opened my eyes and saw nothing but a sheet of red. Blood pouring from my face so thick I couldn't see straight. My hands were stained red. My light purple pants were a deep red. Everything was tinted red. There was nothing else but pure red.

It's funny the things that come back to you while running. I was out slogging through a long run when I remembered that exact feeling of flying towards my impending death. The fear and pain were both palatable, causing my heart to start pounding and my breath to turn shallow. As the tears began to fall, I understood why my mind had returned this memory to my consciousness. Fifteen years later, as I watched Emmett suffer, I was once again flying through the air in slow motion, sure that the windshield of our life that ominously loomed ahead was going to kill me. There were a thousand questions going through my mind. None that could be answered. Things that only time would tell me. *Would Emmett survive? Would he ever be the same? Would Emmett die? Would it hurt him to die? Dear God, I hope he doesn't go slowly and painfully.*

I closed my eyes once again. I waited for it. I invited it in even. I couldn't live like this. I opened my eyes to nothingness, a dull empty world that matched my dull, empty heart. Emmett's MRI was still on the kitchen counter when I got home. The crisp white paper mocked me. Something so innocuous looking that could shatter my entire life. I thought we were just going to fix his skull with this one surgery. The MRI was routine pre-operative testing; they weren't supposed to find anything wrong with his brain. *Where did that even come from? Why couldn't they just fix it and tell me it would all be okay?*

The doctors had found a malformation and lesion in Emmett's brain. A great tangle of veins that weren't supposed to be there. There was evidence of a previous bleed. A large, important vein intertwined with it making removal nearly impossible, or at the least, very, very risky. There were theories of the first seizure corresponding with the bleed in his brain. There was a doctor who said it was really nothing to be worried about. There was another that talked about how dangerous these things lurking can be. We asked for too many opinions until we were overwhelmed and confused about who and what to believe. We finally decided to stick with a doctor that we trusted. He told us there was nothing we could do about it. Nothing at all. We could wait and see. Hope and pray that it doesn't bleed again. Believe that it will be okay. Dismiss the thoughts of irreversible damage, paralysis, and death from our minds. Focus on the now. The present. The gift of today.

I pictured it in my mind. An evil, sinister looking mess that had invaded my baby's brain. It wanted to live and thrive, even if that meant killing him. The air left my lungs. *If I put him down for a nap, would he wake up?* I could feel the walls closing in on me. *How was I ever going to be free of this fear? Would I ever be able to let my guard down because I didn't know what could happen, without warning, forever changing our lives?* At first I was only angry. Angry at God. Angry at myself for not catching this sooner. Angry at the rest of the world that didn't understand. Even angry at other parents with healthy children. I hated everything. I wanted to rip that MRI to shreds, burn the pieces, and then bury the smoking ash six feet underground, but it still wouldn't be enough. There had to be some sort of mistake. There had to be something else they could do. My entire world changed with one piece of paper, why couldn't they change it again?

Once more, I screamed for a God that seemed oblivious to my family's pain and suffering. *Just how much did He think we could handle? Why was this happening? Why was He allowing another life threatening diagnosis for Emmett?* I remember crying out, "Dear God, we've suffered enough. Please no more. Please not this too." Yet I was met with a maddening silence. A silence that roared in my ears and shattered my heart into a thousand pieces. I could see nothing other than the fact that God had abandoned us there. He had left us to flounder in water with no dry land in sight. He left us there to drown. We were all alone, on our own, and we were going to drown there.

Two days later, that wretched piece of paper still sat on the kitchen counter. I refused to touch it. I refused to move it. I refused to add it to Emmett's medical binder. I refused to acknowledge that it was now a part of his medical history. For days, I looked at it with disgust. It made me antsy and anxious. I paced up and down the hallway of my house as the walls closed in on me. I couldn't breathe. There wasn't enough air. I could feel hysteria rising. I had to get out of the house. I had to go for a run. I took off down the road. *How could the sun be shining?* I wanted it to rain. I wanted the skies to cry out for my son. I wanted to see black clouds and thunder and lightning. I wanted the wind to blow away everything I felt. I wanted the sky to reflect that my world was collapsing. I wanted acknowledgement that I was flying towards a windshield again, towards impending death. Still, the sun shone brightly, mocking me with its warmth. I felt only cold.

I ran and I ran. I lost track of time, my phone silenced and stuffed in the back of my running pack. Up and down the same trail I went over and over, willing myself to keep going and willing myself to wake up from that nightmare. If I could just come out the other side of the trail somewhere different, it would all be okay. If I could just alter the world a little bit, swing things a tad to the left or right, then I would feel better. I focused on what I knew, forced away the impending feelings of dread, and ran harder. There I was, a desperate woman sweating, gritting her teeth, covered in trail dust, and hitting the ground with each step so hard it was almost like stomping. Each footfall reverberated back up my leg with a painful force. I was glad. I wanted it to hurt. I wanted to take away the pain in my soul and replace it with physical pain. Physical pain I could deal with. I wanted a distraction.

I don't remember exactly when I came out of my fog. It was the sudden realization that the sun had gone down and darkness was setting in that brought me back to the present. I had been gone for over five hours stomping up and down the trail in desperation. Once I realized it, my mind caught up with me and I was suddenly ravenous and too tired to continue to run. I walked back to our house, each step slightly more painful than the previous. I was hungry, exhausted, and sore, but I was not defeated.

Out on the trail, I caught a glimpse. A small piece of that sunlight, which had mocked me with its warmth, broke through the trees above and slipped into my dark and angry heart.

It was a tiny sliver of hope.

#Kathyfacts

So many times, I have been too angry to seek peace. I have not wanted peace. I have wanted my self-righteous anger. Everything inside of me had been erased. There were only two emotions left; rage and numbness. There was no in between. I couldn't see how these two opposites were linked. The anger kept me from feeling anything else. For so long, I refused the hurt and pain because I was scared of it. It delayed everything: grief, pain, healing, acceptance, and eventually moving forward.

1. Is there something you are afraid of feeling? A pain so deep you'd rather stay angry about it because if you feel that hurt, you're afraid it'll never stop?

2. How could you confront the anger and pain? Could you talk to a pastor, therapist, mentor, or trusted friend? Could journaling help you push past the anger to what's below?

Find just one thing you are still angry about and start digging around for the emotions and feelings underneath that. It's easy to get sidetracked with blame and anger. You must remain open if you want to dig past that anger. Allow yourself to feel what is under the anger, the hurt, disappointment, or maybe bitterness. Feel whatever is there with no judgment of yourself. Confront the things that you've been afraid to before. Turn around to face what you've been running from. If you are ready to let go, you must make a choice to let go of the anger. That choice may need to be made a thousand times a day at first. Keep choosing to let go of the anger until it becomes easier and easier by the day. See how it transforms you.

Chapter 18

Ever since I was a kid, I knew what I wanted to do when I grew up. I wanted to write. That didn't really mean anything way back then. Lots of people wanted to be lots of things, and even as a child, I was a realist. I had my feet firmly planted on the ground. Just because I wanted to be a writer, it didn't mean I was any good at it. It certainly didn't mean anyone would want to read what I wrote just because I wrote it. In elementary school, I wrote poems and little stories that every English teacher I had complimented me on. It was never about me though. I didn't want to talk about me. I wanted to make up stories where I could control the characters and their lives. I wanted to be able to put down where I wanted their lives to go and how things should be. I started keeping diaries and filling them with stories of me leading alternate lives. Things that could have happened or should have happened. I wrote about all kinds of things except for myself.

By the time I got to high school, I could easily crank out page after page of words about nearly anything. It really wasn't work. I liked it. Of course, it wasn't cool to like homework, so I kept this secretly thrilling homework to myself, but I was always penciling something down in a notebook.

When I was in community college, I took a writing class. I had ALWAYS wanted to take a writing class. It was what the lead character did in the movies. Great things happened because of writing classes, or so popular culture had led me to believe. The whole class was essays and stories. It was the just the best thing ever. I had never enjoyed anything school related so much. I was nineteen years old, working part-time at Target, living in someone's basement with no money to call my own, no plan, and no real direction for my life. That class sparked a direction that I had long wanted to travel in but was never brave enough to attempt.

The professor was a friendly, middle-aged woman, with glasses. She carried a multi-colored bohemian bag, or what I would call a "hippie bag" today, because my free spirited friend Pam carries nearly the same exact bag. The professor was excitable and passionate about words. She was enthralled with what one could do with them, what sort of pictures one could paint with them, and how one could make an entire world out of words. I submitted many stories to her about movies and books that I thought were amazing. There were different writing assignments to describe a room to her well enough so that she could picture it and other things like that. The final essay was a big one. She wanted some large amount of pages written about an experience that changed our life in some way. It didn't matter if it was big or small, happy or sad; she just wanted us to write about a change. I racked my brain for an easier one, for something else I could write about with conviction but I kept coming back to the same day each time. There was no other way around it.

I decided to do something brave and something out of character. I wrote about myself. I filled pages about the short yet impossibly long seconds that passed when I was a passenger in an out of control car, flying through the air towards the windshield that I believed would kill me. In the seconds from the driver losing control of the car to my impact with the windshield, I lived a lifetime. In those short, ominous seconds, I aged terribly at the possibility of my own death.

It was the most personal thing I had ever written, more so than any journal entry or scribbling in any of my notebooks. I was terrified when I handed it in. I dropped it on her desk and scurried out of there as fast as I could. Three days later, I got it back covered in red marker. Things were circled, underlined, and there were notes in the margins all over the place. My heart pounded rapidly and I was unsure of what I was about to find. On the last page, there was a single line. A few words scrawled in her fancy but still sloppy handwriting. "This was beautiful Kathy. Please keep writing." My heart soared. As I inspected it further, I saw that all of her red markings were not mistakes or things she wished me to change. She had underlined and circled phrases and parts that she found particularly poignant and added her thoughts in the margin. It was the first time I thought maybe I really could write.

A few years later, I started a blog under a pretend name shortly after I had lost the first baby. I was struggling and I had a lot of thoughts that just had to get out. It was just for me. I had no followers and no readers and that's how I wanted it to be. I wrote and wrote on my quiet little blog. I would re-read it a day or two later and then delete it all. It was too much. It was too personal. It was too dark. It was too everything. I was afraid. I was not only afraid of having people find out about the real me. I was afraid it would impact people's opinion of me. Some of the words I had written right after I lost the first baby were the darkest, deepest, most poetic words I have ever put on paper. I vaguely remember pieces of it, but I still regret I never saved any of it. I deleted it all and tried to white wash over that entire painful part of my life. I had decided I didn't really want to write after all and for many years, I didn't. I packed away my biggest dream. I tried to forget about what I wanted and suppressed the fear of either achieving or failing at it. I thought if I decided to do nothing with it that it would just all go away. I gave up on it. I put my head down and started moving through the life I thought I was supposed to. I kept busy with an office job, raising our oldest son, and taking care of our home.

Two years later, fate seemed to intervene. It was December, Christmas time, and we had been having a very rough year. Just six months had passed since Emmett had been diagnosed with Craniosynostosis. It was only five months since his first major skull surgery. We'd already been through a second surgery for his ear canals and were awaiting a third surgery for his tonsils and adenoids, in the hopes that it would help with his sleep apnea. Hearing your child stop breathing while they are sleeping is a terrifying sound. The surgery was set for mid-January and we'd recently found out about the brain lesion. We were in a bad place: Tony and I. God and I. Me personally. Christmas was coming and I hated it. I didn't want to be happy. I didn't want to pretend anymore. I didn't want to keep up the part I played so well. I was flipping through our little hometown newspaper when I saw something that spoke to me. "Writers wanted!" it proclaimed. Underneath were a few vague details about wanting stories or poems about Christmas, fiction or non-fiction, for a special upcoming section. I wasn't sure what came over me, but I thought about it for just a second until common sense washed over me and I rightfully dismissed it.

I live in a very small town. It's a "go the gas station and see ten people you went to school with," kind of town, where everybody almost literally knows everybody. There was no way I was going to put something I wrote out there where people I went to school with, old neighbors, teachers, and everyone I've ever encountered since I was a child could read it. I threw the paper in the trash and went about my business. Try as I might to forget about it, I couldn't. A couple of hours later, I was digging it out of the trash. I wrote down the provided email for submission. I really wasn't going to do it I assured myself, but it was just in case. It couldn't hurt to have the information.

The next day I couldn't help myself. I got out my laptop and opened a Word document. The cursor blinked back at me rhythmically. Daring me. Taunting me. *Blink. Blink. Blink...Write. Write. Write.* So I did. I wrote about how I was tired of fake holiday cheer. I wrote about how angry I was at a God that I felt had abandoned me. I wrote and wrote and every time I re-read it, I changed something. Over and over, I nitpicked at it without telling a soul. Over and over, I was sure it was awful and I kept trying to make it better. Finally, on the very last day they were accepting submissions, I attached the document to an email anonymously. I asked that, if chosen, my name would not be printed alongside the article. I was too unsure of myself. Besides, it wasn't really that good anyhow. No one was going to want to publish a silly little article I wrote.

A week later, I got an email from the editor, confirming I wished to remain anonymous, because apparently that's an unusual request. I confirmed with a rock of dread in my stomach. I panicked. Waves of self-doubt rushed over me and buried me in its unforgiving waters. *What did I do? Everyone was going to know it was me, even though my name wasn't on it. People would see what a terrible writer I was. People could laugh at me. People could judge my misfortune; tell me to get over it, or to stop complaining.* I wanted to take it back. I wanted to email the editor and tell her I changed my mind, but I couldn't think of a good enough reason to do so. How flaky and odd I would seem if I asked for my article back! Besides, I had read the terms and conditions, all work submitted became their property.

I waited anxiously for the newspaper. I dreaded it like a kid with a secret waiting for their parents to discover it. I felt sick over it. When I finally got the special Christmas edition, there it was on the front page! I held it in my hands, careful not to wrinkle it, as tears streamed down my face. "A Sliver of Hope," by Anonymous. More tears fell. This was big, I could feel it. I was proud and embarrassed. I was happy and ashamed. I didn't really understand it then. I was just so good at pretending. This would change that. This was the truth. I didn't want anyone to know the truth about me. I let it go unnoticed, told only one person to read the newspaper that week to see if they'd recognize anything.

That article burrowed itself into my mind and whispered for more. It picked away at me slowly. "More!" it cried, over and over relentlessly, until I couldn't ignore it any longer. I started writing again, not for anyone else but for me. As I put the truth down on paper or poured it out onto a blank screen in front of me, my burden began to lift. Telling the truth made me feel better.

It would still be another year and a half after that until I started telling the truth on a regular basis. It took some time, but ever so slowly, I tested the waters with an article here and a long Facebook post there. No one seemed to think less of me for it. No one accused me of being a failure even though I felt like one just admitting those things. No one judged me. Well…not very many judged me. People listened. People responded. People thought I was brave when I was sure I was such a coward. People said they were proud of me. *How could I be proud of who I was when I was admitting I have thrown temper tantrums that would put a two year old to shame?* I was sure I couldn't, but others disagreed. Just a little bit of encouragement stoked the flame. It began to burn brighter and stronger. I couldn't stop. I had more to say. I had so much more to say. I was never done. As soon as I was finished with one thought, there was another in waiting. It was just below the surface. Sometimes I would have to spontaneously stop everything I was doing to write an idea down on the back of a receipt or put a note in my phone. The dam had broken and the words were rushing out in waves. I didn't know why, but I felt more like myself than I had ever before in my life. I felt like I was doing what I was supposed to be doing. Like I had finally figured it out.

I began blogging regularly. I put my articles and stories and bits of truth in magazines, newspapers, and on other sites. I got picked up by *The Huffington Post* and became an official blogger for them. I worked on this book, the most self-indulgent thing I thought I had ever done. I worried every step of the way. *Who is going to read this? I haven't lived long enough for a memoir. Do I sound whiny and self-centered in all of this? Who is going to find any of these stories interesting enough to read? What if everyone hates it?* I was scared. I dragged my feet for years, afraid to share so much of my life all at once. It felt narcissistic, which was ridiculous. Why would it be narcissistic to believe in myself or to believe I had potential? Why should I care what others have to say about my words? They are mine, not theirs. If you read this and hate it, that's okay. If you read this and love it, that's okay too. I had to decide not to attach my personal feelings of success to anyone else but me. Do negative comments and bad reviews sting? Sure, sometimes they do. Do positive comments and words of encouragement make me smile and feel good? Of course. But with or without anyone else's perceptions of me, I choose to define success on my own terms. If you are holding this book in your hands, I have succeeded.

Because one day, I decided it was time. It was time to leap. It was time to be brave once and for all. It was time to jump. I jumped headfirst into these pages.

And there would be no going back.

#Kathyfacts

There is a dream, a passion, or a plan in all of us. We all have something we want to do in this life, however big, scary, or unattainable it may seem. The problem is we can let our inner critic talk us out of it before we've even started. I spent too much time refusing and unable to write, for fear of what others would think of me and my work. I tried to bury that passion for words under piles of life, but that fire never went out. It burned bright even while buried.

1. Is there something you feel passionately or strongly about that you haven't done yet?

2. Are you working towards a dream or a lifetime pursuit? Why or why not?

3. Do you think you let fear of failure stop you?

Give yourself a pep talk today. Build yourself up. You will start to believe what you tell yourself regularly. If you've been constantly telling yourself it's too hard, you can't do it, or that you're not good enough; you'll start to believe that. Start telling yourself the opposite. It seems silly at first and may even feel a bit narcissistic but give it a try. Start your day off by saying one positive thing about yourself. Compliment yourself for remaining calm in a stressful situation, for the way you followed through on a tough project, or even the way you look in your new jeans. Start complimenting yourself regularly. Remind yourself you can do the hard things. You can put in the work and go after big dreams. Keep telling yourself that you are brave and capable and can do anything you set your mind to. Then, go ahead and do it.

Chapter 19

On June 20, 2013, exactly one year after Emmett's first surgery, I decided to take to my treadmill once again. I wasn't sure if I was coming unhinged to make that decision or not. All I knew was, as the date approached, I felt all of the things I had felt that previous year compounded and coming at me like an out of control truck. I knew I had to do something.

Because we were overwhelmed with love and support the prior year, I wanted to pay that forward somehow. I decided to collect prayer requests from friends, family, followers on Facebook, and random strangers. I decided that for every hour I ran, I would dedicate it to a small group of people involved in the prayer requests, and I would spend the entire hour praying for them. The next hour, I'd move on to another group of people. It was a small effort and a sentimental gesture, but I was proud of it. I felt strongly about it and knew it was the way it should go. There were parents who had just lost their baby, children in need of surgery, a terminally ill family member, marriages on the verge of divorce, and more. I was honored to be a part of these people's lives, if only briefly.

Every hour, Tony was to give an update and take a picture to document my progress on Facebook. This was as much for me as it was for the general public. If you tell people you are going to do something like this, they first want to know why, and then they want to know if you are actually doing it and not just saying it. We documented it to share with the world and for future safekeeping.

The kids were home and Tony was upstairs with them. Of course, they wanted to be downstairs by Mom. Tony put up the baby gate all the way around my treadmill to keep the kids away so they wouldn't get hurt but could still be downstairs and play. It was like running in a cage, tied to a treadmill, but I was ready and willing.

Hour 1: The beginning of a long run is usually pretty uneventful. It went off without a hitch. It was still early and I was feeling strong. I patted myself on the back for the journey I was about to endure. I was proud of my decision to do this and to continue raising awareness for Craniosynostosis.

Hour 2: This was a bit more exciting. Just a few minutes into hour two, my treadmill abruptly flashed "lube belt" and came to a grinding halt without any warning. I crashed into the front bar and took a handle to the side pretty hard. Instant panic welled up in me. *I had to do this today. It was too important. I had to do it today.* I yelled for Tony and he came downstairs to take a look at it. He quickly greased the belt for me and turned it back on. All seemed well and I had only lost a few minutes. I jumped back on and restarted cautiously and slowly so as to not crash back into the bar if it locked back up on me. After a good ten minutes, it still showed no signs of shutting back off, so I ran on and got back in the zone. Because of my obsessive tendencies, I was keeping track of my hourly progress on paper as well, even though it was right in front of me on the treadmill, so I never lost any time or mileage totals.

Hour 3: I started to get into my own head. We had a laptop sitting on the bookshelf opened to a page on the internet with a large stopwatch on it. I kept looking at it. It seemed to be barely moving and it was very disheartening to see only a few minutes had passed each time I found myself checking it. Tony moved the laptop to the other side of me and faced it away so I couldn't see anymore.

Hour 4: The entire hour went by quickly and my spirits were high. I was happy and felt like I was practically bouncing with each step I took. I was in pure joy mode as I ran.

Hour 5: This hour put me back in my place. I had officially run a marathon at this point and still had plenty left to go. I turned my thoughts inward, thinking about all the reasons I was there and doing this; all of the people who had helped me along the way that I wanted to help however I could.

Hour 6: I had yet another huge resurgence of energy, the ever sought after second wind. I found myself pushing the up arrow to increase my speed and singing loudly and off key. Young the Giant popped up on my playlist and I sang along to the song "My Body," until it got hard to sing, scream, breathe, and run all at the same time. Over and over, I sang "My body tells me no, but I won't quit cause I want more, cause I want mooooooore," with all of the windows open. I'm not really sure what the neighbors must have thought, but I continued onward.

Hour 7: The last hour is always a reality check. I shouldn't have sped up the previous hour when I was feeling good because now I was hurting and really wanted to stop. I was ever famously gritting my teeth, which I do so often and every running coach will tell you not to. I kept going, knowing I only had a few more minutes to go. Just twenty-six minutes. When I hit seven hours and twenty-six minutes, I had run just over thirty-eight miles. I was ecstatic with my pace and distance but felt like I wasn't done yet. I was so very close to forty miles. I decided not to stop. I decided to dedicate the final two miles to two-year-old Emmett. I prayed, gasped, and ran.

Finally, gloriously, I was done. I breathed a sigh of relief and started crying. It's my go to response when I run long, and especially when I run for a reason. These days, every run has a reason, so I am always crying. I ran forty miles in seven hours and fifty-two minutes. I stood bent over on the treadmill, trying to catch my breath and calm myself down when Travis and Emmett both jumped on my treadmill with me.

I looked to my left and saw the flight of stairs I had to climb up to get back upstairs and sighed. This run was all about hoping and praying, and now I hoped and prayed I could get back up the stairs. But more importantly, I prayed that this passion I felt surging up inside of me would stay.

I felt alive and like I was making a difference and I hoped that would never stop.

#Kathyfacts

People talk a lot about paying it forward and doing something for others. It can be easy to get discouraged and believe we are only one person. It's easy to see all of the needs in this world and realize you can't make a dent in all of them. I'm a big believer in small acts of kindness. People have overwhelmed us with both small and large acts of kindness. We have been on the receiving end of things which we can never repay.

1. What is one time in your life someone stepped up to do something for you?

2. Have you ever paid in forward? In a big or small way? How so?

3. Do you think even a small act can have a big impact? Why or why not?

We can talk ourselves into being sure we don't have anything to offer others that are hurting. The truth is, when we do things for others, we benefit as well. I believe one of the greatest things you can do for your self-esteem is to start helping others. To stop focusing on you and start focusing on others can be an instant boost of confidence and meaning in your life.

Perform a small act of kindness. Buy the person coffee in line behind you, drop off flowers for a friend, bake cookies, or anything you want. When you do something to make someone else happy, it will make you feel happy too.

Chapter 20

When I think back to the most difficult circumstances I've ever found myself in, I can see a pattern. Of course, this pattern always comes in hindsight; I'm never smart enough to figure it out as it is happening. It was when there was nothing happening that I was the most helpless. No answers, no progress, no plan, no direction, nothing. It was stagnant and stale, which was harder for me than actually facing something scary. It was hard to face a surgery, hard to face test after test, more medications, another surgery and more, but at least we weren't standing still. Standing still was so much more excruciating to me than movement, even if that movement wasn't in the direction I wanted it to be.

After Emmett's first surgery, things didn't improve. Emmett was still in so much pain. He'd hold his head and cry. He'd abruptly drop to the floor, losing the ability to stand, and roll around screaming hysterically in anger, frustration, fear, or pain – we didn't really know back then. Emmett couldn't speak then and we were simply guessing. All we knew was that he physically couldn't stand back up during these times. Sometimes he would try to pull himself up to his knees but every single time it resulted in him falling back flat on his face. So mostly, he'd just roll around on the floor and scream.

The doctor dubbed these "episodes." He didn't know what these episodes were or what they meant but urged us to start recording them on our phone and keep track of them in a notebook. Frequency, length of time, what was happening before that, and what happened after. We started tracking them. Sometimes it would happen fifteen times in one day. Other times just once a day or every other day. Sometimes it would last twenty minutes. Other times it would last five minutes. Sometimes it was first thing in the morning. Other times it was all through the night. There were no patterns that we could find. Emmett stopped sleeping, for real. He would scream frantically for hours all through the night. I was lost. I would hold him tightly in my arms and cry right along with him. I'd beg for relief. *Dear God make it stop. Please. Whatever it is, make it stop. I can't watch him suffer any longer. While you're at it, make the crying stop too. I'm so tired. I'm just so tired. Please make it stop. Please.* It didn't matter what I begged for. Emmett would just keep crying in pain and everybody's pain intensified with his.

We had more tests done. EEG's, EKG's, CT's, MRI's, X-rays, blood work, sleep studies, and more. No one could figure it out. We were so helpless in watching him suffer. It made me feel small and useless to watch him so desperately need something but not have a clue as to what that something could be. Every cry and scream tortured me. *Did his head hurt? Was it because of the lesion? Oh no, did it bleed again? Was he about to die?* We just had no clue about any of it. There were nothing but long exhaustive days followed by long exhaustive nights.

One morning, I was getting ready to go grocery shopping with Emmett while Travis was in preschool. I was in the kitchen gathering up my purse, coat, and Emmett's shoes when I heard the telltale *thunk*. Emmett had dropped to the floor. I grabbed my phone and went to the living room. I'd grown accustomed to it. We'd been recording the episodes for a while now, amassing hours of footage of the same exact thing. We had to do it with seizures too: watch him through the screen of my phone while I recorded everything. Emmett grew more and more hysterical as time went on. I wanted to scoop him up in my arms and hug him but still I knew not to touch him. When anyone would attempt to even lay a finger on Emmett during an episode, he would recoil, try to crawl away in a panic, and continue to scream even more intensely. It made no sense to his doctor, but we were advised to let him be. If touching him made it worse and didn't comfort him, then we didn't want to do it. It broke my heart into a thousand pieces to see him in such pain all alone. I wanted to do something, anything, but was utterly powerless.

When my video hit the twenty-three minute mark, I hit stop. Emmett was on the floor sobbing and screaming. I lay down next to him and stared into his frightened face. He was just as helpless as I was. I cried with him, face down on the floor. The two of us lost together in a confusing world of pain and anguish. The air devoid of hope. It went on for over forty minutes. I had called Tony and was considering bringing Emmett into the emergency room because it had never gone on that long before and I thought maybe it was his brain, when it stopped. I scooped him up in my arms and sobbed, rocking my baby boy back and forth while he lay limply in my arms, all tired out from the huge episode.

It was close to eight months of this agony. We asked every single one of our specialists. I asked support groups. I researched obsessively once again, sure that if I had found an answer before, maybe I could find one again. We put Emmett through more testing, compounding his suffering, but we were desperate for an answer.

Standing still was so much harder than moving anywhere. I've often thought the same of running, although it seems counterintuitive. For me, it was always easier to run away. I would run down the road and attempt to outrun the baggage that threatened to bring me to a standstill. That was always the gauge. The way I knew something was really, truly wrong was when I just didn't want to run at all. Standing still was so much harder for me. When I couldn't run, I couldn't escape my own head. I was really good at running away and escaping until I wasn't.

In the midst of Emmett's ongoing suffering, I was out running one of my favorite trails. It had been long run day and I was tired. I was minding my own business, opening up a super crinkly energy packet to sustain me and my stomach for the duration of my run when I heard it. There was something moving through the brush. It sounded like something big, moving very quickly. I looked to the left and then to the right and saw nothing. Every single episode I had ever watched of *Law and Order* flashed through my mind. I was about to become a statistic. I held up my mace in one hand and opened my feet to take a defensive stance and brace myself for an impending attack.

Later, I mulled over the situation and was surprised. I had always thought I would be a flight kind of person when faced with a fight-or-flight situation. It made sense, I was a runner. While I was not particularly fast, a good boost of adrenaline could really help put some pep in my step and I most likely could outlast and outrun a pursuer on foot. None the less, there I had stood; preparing to fight whatever was coming straight for me from the thick trees. That's when I noticed them. First one, then another, and another. Deer had jumped out from the safety of the trees and crossed right in front of me, onto the trail and then back into the shelter of the forest. I stood back and watched them in fascination and relief. My heart was pounding wildly and my legs were like Jell-O, but I was relieved. They had almost run right into me. They didn't even seem to notice me, the trail I was on, or the way our paths intersected. They just kept their heads high and ran with wild abandon on their own trail, cutting through the woods. A shortcut.

Help for Emmett came in the form of a wonderful ear, nose, and throat doctor. We were finally able to put a name to these episodes. Migraine Associated Vertigo. It can be a debilitating disorder, as we had already seen. The vertigo can be so severe; it can drop a person to the floor and keep them from being able to regain their balance. The migraine brings with it pain and throbbing in a head that's already extra sensitive and leaves the sufferer feeling sick and nauseous. In some cases, it can be accompanied by hallucinations or disturbances in sight and sound. It all made sense. The drop to the ground. The inability to stand. The screaming and crying. The pain. The fear. It was all connected.

We began treatment, increased medication, and developed a plan of action for what to do the next time it happened. With these measures in place, things changed. We were able to understand what was happening and how to help him.

How I had wished for a shortcut so many times. So many times with Emmett's diagnosis, I could clearly see what I wanted off in the distance. I could see where I wanted to go, but it was so far away. I could steadily run towards it, sometimes sprint with all my might, but still it remained off in the distance. The further I ran, the further away it got. It was a mirage. It wasn't really there. That's because I was never going to get to that point. I didn't understand at first. I was on the wrong path. My path would never meet up with that place far off in the distance. The best bet I had was to start cutting through the woods like a wild animal, making my own path and looking for a new destination.

When I stopped mourning what could or should have been, it was easier to see the separation of these paths and this new place. I had been wishing away the battles Emmett was facing. I had been trying to imagine a life without these fears and struggles, desperate to go back to when we were happy and carefree. But there was no going back. I had to do something. I had to decide it was time. I couldn't just stand still any longer. So I started down the path of acceptance. I wasn't just standing dead still in my tracks. I was moving again, towards an unknown destination, and it was different. It was more different than I ever could have imagined, but it was better this way. It was easier to accept something rather than nothing. Whatever it took, that was the new plan.

Watching Emmett suffer was like being lost in the woods during a long race, which I have also experienced. It was scary cutting through the nothingness, being smacked in the face with branch after branch, my legs cut and bleeding from the brush, and the going was slow. It was so slow, at times I wasn't even sure I was moving, but still I went. I ran off into the distance, towards what I didn't understand, towards what I didn't plan on, and towards life again. There was only ever one way it was all going to go. It didn't matter if I dug my heels in. It didn't matter if I wanted to live in denial. It didn't matter that I didn't want it to be happening. I had to get on board or get left behind. That was the way.

A few brave steps here and there and I was moving once again towards hope.

#Kathyfacts

I think it's the hardest to not know. When we know what we are up against, we can at least attempt to either face it or run from it. The same is not true when there is nothing to face, when the answers run dry, and all progress comes to a screeching halt. You are left with little choice because there is no "it" to face or run from. For me, that is a leading cause of hopelessness and despair.

1. Have you ever found yourself stuck in a situation without all of the facts?

2. How did you move forward without knowing what may lay ahead of you?

3. Have you ever known so clearly where you wanted to go but couldn't get there?

I think that we tend to look for the easy way out a lot of times. It's human nature. If something seems too hard, maybe there is a better way to achieve it and a way around all the hard stuff. In hindsight, I can see the progress that is made in the journey. If there was a shortcut through all of the messy middle, the journey wouldn't matter as much. It wouldn't be the same.

Look at one difficult situation in your life where you became stuck and didn't know what to do next. Examine what came next. Even without knowing what to do, you did something. Even without all the answers, you kept getting up day after day and trying. Look for the progress you've made with even small steps. Acknowledge your hard work and give yourself some credit for trying even when it was hard. Keep trying.

Chapter 21

There is an invisible line that can separate parents of sick children from parents of healthy children, further adding to the isolation that we can often feel. As a parent of a sick child and speaking for others like me, we are the parents drowning in medical jargon and fading into the hallways of the hospital. We are permanent fixtures in the specialist's offices. We are buried under mountains of insurance paperwork and being suffocated by red tape. On this side of the line, there are no "normal" problems. Here problems are organized, compartmentalized, and placed into a hierarchy of importance. Most often at the top of this hierarchy, our suffering child. Parents on the opposite side of the line are there by no fault of their own, just as we are not here by any fault of our own. No one side is better or worse than the other, just different.

Sometimes those differences are so stark that it's hard to relate to one another. It's hard to not feel a twang of jealousy at how easy we believe someone else's life to be. I've known people who want to pit these parents against one another. People who want to compare everything they can, to always win the competition for whose life is harder. It's not a competition though. We may not live the same lives or suffer the same way, but everyone suffers. A competitive spirit derived by making light of others' problems is not an attitude I want to have. Now that's extremely easy to say, but sometimes very hard to do.

There are some parents who make it even harder. You know who I mean. The dramatic ones, the over-exaggerators, the "it's all about me," ones. The ones who make you feel like you don't really exist in a room or sometimes even in this world, except to listen to them. Picture this:

I have been pinning down two-year-old Emmett on the floor for the last fifteen minutes, trying to get him to swallow his seizure medication as he kicks and thrashes, vehemently protesting. Prior to this, I had another ten minutes invested in trying to get him to take it any other way but the hard way. He's screaming, crying, red faced, and full of hysterics, gasping deeply and loudly for breaths of air. I see my chance and quickly shove the syringe full of medicine down his throat. He's gagging but then stops. I breathe a sigh of relief with my success. *Thank God that's finally over.* Before I'm even finished patting myself on the back, Emmett proceeds to throw it all back up, all over him, me, and the floor. I look down at my soiled shirt. *I'll have to take a shower, give him a bath, wash all these clothes, get out the carpet cleaner to clean up the floor, and then I'll have to start again with the medicine.*

He's still crying, rolling around on the floor in a fit of panic at having thrown up. I have collapsed onto the floor beside him. My frustrated, angry tears spill down my face as I lie next to him and plead for this to get easier, at least once.

This battle with his medication has been constant and ongoing for months. Ever since he was diagnosed with Epilepsy, twice a day, we do this with his medication. Sometimes he throws it back up and more often than not, we both end up crying afterwards. I am begging for relief from this, for both of us, and looking for a distraction. I grab my phone out of my back pocket and scroll mindlessly for anything to take my mind off of the current situation.

That's when I see that little Johnny has come down with a cold, and it's apparently the worst cold the world has ever seen. His parents don't know how they will get through this terrible trial. It's like a slap in the face. It's everything I have wished our life could be and everything I feel immediately guilty for wishing because my child is amazing, wonderful, and the best thing that's ever happened to me. I just want it to be easier. I just want the pain and suffering to stop. How I desperately wished Emmett could just go play with cars and blocks like other kids his age. I so desperately wanted to take it all away for him and to make his life easier. I wished it were just a cold with an end in sight and not this ongoing battle that will plague him for the rest of his life. It's so easy to wish we could trade places so that others would understand or so that we could have a break. It's easy to wish for that easy life and then be washed away by the guilt that rains down on you.

It's a real thing. The "us versus them" parents. I don't believe in people who feel the need to tear down others to make themselves feel better. I distance myself from that type of person. I don't want to make comparisons, I don't want to be compared, and I certainly don't have any desire to play the "whose circumstances are worse?" game. Parenting can be such an isolating job, even in the best of circumstances. Throw in some circumstances that very few around you can understand and you may as well be stranded on a desert island. You are a voice that no one hears.

When Emmett was first diagnosed, I had a few people who I thought were my friends. Those people just kind of slowly faded away, backing farther and farther away from our family. There were no words spoken. They just disappeared from our lives for good. There were also people who came out of the woodwork; people I didn't really know that well who were suddenly my biggest supporters. Other mothers of children with special needs rallied around me. Yet, I couldn't help looking back to the other side of the line, where all the other moms were. That was the side of the line I had been on for so many years, blissfully ignorant of things on this side.

It didn't take long to notice them. Some family and a few close friends who were left, attempting to leap over that line. Getting a running start and jumping over and over again, trying to make it. The line was not thin but miles wide. They were waving their arms desperately at me in an attempt to get my attention. "We have not abandoned you," they yelled. "We are still right here. Stay there, we're coming over!" Again and again, they tried. It must have been hard and uncomfortable; like crossing over into another dimension at times, but they didn't give up. Their legs grew stronger with all the practice jumps, and they finally leaped victoriously over that line, into the great unknown. Over here, they were now the odd ones out, not me. They saw the line and didn't care. If that was where I was, then that was where they were going to be too. Their hands tightly held my arms and reassuringly patted my shoulder. They wiped tears from my face, only to have a rush of tears fall even faster at the gesture. They settled on my side of the line and immersed themselves in things I tried to explain but couldn't quite understand myself. It didn't matter. They wouldn't abandon me no matter where I went.

I know I'm lucky. I know quite a few families who have been in crisis. I know even more who haven't had the same experience as I have. There were no friends who came barreling across the line swords drawn, preparing to fight this battle with them. These families shared the experience of the world backing away from them. The people in their life didn't want to say the wrong thing so they just didn't say anything at all. They had friends who suddenly thought they were no longer fun, and so they were no longer invited along Their people left them high and dry and alone, which is heartbreaking. I've known some of those people too in my life. Although, I don't know them very well anymore. An awkward hello and head nod when we bump into each other in public is the extent of that relationship. That's okay. Those were never the kind of people who we needed. Those were never the kind of people who were going to make it in our new life, on this side of the line.

I know I've explained it like we are on different sides of the line, and that may seem a bit like the "us versus them" mentality, but I don't intend it to be. We can't help where we live. We are irrevocably on this side of the line now, and there's no going back. Where we once lived, that seems so far gone now. I don't remember who I was on the other side of the line, before Emmett. That doesn't seem like the real me. The real me; she is the person who learned to thrive in her new home. I can still look fondly to others on that side. I'm glad they are there. I'm glad they don't have to know or live the soul crushing experiences that many of us do on this side of the line.

I use the word gratitude a lot because it's hard to describe. It's the way that people can change your life a text at a time, a laugh at a time, and a meal at a time. It sneaks up on you. All those acts of kindness and caring when you are floundering. It's hard to notice it when you are there and living through all of it. It's a surreal pushing through the fog kind of feeling. Then all of the sudden you realize you are not in it alone. You have not been abandoned. There are people right there. They keep checking in and they keep doing things for you when you haven't asked. They keep making sure you're okay. They continue to step in when everyone else steps out. They radiate love. They radiate concern. They radiate light. They radiate hope. That's the kind of person I want to be. That's the kind of person I want my children to be. The love, the concern, the light, and the hope; sometimes it's all you have to hold onto.

When everything of yours is gone, someone else's hope can make all the difference.

#Kathyfacts

It is so easy to draw lines in the sand, take sides, and compare yourself to others. When your life suddenly looks different from those around you, it can be isolating and lonely. It can feel like you are on your own, pushing through uncharted territories while everyone else enjoys their clear cut path lined with flowers.

1. Have you ever felt like you've been abandoned in a certain situation?

2. How do you find common ground with those whose life differs greatly from yours? Is it easy or hard to accept those differences?

When we focus on what makes us different, we lose track of what makes us the same. We are all human. We are connected together on a much larger scale. When we only look for the differences that separate us, we lose track of what binds us together. The human experience of love and life is proof that we are not that different after all.

I believe it's important to have people who have had the same experiences as you. It can make you feel less alone and more understood. Alternatively, I also believe it's important to have people who have not lived the life you have. Different life experiences bring in different perspectives and different ways of seeing hope in a situation. People can surprise you. Try to find common ground with someone who you may have written off as too different from yourself. Look for the small ways you could be connected and appreciate the other's perspective.

Chapter 22

I've always been a bit prone to not sleeping well. I am restless. I have nightmares. I wake up and can't go back to sleep. I lay in bed awake, my mind always churning with a thousand thoughts. When Emmett first became sick, the sleeplessness turned extreme. I evolved into an insomniac. It's funny, not ha-ha funny, but funny in the cosmic kind of way. I had naively always thought insomnia was highly exaggerated. I mean, come on. We're all tired. Everybody has trouble sleeping from time to time and yet we manage. Then I stopped sleeping, like, really, truly honestly stopped sleeping. Not tossing and turning, not waking up every hour in broken up bits and pieces of sleep that leave you more tired each time you wake up. It was none of that. This was middle of the night, wide eyed, mind awake, serious un-sleep. The first few nights of it were hard, but I was sure I would be so exhausted soon enough that I couldn't help but have to sleep. I was wrong. So very wrong. As time went on, I still didn't sleep. I was awake throughout most of the night. I would say on average I was sleeping three to four hours a night, if that. Some nights, there was a touch more or less. When morning would come, I would step out of bed feeling hung over, lethargic, ridiculously exhausted, and have no choice but to get on with the day.

At first, I just laid in bed, waiting to fall back asleep. It didn't work, so I explored other avenues. I read books, I listened to calming music. I tried yoga. I drank tea. I took a bath. I did all of those things that are supposed to help, but nothing did. Eventually, I gave in to it. Instead of trying to sleep and getting frustrated that I couldn't, I got out of bed and started to make myself useful. 2 am seemed like the perfect time to rearrange the kitchen cupboards. A 4 am run downstairs on the treadmill was nice. Jumping around and dancing in the living room at 3 am with my headphones in killed some time. I was making cookies at midnight. I was writing furiously in my journal all hours of the night; sleep deprived rantings that are actually kind of scary to read now.

I thought I was handling it pretty well until I took a long, hard look at myself one day. I had gained quite a bit of weight. I thought I would lose weight with insomnia. The movie *The Machinist* portrays a man with severe insomnia wasting away. Of course, things would swing the opposite way for me. I couldn't even take away that one small perk of insomnia. It looked like I had purple bruises underneath my eyes. The circles were deep and dark and required makeup caked on with multiple layers to look even remotely okay. Even then, with five layers, they were visible. I looked haggard. Everything on my face kind of sunk downward. It was the most depressing thing I had ever seen in myself. I sighed with self-loathing. What on earth had I let myself become? What on earth had I done to myself?

I lost my phone and found it three days later in the refrigerator. I put the dirty clothes in the trash can. I forgot what day and month it was multiple times a day. I did things I couldn't explain. *Why would I put my purse under the bed? Why did I put my headlamp in the cupboard with the cereal? What happened to my car keys? Oh, they're in the bathtub. That makes perfect sense.* I began to screw things up at work, making all sorts of simple mistakes. I was losing my mind. I could feel it. I was on the edge of that delirious laughter that would come at inappropriate times. I alternated between delirium and a numb, wordless state, just going through the motions.

After much pushing and prodding from a few friends, I went to my doctor. My doctor gave me a couple of prescriptions. *The things I wish I could go back and redo.* What a stubborn, stubborn ox I was. In one week, the only thing the pills made me do was feel even more sluggish and foggy. There wasn't much sleep going on and I certainly didn't feel any better. In all of my infinite, stubborn wisdom, I threw the pills away and continued to white knuckle it on my own. I was miserable, but I was surviving.

Things changed the day we got back home from being in the hospital for Emmett's third surgery. I was lying in bed. I tried to ask Tony for my favorite lotion because it had been so dry in the hospital and my hands were suffering. He just stared at me like I had grown a second head. I kept talking as he continued to look at me strangely. That's when the room turned yellow and tilted up at me. I felt sick to my stomach and heavy all over; like my arms and legs were pure lead and moving them would be impossible. About a minute later, it had passed. *Weird.* I closed my eyes and took a few deep breaths and felt better, but still strange all over. The next day Tony took me into the doctor who suggested I had something called a Transient Ischemic Attack (TIA) otherwise known as a mini stroke. I almost laughed out loud. A stroke. I was thirty years old. I was running twenty-five to thirty miles a week, I lifted weights three times a week, and except for my overindulgence in chocolate, I ate pretty well. There had to be a mistake. As time went on however, things in my head were still cloudy. I forgot how to get to work and words wouldn't come out like I wanted them to. I began to believe maybe it was possible.

Now it was serious. There were no more gentle suggestions from my friends and family who were witnessing my steady decline. They demanded action. I needed to do something to get this under control. It was obvious I was not handling the stress and sleep deprivation in even a remotely good way. I was scared but spurred into action. Fear can have that affect. It can paralyze you in place or light a fire underneath you. This lit a fire under me. *Wake up,* it screamed. I went to a few neurologist appointments and had scans and tests done to make sure everything was okay. When everything came up clear, I knew it was time. I needed to make drastic changes. No more 3 am dance parties. No more fifteen mile training runs in the middle of the night. Sleep. That's what I needed. The genuine fear I felt for my health and well-being broke down the walls I had put up, and I was ready to face my fears.

I sought out a therapist, Dave. As the months passed, things started to make more sense. Dave was able to cut right through the heart of everything. The more he talked, the more I knew he was right. I knew what was wrong all along. I had always known. I just couldn't bring myself to admit it. I couldn't bring myself to do it. I knew why I couldn't sleep. I knew why I was miserable. I was at war. God wanted Emmett and I said no. *No. No. No. You can't have him. He's mine. You gave him to me. You can't take him back now.* That nagging voice in the back of my head that I couldn't escape, it just wouldn't quiet. I couldn't outrun it. I couldn't outsmart it. I couldn't outthink it. It was always there. "Let go Kathy," it told me. "Let go." I screamed in defiance. I threw my head back and raged at the sky. I dug my heels in even harder and clung tighter. *He couldn't have him. No. I was not going to be okay with that.* That voice was there still. "Trust me. Trust me," it beckoned. My therapist kept pushing me toward that voice, while I kept trying to run the other way. I didn't want to. I didn't want to be okay with it. If Emmett died, I would never be okay. I was sure of it. I couldn't silence that voice no matter how hard I tried. It was breaking me. I was broken. I was falling apart. I was losing myself. I was all out of options. I was all out of ways to make it through another day.

There was no other way around it. I just didn't have the energy to fight it anymore. I cried face down on the floor. *Okay God. You can have him. If You have to take him, You can have him. As if You ever needed my permission anyhow. Do what You will. He's Yours, but I would really like it if I could keep him around for a few more years. I'm not ready yet. Please God. Please.* I cried and cried, feeling like less of a mother to offer her child up at the altar of sacrifice. When I calmed down, that burden I was carrying, that impossible weight in my chest was gone. I cried some more.

What had I done? I'd given Emmett up. If I loved him, I wouldn't have been able to do that. I burned with shame. What was I doing? This was wrong. That voice in the back of my mind, even more stubborn than me, said "No. Let go. It will be okay Kathy." So I did - I let go. I made my peace with whatever was going to happen with Emmett. If God was going to take him, there wasn't anything I was going to do about it. Obsessing about what might happen or what was going to happen was doing nothing but robbing today of its joy. I had to believe that, for whatever reason, whatever was going to happen next was going to be okay. Of course, it wouldn't be just fine if Emmett died, but I couldn't do anything about the unknown future. I relinquished control. I was not in charge of healing Emmett. It was not my personal failure if I could not take away his pain. I was not a bad mother if I couldn't find the answers that even the doctors couldn't. I let go. I let God have it.

Maybe that sounds morbid. Maybe that sounds cold-hearted, but I promise it's not. I would throw myself in front of a moving bus to heal Emmett. I would die in a heartbeat to make it all go away, but I couldn't be responsible for it any more. I couldn't carry that with me. My fragile heart couldn't take on all of those things I couldn't fix. God could though. I will love and cherish both of my boys every single second they are here. Someday, if God does take Emmett, it will be the most devastating blow of my life, but I believe I will find my way back. I will, because I believe His promise. It will be okay. I will be okay. I believe in the hope of today and the hope of tomorrow. I believe Emmett will be okay, whatever that means in the grand scheme of things.

I thought I had life figured out. I could see things more clearly and feel things more deeply. I had come out on the other side of it. I patted myself on the back for the hard work I had done, pleased with myself that all I had needed was a little bit of perspective. I deemed myself successfully intact. I had overcome my issues and now I could get on with the business of living. I didn't realize how naive and clueless I still was then.

The train was still barreling down the tracks at me, I just couldn't see it with my head in the clouds.

#Kathyfacts

I think many of us are reluctant to ask for help and receive it. Maybe you don't want to be a bother or hassle. Maybe asking for help feels like an admission of defeat. You might feel like you are putting your weakness out there for the entire world to see. It can be embarrassing to feel like you can't hold things together or do them on your own when it looks like everyone else can.

1. Have you ever needed help but couldn't bring yourself to ask for it? Why or why not?

2. What is one area in your life you could use some help with right now? Can you ask for help? What would that look like?

Sometimes we don't realize how bad things have gotten. When you are overwhelmed and struggling, it's hard to see where you are and recognize you're in a tailspin. Others may be able to see it, but often, we are blind to our own circumstances in that area. We can sometimes feel something is off, but not quite grasp the extent.

Take a few minutes to take stock of your current situation. Are there things that you could eliminate to relieve your stress? Are there things that you could delegate to others so as to lighten the load? Are there things you need to accept and heal from in order to move forward? It's time to start. Pick one area in which you can start to alleviate some of the stress associated with it. Ask for help. Give up on the idea of doing it all on your own. Let go of perfection. Dump some of the stress and start to invest in yourself more.

Chapter 23

Before I had Emmett, I had never known anyone that dealt with depression, or so I had thought. I had heard quiet whispers of postpartum depression among a few friends, but I really, truly had no experience with it. I didn't understand what it could do.

When we were deep in the trenches with Emmett, just completely submerged and drowning in sleeplessness, worry, pain, and suffering; that is when it must have set in. Like so many other things, it was gradual. I didn't recognize it at first. Everything I knew about depression, I knew from television commercials; the sad tomato all by himself and the lady lying on the couch unable to get up and do anything. I didn't see myself in either of those scenarios at all. I just didn't realize all of these small changes together were setting in for something bigger.

I couldn't sleep. Of course I couldn't, Emmett stopped breathing during seizures and in the middle of the night. It's understandable that I couldn't sleep through the night.

I couldn't eat. Well, obviously I was heartsick. I was in a constant state of preparing for the other shoe to drop. I just wasn't hungry. I didn't care about food.

I was eating way too much at once. I rationed this one away. I didn't eat breakfast or lunch. Of course I could eat an entire package of cookie dough as is. I was hungry. It was going to make me feel better and if I could glean any small bit of enjoyment during this awful time, even from food, I was going to take it.

I didn't want to run anymore. I was too tired. Of course I didn't feel like running. I was exhausted.

I started having panic attacks. It was just the sleeplessness. I was so sure. I was terrified of what was going to happen. Whose heart wouldn't start pounding erratically when faced with how helpless they are in what is happening to their child?

I wasn't crying. This one, I patted myself on the back for. I was strong. Look at me, so stoic and proud. I could cry in certain situations but other times, when I should have been feeling any sort of emotion, there was nothing there. I was numb.

I was only angry. I was flying off the handle at Tony every chance I got. I directed all of my pain and anguish and things I couldn't say and things I didn't understand at him. I became a different person, a mean spirited woman who didn't care. I could see that I was hurting those around me but it didn't matter. It didn't compare to the pain I was in. I didn't feel anything but anger. There was no guilt and no empathy. Movies that used to make me cry did nothing. Things that used to make me happy didn't matter to me. There was just nothing. There was only anger and then numbness. Complete and utter numbness. I knew that it shouldn't be that way but I wasn't sure what was wrong.

In hindsight, I can see it so clearly. When I was in the middle of it, I just didn't understand. After a particularly bad batch of days, the proverbial sky started falling and friends were there to witness it. I promised them I would seek out help. I would go to the doctor, I conceded. I was convinced the root cause of everything was that I was suffering from insomnia. I was sure that if I could sleep, everything else would just fall in place. I was so naive.

I went to our family doctor and explained about my sleepless nights. She was very familiar with Emmett and all of his medical issues as she had been signing off on referral after referral and amassing all of his results and write-ups from different specialists. I knew she truly cared which is why I was taken aback when she explained why she wanted to put me on anti-depressants. I completely disagreed with her. I began building up my argument in my head. *That was ridiculous. I wasn't depressed. I was tired and maybe a bit overly anxious. Fine. But depressed? No. I wasn't depressed. I wasn't lying around on the couch. I was dressed. I was still running even though I didn't feel like it. I was working. I was doing all the things that were expected of me. I wasn't depressed. I didn't even feel sad! Just ridiculous.* She wrote me a prescription for an anti-depressant and something to help me sleep. She looked me in the eye, talked to me honestly, patted my knee in a motherly gesture, and sent me on my way. I chalked the whole appointment up to a giant waste of time. I knew I wasn't depressed. She was just plain wrong.

I took the pills for a week, then abruptly stopped, and never touched them again. They made me feel weird, like I was on the outside looking in. I had read all the fine print that came in the twelve page insert. I knew it took time, but I didn't care. I didn't like it. Whether right or wrong, I do things my way. I do things the hard way and learn all sorts of lessons that could have been avoided if I'd just do what I was told.

I went back to trying to manage it all on my own until I couldn't possibly another minute. Again, I promised a couple of close friends I'd look for help. The problem was I didn't really want to. I was afraid. Something was wrong with me. *What if I was never the same again? What if I was always going to feel that way? Would I always feel dead inside like nothing mattered? Why was there no joy, no happiness, no sadness, no nothing?* I was just a blank slate with occasional anger boiling at the surface. I felt like a terrible person. I didn't want to know why I was this way. I just wanted to make it stop all on my own. I didn't want to have to tell somebody else about it.

In the end, Tony convinced me to seek help after I had the mini stroke. Tony called a therapist and made an appointment for me. I wouldn't do it myself. I already knew this therapist, so it made it a bit easier to go in and admit failure and defeat. I was sure that was what this meant now, that I had failed. I talked a mile a minute at the first appointment with my therapist, Dave. I laid out absolutely everything that had gone wrong, how God had left me high and dry, and how afraid I was at the possibility of outliving my child. I told him if one more person told me that "God only gives you what you can handle," or "God would see me through it," I was going to scream. I was tired. I was afraid. I was anxious. I sat there with my knee bouncing to and fro and unloaded a thousand fears all at once.

Somehow he got through to me. Dave was a voice of reason that persistently chipped away at the tip of the iceberg. He made the nonsensical make sense. Dave helped me see God for who He was, not who He wasn't. Dave helped me look at both my actions and inactions and measure what effect they had in my life. He had me considering things like: what was I going to do if God didn't heal Emmett? How was I going to change anything by simply punishing myself? Was that how it worked? Did God negotiate in a hostage situation? Would God finally give in to my demands if He saw how I blamed Him and how miserable I was making myself? What was I going to change by planning out every single outcome there was? Was it going to make it any better if I worried about it before it happened? If there were additional surgeries, if Emmett would continue to be in pain, if he had more seizures, if other kids would see him as different and be mean to him? How was I going to do anything about those things by simply worrying right then? I wasn't going to change any of that. There was no way to plan for the future, no way to know what was ever going to happen, so what did I think I could really do about it?

After we studied the absurdity of my behavior, my therapist started in on the even harder concepts. Who did I really think God was? What did I really think God was doing here? Was God punishing me by making my own child suffer? Was God disappointed in me and trying to teach me a lesson? Did God not care what I wanted? Did God turn a deaf ear to my desperate pleas and watch me go down in flames without ever intervening because I had to learn the hard way? No. Although I didn't understand it, I didn't have to.

Why does God allow our children to suffer? I don't know. That's the truth. I don't know. I don't understand it. If watching my baby suffer was to learn some sort of a lesson, to come out of something stronger, to be able to empathize with another group of people, or any of the other good things that can come out of hardship, I am sure there was another easier and better way. I don't know and I don't have to. It's not for me to figure out. It's not for me to unravel the mysteries of this life. Bad things happen. It's true. It doesn't matter why anymore. Asking why was destroying me. The more I looked at the way I felt about things and learned about myself, the more I realized it wasn't about any of that.

Trust. That is what it was about. Trust that this was not all in vain. Trust that this was the only way. For whatever would happen or needed to happen, this was the only way to accomplish it. It was about trusting what I didn't agree with. It was about making peace with what I didn't want to see happen. It was about accepting what I had refused to accept and what I wanted to change. It was about facing what wasn't fair and understanding I could still be okay. You can trust that there are things happening behind the scenes that you can't even comprehend right now. Those things are going to weave together a rich tapestry of hope. Trust and hope. That was the lesson. That was what I had to face.

After a few months, I was on the track to reclaiming my life. I felt older, wiser, and like I had lived a lifetime during such a short period of time. I couldn't understand my previous behavior. I couldn't believe how I didn't see it then, when it is all so clear to me now. I think that is how depression feels. It feels like you are finally walking out of a thick, blinding fog. Once you can see again, you can hardly remember why you were so scared in the midst of that fog. Surely you couldn't have lived in that fog for the rest of your life. How could you not realize or see that eventually, there was going to have to be something else? That's what depression does. It eliminates all of the good. It makes you forget about the possibilities of tomorrow. It makes you forget about the joy in yesterday. It holds you in the fog and fills you with nothingness. It's a scary feeling – complete and utter hopelessness, like nothing would ever matter one way or the other. It's hard to see hope when you can't see life around you. It can be so easy to get stuck in an immobile state. You can get comfortable there. It's old and familiar, it's what you recognize. The chaos can be comforting. Even when you know it's not right, when it doesn't feel right, and it doesn't look right; it can be hard to find the will to break out of it.

For me, that was all I needed to get myself back at that time, but that is me and only me. Many people have serious chemical imbalances that require medication and I believe that anyone struggling with depression should seek medical help. I do the wrong thing all the time, so whatever you do, do not attempt to follow in my footsteps! I guess I'm just as guilty as the rest of the world is in sweeping depression under the rug. I was embarrassed. I was ashamed. I was afraid I was a disappointment.. I was just afraid in general. I thought I could control it through sheer will power. I thought I could fix it myself by trying to focus on the good. I thought I just wasn't strong enough or intuitive enough to see the big picture. I was disappointed in myself. I wanted to be a better person. I wanted to be a better mom, a better wife, and a better friend. I didn't want to admit I'd selfishly disappeared into nothingness. I didn't want to face the fact that I had lost all that time being stuck.

Sitting here now, I can see it wasn't a waste of time. I grew up. I had always thought I was an adult. I was naturally independent and very responsible even at a young age. I knew it then and I know it now. It may sound arrogant, but I was years ahead in this area compared to others my age even way back then. I knew how to take care of myself. I knew how to take care of others. When I had kids, I thought that was when I was officially an adult. I had been married for five years prior to Travis being born, but having a child cinched it for me. Now I was a real, live grown up. Really though, I wasn't. I didn't realize it until Emmett.

That day sitting in the back of the ambulance with Emmett after his very first seizure, I was a scared little girl. I wanted to call someone in charge. I wanted someone to figure out what I should do next. I wanted someone else to fix it. I didn't know how to do it myself. I had never been an actual adult until I stared the truth in the face. When I looked at what I wanted so badly, what I wanted to fix so much it hurt, and instead stood by helplessly. That's where I grew up. Maybe it wasn't so much growing up as it was seeing the world in a completely different way. As much as I wanted to wish that time away, I couldn't. It wasn't a waste. I was down in the pit. I was screaming in agony and hopelessly lost. I thought I was nothing and no one. I came out of that experience different in every way possible. This is who I am now.

I am grateful for the experience. Yes grateful. I was missing out on so much before that. I was surviving life and not living it. I was moving through the motions and doing all of the things I thought I was supposed to. The depression kicked me out of that rut. I was ordered to take better care of myself. I was told to do something I wanted to do. I started writing more. I started running longer. I made new friends. I left the house by myself every once in a while. I found a passion for the things I wanted to do. I could see purpose again. I could see the slow wide arc that I was making, swinging from one direction to a completely new one. It was where I had always wanted to go but was always afraid to. Now I had nothing to lose. Now I had much bigger things to fear than just failure. It was now or never. It was sink or swim.

It was give up or hope.

#Kathyfacts

I could easily lie to myself and make myself believe whatever I wanted to. I could tell myself I was just fine despite the overwhelming evidence that I wasn't. I could keep going assuring myself that everything was going to be okay eventually. I could remind myself on a daily basis that I didn't need help and could do it all on my own. I was convinced I could do it ALL on my own.

1. Do you try to do it all on your own?

2. Has there ever been a time when you have lied to yourself so convincingly you believed it?

3. Why do you think we are reluctant to admit we can't do it all on our own?

When enough is enough, your body will tell you. You can lie to yourself but your body will not keep up the facade. You won't be able to ignore it forever. Try checking in with yourself more often. Are you feeling overwhelmed, stressed, exhausted, or ready to burst? You don't have to do it all. You don't have to be perfect. You can leave things for later, you can ask for help. You can give yourself a break. You deserve a break. Be as kind to yourself as you would be to others.

Give yourself some down time because you can't operate at full speed all of the time. Slow down, cut yourself some slack, and just breathe. Acknowledge your hard work and constant efforts, but also realize that you need rest and recovery during those efforts. Even a few minutes at a time can have restorative effects on your life.

Chapter 24

My oldest son Travis is just simply amazing. I spend a lot of time on Emmett, with Emmett, and talking about Emmett's struggle as my motivation to dig deep when I want to give up. The reality is that Travis is just as much of a part of it as his little brother. Travis wasn't like other six year olds. He could say the word Craniosynostosis correctly. He knew what happened to Emmett's head and what they had to do to fix it. He helps cheer up his little brother when he is getting medicine. He holds his hand when Emmett is lying on the floor in pain. He sits at Emmett's bedside in the hospital with a picture he colored and makes funny faces and silly noises for his brother. He is educated in seizure safety. He knows what to do in an emergency.

I remember Emmett's first seizure, how scared we all were, how that must have been for then three-year-old Travis. He was wrapped around my leg holding on tightly when the EMT came in. He recoiled against the back wall, afraid of this strange man with all of his gear. Travis wanted me to stay with him, but I couldn't. I kissed his cheek and told him it'd be okay before climbing into the back of the ambulance with Emmett. Tony tossed Travis in his car and they followed us up to the hospital until our friend Jacci came and picked up Travis. As I sat in the back of the ambulance and stared at my little boy, lying limp and hard asleep, I felt guilty. Travis was afraid. He wanted me to be with him. I had to pick one over the other.

Over the years, I would be plagued by the fear that I was doing Travis an injustice. I couldn't spend as much time with him as I wanted to. He had to miss out on parties, fun trips on the weekend, and doing things he wanted to because Emmett couldn't go anywhere. He got left out and shuffled around to and from the houses of his grandparents, aunts and uncles, friends, and more. We were often gone due to appointments for Emmet, long days spent in the hospital for testing, surgeries, and subsequent recoveries. There were last minute cancellations of our plans and early mornings spent shipping him off so we could make the long trip to the hospital. *Was I a better mother to Emmett than Travis? Just because I was so scared?* I didn't know. Travis was so smart and so self-sufficient, I rarely worried about him. Except when I worried he wasn't get his fair shake of this life. *Really, who was getting their fair shake in this life? Certainly not Emmet, not me, or Tony. This wasn't fair for anyone. This wasn't the plan for any of us.*

I was this weepy woman walking around like a zombie, too tired to play. "Watch another movie baby," I'd say in those first few hazy months after Emmett's diagnosis. I'd lay on the couch, anxious and afraid, half awake, half asleep and hating myself for not trying harder. I hated myself for not being better. I wanted to play games. I wanted to build Legos. I wanted to race cars and do all those other things that boys his age want to do, but I just couldn't. The insomnia and anxiety had worn me down. Although I would be adamant for so long I wasn't depressed then, I was in denial. It wasn't until much later that I could see a difference, that I could feel a difference, and realized I must have been depressed. I just thought that was how a diagnosis for your child feels, like impending darkness and doom with no way out.

One day, Travis asked me for a picture of Emmett from his surgery. He wanted to bring it to show-and-tell at school and tell everyone about his brother and his big surgery. He wasn't embarrassed, he was proud. I was so proud too. I was proud that Travis could tell people about the triangular bones his little brother had. I was proud he could tell them all about how they cut it all apart and put it back together like a puzzle. I was proud he could tell them about what a seizure looks like and what you are supposed to do if it happens. He was wise beyond his years and more compassionate and understanding than some adults. He was a light in the darkness for all of us, always laughing, smiling, being silly, and wanting to take care of not just his brother, but all of us.

In hindsight, as with so many things, I can see it so much clearer. I can understand it. I was focused on research; I was buried in my laptop obsessively searching for answers. I wasn't sleeping at night, so I was exhausted and barely able to function during the day. I've often wondered what Travis will make of this when he grows up. With Emmett being front and center, will Travis feel like his life constantly and continually comes in second place as the necessities of Emmett's life ebb and flow? Will he resent us or me especially? Will he think I have loved him less? Cared for him less? Taken an interest in him less?

It's something that I regularly fight with, so I try to go above and beyond to do special things with just Travis. It's easy for an adult to understand. We can see one child just needs more in this season of their life, especially when those needs are medically based. For a child, it doesn't make sense. There are so many questions: "Why can't he play like other little boys? Why do we have to go to the hospital again? Why do I have to be quiet because Emmett doesn't feel good?" If I only had the answers and a way to make it all right, for both of my boys.

There's a quote that I've seen multiple times that says "Behind every great kid is a mother sure she's screwing it all up." I love it because I've been so sure, so many times, that I am just irrevocably screwing everybody's life up. I have felt certain that I am ruining their formative years or that I am scarring them for years to come with my previous behavior. But then I see Travis reading to Emmett on the couch. He kisses Emmett's head that hurts and tells him that it's going to be okay. He puts his arm around Emmett and goes back to reading a book to him. As I watch from the kitchen, I am overwhelmed. So kind, gentle, and reassuring to his little brother who is so afraid. How did he get to be such a person? He grew up when I wasn't looking and when I wasn't paying close enough attention. He became this amazing little man that loves deeply and wants to take care of his little brother. I find myself smiling at the scene in front of me, feeling hopeful that maybe I haven't screwed them both up. I can see what wonderful people they are becoming and know I must have done something right amongst all of the things I've done wrong. Travis is too loving and too compassionate, he won't resent us. These two brothers truly love one another and take care of each other. I don't have to worry anymore.

In groups of parents who have medically fragile children, there's even more guilt to be had though. Some worry, wonder, or blame themselves that they might have caused their child's disease or condition. Many mothers theorize that if they could have done something different in pregnancy, maybe it wouldn't have turned out like it did. There are varying degrees of guilt. Some have made their peace. Some never need to know, standing self-assured with the way things are. Others are buried under a mountain of guilt; guilt so deep they don't dare even speak a word of it, lest someone confirm their deepest, darkest fears. I have felt that guilt buried down deep in my gut, burning in my throat, always at the tip of my tongue, but too afraid and too cowardly to ever let the words go. *Did I do this? Do you think it had anything to do with me?* Questions that I never wanted answered. Questions that were so loaded, they could bring up a nuclear wall of defenses if someone even so happened to breathe a little too close to that line.

Then someone did. Someone unleashed the demons that nearly every mother of a child has felt to some degree, at one time or another. They looked to blame the diagnosis on something I had done. "Did the doctor say it had anything to do with your running?" Whether it was supposed to be an innocent question or not, whatever they truly meant by it tapped into the part of me I didn't want to see. I had already asked the doctor even though I already knew the answer. I had researched running and pregnancy, read many studies, bought a few books on it, and talked my OB/GYN about it. I knew it was okay. I knew the history. I knew everything. I knew it wasn't me. It was genetics. It was statistics. It was God. It was fate. It was "one of those things." It wasn't me but as the person who carried him for nine months, I couldn't help but feel more responsible than anyone else. My fragile psyche broke. *Is this what everyone else thought? That I was an irresponsible mother who did this to her own child?* I tried to dismiss it, but the guilt ate away at me. I knew I wasn't to blame, but others didn't. I was going to have to make my peace with it, which turned out to be a lot harder than I thought it would be. I had to dismiss what other people thought of me. That's asking for a lot from a people pleaser.

I wrestled with it. Read more about Emmett's conditions and health history. I prayed. I polled others on what they thought. I wrote about it. Eventually, I dismissed it. I decided that the opinions that matter the most to me come from the ones who love me and aren't interested in hurting me with their harsh judgments. Who do I want to be proud of me? Whose voice matters the most? Who is in this with me? Really all in with me and my family? Those are the voices that need to be heard and respected. Regardless of any fault, I want my boys to see how hard we have tried. I want them to understand how we've all suffered together and done the best we could. I know the love my boys have for each other will be a lifelong bond.

All I can hope for is that they see my love and devotion to them even in the midst of pain.

#Kathyfacts

Sometimes it feels like if we are succeeding in one area, we are failing in another. That doesn't necessarily mean its true, only that guilt has taken hold.

1.   Have you ever felt like you've failed your child or someone else that was counting on you?

2.   Have they surprised you by being more gracious towards you than you have been towards yourself?

So often we expect too much from ourselves and have unrealistic expectations. We see the pretty, polished, and seemingly perfect life someone else is living and can feel guilty that we aren't there too. I don't like comparison. I don't want to compare my progress, my life, or my struggle with someone else's. When we look at someone else's life, we don't have all the information needed. We often don't see the messy details that we know exist in our own life. This is what makes it an unfair comparison.

Live each day as best you can. Know that we all make mistakes with our children, spouses, friends, and family. Most of us are doing the best we can so try to be more forgiving of yourself and those around you. If you are living with love in your heart and trying to do right by those around you, then it is enough. They don't need or expect complete perfection from you. We are all imperfect people, each and every one of us. Make peace with these imperfections, embrace them even. Remind yourself over and over that you have done the best you could. Keep telling yourself it until you begin to believe it.

Chapter 25

Relationships are hard, and marriage requires a lot of work. A marriage can buckle under the stress of everyday life. Sometimes a marriage can blow up without any warning for a number of reasons. Throw in incredibly difficult circumstances with no end in sight, fearing for your child's life, and money problems because of a sudden influx of hospital bills, and you have a recipe for disaster; especially if you are married to someone like me. I was someone who wanted to control the entire world, someone who had their entire life mapped out ahead of time. I was an obsessive planner, a scheduler, a non-spontaneous person who was thrust into pure chaos.

I had a hard time finding my way in this new part of our life. Doctor's offices didn't call when they said they would. Waiting times were always longer than I thought they should be. Test results didn't come quickly enough. Neurosurgeons couldn't give us any absolute guarantees. There was no sense of stability when dealing with our insurance company and the bills they were refusing. There was no timeline on when Emmett would get better, if he would get better, how long it would take, or how long he would continue to fall behind. Nobody could tell me anything. I was overwhelmed and terrified without a clue what to do next.

My father-in-law, Brent, once explained me to a group of friends with this observation: "I've never seen anyone try to control gravy." In my younger days, I was a much pickier eater. I didn't really like my food to touch back then. Maybe I still don't. When I was all of seventeen years old, I had a nice dinner at my boyfriend Tony's house with his family. My future mother-in-law made some fantastic multi-course meal with mashed potatoes and gravy. When I poured my gravy over the mashed potatoes, it started seeping down and slowly moving too close to my meat and vegetables like always. I thought nothing of my behavior because I had done it so often. I kept pushing the gravy back towards the potatoes with my spoon, a never ending job as the liquid continued to spread out. Over and over again, I tried to bend that gravy to my will and continued to fight a losing battle. That silly little story offers a bigger narrative as to who I was for a very long time. I needed to be in control. Having control of a situation made me feel safe. I could breathe easier if I could just make things go my way. It didn't matter how impossible it seemed to regain control of a situation, or whether or not it was even in my ability to change the outcome. I only knew I had to try.

As one might expect, being thrown into such chaos with Emmett's diagnosis made me a less than desirable person to be around. I used to think that big romantic gestures meant love. Super thoughtful, amazingly planned surprises, a small present, a weekend trip, or a card full of eloquent words. I used to think I knew who I was, who Tony was, and understood how our marriage worked. All of that changed when Emmett was diagnosed. The world spun out of control and I went with it. Tony and I were at each other's throats all the time about everything as life continued to fall apart. We could not get on the same page, turning an already terrible situation into an even more desperate place. I've got nothing left to lose at this point, so I can admit it was mostly my fault, because of my behavior. I turned into a bit of a volcanic person. One minute I was serene, still, and unmoving. The next I was erupting in rage, spewing red hot anger in every direction around me. I was poisoned, truly I was. In bits and pieces I would douse those around me, mainly Tony, in poison too looking for relief in any way I could find it.

Tony was everything I was not. He was patient, understanding, go with the flow, and a perpetual optimist. He was stronger than I was. No doubt he was just as scared, confused, and overwhelmed as I was, but it was me that couldn't hold it together. It was me that took out all of my fear and frustration on him. He took all of my irrational, out of control melt downs. He helped me pick up the pieces to something I had broken in a bout of anger numerous times. He forced me to eat something when I was refusing all food.

He would cover me up with a blanket in the middle of the night as I lay on the floor in front of Emmett's crib. He would come find me when I'd been running for far too long with food in hand. He was always taking care of me, standing by my side, even when I didn't deserve it. It turns out I never knew who I was and I didn't really know the depths of who my husband was either. I most certainly didn't understand our marriage or how it worked at all before this. He was willing to meet me not just halfway, but ninety five percent of the way. When I couldn't do anything, when I couldn't be anything, he did it for me. If it were on my shoulders, everything would have crumbled to ashes.

After I sought counseling and had begun making peace with the things I couldn't understand or control, I started to emerge from the terrible place I had been in. I was able to open my eyes for the first time and see that Tony had been single handedly keeping us afloat. I could see my past behavior for the unreasonable and out of control mess it had been. I was embarrassed and ashamed of who I was and how I hadn't been able to handle Emmett's diagnosis the way I thought I should have. I wasn't sure how I would make my amends, but there was Tony holding his hand out to me and smirking triumphantly just like he did back when he was a sixteen year old boy. It made me love him even more. That's what love does. I needed someone to wait for me. I needed someone to see me through the hopeless depression I had found myself in and not give up on me. I needed someone to love me when I couldn't love myself, and that's just what he did.

For everything that had gone wrong, there were things still going right. I just couldn't see it then. Day by day, my mind started to clear and I began to do things differently, see things differently, and feel things differently. I realized that whatever life was going to throw at us could either drive us farther apart or bring us closer together. It was our choice. It was my choice and so I chose. I chose my best friend. I chose hope. I chose to laugh instead of scream. Some of that laughter was crazy; hysterical on the edge of delirium laughter, but it was still laughter. I chose to scream instead of break things. I saved my remaining picture frames and screamed into my pillow until my throat hurt when I was on the verge of losing it. I chose to run rather than to stay unmoving in my despair. When I ran, I left behind the urge to wallow in pity, to destroy my house, or to blow up and lose my cool. I chose to live again and it was the right choice.

These words would not be here if it weren't for Tony. There wasn't anyone that could reach me. I couldn't see God anywhere. I wouldn't let anyone in. Instead of breaking down the door and barging his way in, Tony waited on the other side of that door. He brought me the good Kleenex with lotion because my skin was rubbed raw from wiping away a steady stream of tears. He even fixed my treadmill once in the middle of the night when I couldn't sleep and wanted to run. At 3 am, when I was crawling up the walls in a terrible state but couldn't get my treadmill to turn on, I woke him up and he fixed it without complaining once or including one word of judgment. He rearranged his entire schedule over and over again, all so I could have a moment to myself during the day or so I could go sit by the lake for an hour quietly. He saw me when I couldn't see myself.

He gave me hope when I was hopeless.

#Kathyfacts

So often, we take our anger and frustration out on those closest to us. In my case, it was Tony. I knew he wouldn't leave. I knew I could throw myself down into that pit and suffer as long as I needed to and he'd still be there. It wasn't what I had thought our marriage would be, but it was what happened.

1. What does your love story look like?

2. How is it different than you imagined?

3. Have you found yourself really surprised by a spouse or even a friend in the midst of your turmoil?

Even in the midst of undesirable circumstances, we can still nurture our relationship(s). I'm not saying it's easy or even fun at times, but when things are hard, that's when we need each other the most. One person may have to give more than their fair share for a period of time, but it's worth it. I believe that relationships grow in the dark and in the struggle. It's easy to love one another when life is going great and there's nothing but light and joy all around us. It's much harder to love one another when life falls apart around you and the person next to you feels like a stranger.

Try to appreciate the struggle just a little bit. See how joy and heartbreak are both there. Look for even the tiniest bit of good that has come from the bad. When you change your perspective, you can change your life. Keep looking and striving for ways to change your perspective and your life. Keep growing from it, every day.

Chapter 26

As the second anniversary of June 20th began to approach, I wanted to do something big. I wanted to do something more than just run in my basement for seven and a half hours. I wanted to involve other people. I wanted to run somewhere public to raise awareness of Craniosynostosis. My first most obvious choice was my favorite local running store, Gazelle Sports. I crafted an email, deleted it all, rewrote it, went back and fixed it, and fussed with it for weeks until I finally got up the nerve to send it. Being highly involved with the running community, I knew many people who worked at the store, so I sent it to a contact and asked that she send it along to someone who could make the decision.

After the email was out of my hands, I promptly went to work with a Plan B because surely they wouldn't agree to let me do this. It was strange. I was just this random person who wanted to hog their treadmill for nearly eight hours. I dismissed it without a thought but much to my surprise, I received an email back. The powers that be at Gazelle Sports thought it was a great idea and wanted me to confirm a date to meet and talk about it in person. My little dream had been lifted off the ground.

Around the same time, I had also emailed Fellow Flowers, a running community and company. I just absolutely love them and their positivity, heart for others, brilliant words, and support of connection. I sent them a note I had been meaning to for a while. I wanted to tell them that one of their people originally posted to my page the morning of Emmett's first surgery. It was a picture of numerous women with flowers in their hair and beautiful words of courage and bravery were spoken. It made an impression on me even then, when I had no idea why they were wearing flowers or what it was all about. It took me some time to figure it out, to eventually connect the dots later that these were the Fellow Flowers people. My email was just to thank them for doing what they do and a note about how their mission has impacted me, along with why I would wear their Silver Lining flower for my run. The Silver Lining flower was about hope and picking up the broken pieces. It was so fitting, it felt like it had been written for me.

Fellow Flowers responded. They remembered my story well, having gathered for their own little run that morning to support me. The owners of the company then proceeded to ask for my phone number because they wanted to talk to me. Little old me. To say I was nervous was an understatement. These were, in my mind, high powered, important, super amazing women doing all kinds of inspirational things. *What on earth could they have to say to me? More importantly, what on earth was I going to say to them?*

When my phone eventually rang, I nervously answered it on the third ring because I didn't want to seem too eager even though I had been holding the phone in my hand with the volume turned all the way up for the past forty-five minutes. None the less, they were both on the line. A conference call with Mel and Tori, the two owners whom I both admired and looked up to! Now I was seriously intimidated. We chatted for a few minutes and their easy going nature put me at ease, until they were ready to tell me just why they were calling. They were going to make the long drive from Wisconsin and Michigan's Upper Peninsula to Grand Rapids to be there for Emmett's Endurance Event. They were going to run with me in person. They were going to bring all of their stuff with them, set up shop, and just be there. I was too stunned to say anything intelligent or react appropriately. "Oh my gosh. Really? Thank you. Really? Oh my gosh. Thank you. Really? Oh my gosh. Thank you!" I'm good like that under pressure. It was a turn of events that just felt like the world was clicking into place for me.

I began coordinating with Gazelle Sports for the event and the plans just kept growing. I was going to be running on one of their treadmills the entire time with an extra treadmill right next to me so anyone could join me for however long they wanted. I wanted to raise money and collect donations for Cranio Care Bears. Cranio

Care Bears is a charity that sends out free care packages to children undergoing surgery for Craniosynostosis. The care packages include everything from hospital necessities for parents, small distractions for baby, zip up pajamas (because the head swells significantly after surgery and putting a shirt over it can be impossible), and my favorite item, a handmade prayer chain. Volunteers write prayers, quotes, and well wishes on a length of ribbon. Cranio Care Bears then assembles the chain so that it can be hung over a child's hospital bed. In addition to these loving care packages, Cranio Care Bears also provides support, education, and hope for newly diagnosed families.

For a donation to Cranio Care Bears, it was decided the giver would receive a coupon to use at Gazelle Sports. There were fliers and giveaways created as it was becoming more and more of a "real" event. I was beyond thrilled. On top of that, Fellow Flowers was going to show up later in the afternoon and their presence was sure to bring a huge fan base. More people meant more exposure and more opportunities to share about how Craniosynostosis has affected our lives.

June 20, 2014 was a Friday morning. We set out for Gazelle Sports with all of my gear. Tony was going to be there the entire time as my point person. He would get me food and drink, essentials from my bag if I needed anything, talk to the people who showed up, and kind of be the voice of this whole event as my voice got quieter and filled with less words the longer I would run.

I almost cried at the beginning of the morning as the events coordinator told me they'd had an impromptu staff meeting that morning, where they briefed all the workers in what I was doing, what Craniosynostosis was, and why I was doing it. I squashed the tears I felt forming and just smiled in what I hoped could convey the depth of my gratitude.

The hours spent on the treadmill blurred together beautifully. I started running and people just started pouring in. The very first runner to join me was my coach Joann from my days as a Fifth Third Riverbank Run Road Warrior and I was delighted to see her. She started things off well, and from then on, we had a steady stream of people coming in. Friends, family, acquaintances, running partners, people I only knew from Facebook, people I didn't know at all, friends of friends, and more filed in one after the other. People shopping in the store joined me. A few workers ran with me on their fifteen minute break. Non-running friends showed up and filled out piles of ribbons for Cranio Care Bears to use in their prayer chains. The collection jar filled. Bags and bags of donations for care packages for Cranio Care Bears kept growing in a corner. So many familiar faces, so much love, and so much support that, once again, I lacked for words. *What had I done to deserve such devotion in this life? To draw all of these people from their homes and jobs and everyday life to show up for me?*

In a whirlwind came my Fellow Flower heroes, Mel and Tori, bursting through the doors. They brought their kids, friends, food, and their wares. I not only got to meet them in person but I was also able to meet the amazing Sarah. I had talked to Sarah extensively on Facebook in the days before and after Emmett's surgery. She has a daughter who has dealt with many surgeries and procedures and offered me a voice of hope and compassion from a place of genuine understanding. I was able to put real faces to these names and I was so unbelievably honored. With a constant stream of people keeping me company, it was pretty hard to get inside of my own head and worry about how tired I was or how long I had to go. My legs cramped up for a bit, but surrounded by many, many runners, I had a good leg massage and delicious food. I had great company the entire time I was running.

Hour 7 went as it usually does, by the wayside. I was tired. I was ready to be done. I was struggling. I had evaded all tears up to that point, trying to be positive, brave, and strong in front of everybody. When my friend Kelli got there, she knew right away I was in a bad place and gave me permission, as if I really needed it, to not be okay. She was my voice of reason. She assured me it was okay to cry even in front of everyone else and it was okay to be sick and tired of running. She reminded me it was okay to feel awful and just want to stop, as long as I didn't actually stop. She ran alongside of me and encouraged me greatly to keep going.

When I started crying about how I couldn't do it anymore, Kelli reminded me that I only had a half hour to go, to which I promptly started crying even harder. To distract me, she started singing Gavin Rossdale songs. We were both nineties kids and shared a deep love for the band Bush growing up. I believe, although my memory gets fuzzier by the minute, this tradition started during one long winter run. We were both especially hating the run and struggling through it when Kelli decided to start belting out some encouragement in the form of song. That is what Kelli does when I am struggling. She sings me Gavin Rossdale songs and sounds lovely doing it. I have never, ever returned the favor for her because I'm pretty sure me singing would just make her want to give up and quit whatever she was doing just so I would stop.

As I neared the end of the run, Amy, our friend and a mutual Road Warrior from our days with the Fifth Third River Bank Run, joined us and ran in place in between the two treadmills for the final minutes. The last fifteen minutes dragged on beyond what I ever thought was possible and then the crowd behind me was counting down. Ten…Nine…I was crying. Eight…Seven…I told myself I could do it. *Just hang on. Hang on.* Six…Five…Out of the corner of my eye, I saw everybody gathered together around my treadmill. My heart swelled with pride and gratitude. Four…Three…Emmett was there. Standing at the side with Travis and Tony. Two… I took a deep breath. *Any second now.* One… I took one last stride forward. "And she's done!" Tony yelled. The place erupted with cheers and loud clapping. I pressed the stop button and began sobbing tightly locked in Kelli's arms. Thirty-five point nine miles total, but much more importantly, money raised, donations collected for other children, and people educated. At the end of the night, as I reflected on all that had been done, I was overjoyed but also, not finished. I wanted to do even more.

I had a list of hopes and dreams that seemed audaciously bold and scary.

#Kathyfacts

Sometimes we can dream so big, it scares us. It seems like we are about to take on this huge endeavor and maybe it's too much. We can doubt ourselves and wonder if we can really pull it off.

1. How have people shown up for you?

2. Were you ever surprised by the amount of support you received for something you felt was a long shot?

3. What good has come from something you've done that you almost talked yourself out of?

When people believe in you and your dream, it can empower you to believe in yourself as well. You can dream bigger and seek more knowing you have the support of those around you. You certainly don't need a huge rallying circle of support but even one or two trusted people can make the difference between wanting to give up or to keep going.

Take a moment to be thankful for your crew and let them know how much you appreciate them. As someone who has been on the receiving end of this support more times than I can count, I am genuinely amazed each time it happens. I want the people around me to know what a difference they've made in my life and I tell them often. Don't let your words be wasted. Use them to build others up and thank them for their love and support.

Chapter 27

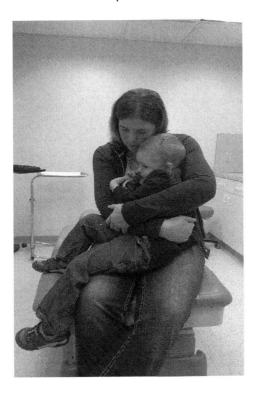

I wanted to fill this page with words that could make you understand, but truthfully, you cannot fully understand it unless you too have survived it. Watching your child suffer is unlike anything else you have ever done. It is endured with both hope and abandonment. The flood of emotions that encapsulates you is extensive. There is a pain so deep and so raw, sometimes it hurts to breathe. There comes a point of hopelessness so severe words can't possibly paint a picture. The walls close in on you and you are a caged animal that can't get out. You are trapped in this turmoil with no foreseeable end in sight. The world spins out of proportion. Five minutes feels like five hours and vice versa. You can cry, yell, pray, scream, or have a meltdown of epic proportions, but it changes nothing.

It has been during those times that I have bargained with God to spare my child and strike me down instead. Of course, it never worked. Life doesn't work that way. God doesn't work that way. There is a rock bottom that some must hit in order to climb up out of that pit of despair. Sometimes you bounce back and forth in that pit, hover just above the bottom, shoot back up, and are thrown back down with no warning. It's not always as simple as going down to the pit and choosing to come back up and back into the land of the living. The only thing you can do is hang on. Minutes, hours, days, and months cease to exist at times. The only way out of that despair is hope. Hope in the face of hopelessness. It's easier said than done. There is always hope; no matter how slight or how impossible it may seem. It's up to you to find it. It's up to you to see it. It's up to you to use that hope, harness its power, and start moving. For me, God was that hope.

How and why? Well, it's not that easy. I have no five step program to trusting God. I can't offer you any failsafe tips for digging yourself out of that pit you are in. I can only tell you what I have done, both what I have done completely wrong and what I have tried to do right. Being a believer in God and struggling with faith is normal, so say numerous books and famous speakers I won't cite here so I don't have to do the research. The point is, you can still believe in God and question what He is doing. You can still be of strong faith and not agree with what is happening.

There have been many things in my life that I have flat out not agreed with. I can't understand even now what God was doing with some of it. It's not for me to figure out though, which is where faith comes in. Faith is a funny thing to hold onto. It's invisible. It kind of makes you feel a little crazy at times. People who don't believe in God start rolling their eyes at this point usually. The ever omnipotent pie in the sky faith makes no sense to them. They want real examples. They want to know what actually made a difference in my life. If I just mention the word God, some people begin to squirm. It's like a four letter word. I promise I don't do it on purpose or for entertainment value but it does make me smile sometimes. I was that person. That used to be me. Whenever I heard someone talking about God, I immediately checked out. Now, I know if I didn't believe in God, I would have had to find another way to make my peace with it. I'm not sure how I would have done that without faith. It would have been similar to this road, fraught with pain and uncertainty and no shortage of tears but without the hope I have found in God.

Having faith saved me from a barrage of what-if questions. What-if questions are toxic. What-if questions lead you nowhere but down. You cannot live your life worrying about all the different what-ifs. When it is your child that is sick, believe me, I understand how many questions there are. In fact, I used to have not just a Plan B, but plans all the way through Z. I like to be prepared. I don't like surprises or to be caught off guard. Ironic that I found myself in that situation.

Life with a sick child is nothing but surprises and being caught off guard. No matter how hard I tried, I could not make our new life fit into any of my ridiculous lists. The lists that I would write out not just once, but again in neater, more concise handwriting. Fellow Type-A people, I know you sympathize with this plight. If I was going to choose to trust God, trust His plan for my life, trust Him with my child, then I knew everything I needed to know. I didn't need to go through scenarios A-Z and come up with responses to all of them.

I really did do that. I had dreamt up a world that didn't exist, many multi-faceted universes where the situation went just a little bit different each time and then I pondered what I would do in each situation. I didn't have to figure it out, but I kept trying. It was exhausting and emotionally draining. If you can banish the word what-if from your vocabulary, then this is the first step towards peace. This is not my own personal wisdom; it actually belongs to my very wise therapist, Dave. He is the one who pointed out this very small step that helped me change my thinking. If you can control your thinking, you can control your feelings. That's another tidbit from a man that knows a lot more about this than I do. While he could give me suggestions and coping mechanisms, only I could follow them. Only I could choose to do something with it.

It was the unhealthy coping mechanisms that I had found on my own. They were only setting me up for more worry and more anxiety. I had always thought feelings were unpredictable, which is kind of why I didn't like them. I wanted to be in control. I wanted to do things my way. I was disappointed because I had set such high expectations in my head. I was scared because I was going through all the terrible things that could happen. Things changed once I stopped obsessing over those thoughts. It's not foolproof. It can, by no means, take it all away. I was still scared, I was still disappointed, and I was still overwhelmed at times. That was the key: at times, not the whole time. When I stopped trying to solve it like a puzzle that sat out on a table in front of me, I could think once again.

It's a wonder that something so simple and small can make such a big impact, but it can. It snowballed. One good day turned into another and another. Soon I wasn't pretending. Soon I was doing it on my own, without counseling and without having to remind myself thirty times a day that it was going to be okay. I suppose it was the only way.

In the middle of despair, there is nothing. There is no one. If feels as if there is no way you will ever be okay again, and that's okay. Despair has its place at times. Sometimes you need to fall apart so you can pick yourself back up and move on. However, despair is not a place meant to be lived in. You can't stay there. It will eat you alive. It will strip your spirit of hope. It will blacken your heart towards others. It will make you unrecognizable. Take it from someone who couldn't recognize herself far too many times. You don't want any part of that.

Out of darkness, comes light.
Out of despair, comes hope.

#Kathyfacts

I have lived too much of my life in the land of what-if. I have spent hours and hours focused on what could happen, what I would do if it did happen, and how I would go on afterwards. I lived in worlds that never even existed. It was exhausting and honestly made me feel a little bit unhinged.

1. What is one thing you spend too much time worrying about that might happen?

2. Do you find yourself fixating on things you can't change? Does it ever help you and make you feel better? Or does it just hurt?

Letting go of what you can't change can be terrifying at times. Especially when what you can't change breaks your heart. On the flip side, holding on to what you are desperate to change and trying to will it into happening by sheer force can destroy you. If willpower and the true depth of our hopes could change the unchangeable, there would be a lot less tragedy and loss in this world. The best we can do is to attempt to make peace with what we don't understand. You can let go of what is actively holding you down and move forward with caution.

Letting go or accepting something does not mean you have to like it. I was caught up in that detail for a long time. I don't like it. I actually hate it. I can't accept it. I refuse to accept it. Accepting it doesn't mean it's magically just fine, it means you realize there is no other way. This is the way it has to be. You accept it even when you don't agree with it. You do so because you can't change the unchangeable.

Chapter 28

It was about 8:30 pm on a steamy Saturday in August. I was doing my first fifty mile run. It hadn't really gone as well as I had hoped. The first thirty miles were something; they practically flew by. My running partner Adele and I had talked and talked, laughed, and almost cried over the hours. Then we did it all again. There's something cathartic about stripping away all of your defenses while you run with someone else. There is no need to impress anyone there. You are both sweaty, tired, and look like crap. There's none of the drama that women so often get sucked into about competing with one another. You are running together and in it together. You are on the same team. There's no energy for egos when you are running for that many hours. That's just the way it is.

We made small talk and we delved into our past histories. We talked about dreams for the future, family, friends, running goals, and so much more. It was the most fun I'd had running in years. I was usually a solo runner, which was good for me and my emotions that were always bubbling just under the surface. I could be a bit volatile when I ran, so it was best just to steer clear, but I forgot how much better it was to not go it alone. Just as in life, I suppose. You get used to doing it alone and forget about that important human connection.

We ran and had a great time until we hit about thirty-one miles. Then, the wheels started to really come off for both of us. We struggled together for what felt like forever. I felt an irrational but ever rising desperation that I would never be done running, that I would never get to fifty miles. I'd just be stuck perpetually running forever, which is ridiculous because we were slowly but surely closing in on that finish. None the less, I couldn't squash the feeling. I was antsy and just dying to run as fast as I could and be done with the whole thing.

We parted ways around forty miles because I just had to be done. Adele was struggling and so was I, but our stress responses were different. I wanted to be the person who stuck with her, who saw the big picture, and didn't selfishly abandon her, but I was fried. All I wanted was to be done running. I had less than ten miles to go. I just had to go faster and get it done sooner. I would feel guilty about this for weeks, afraid to even say anything to her. Finally, I would throw myself at her mercy and beg for forgiveness for my selfish behavior, which she graciously and adamantly swore was not necessary at all. Adele is cool like that. I will obsess over something and she will just shrug it off, with a nugget of wisdom like "We all run our own race."

Extreme exhaustion will find you missing all sorts of manners and behaviors that you would normally have. You don't really know who you are until faced with situations like that. If you want to know what a person is really like, suffer with them. There is no quicker way to peel back all of the bravado and the facade that people put up. Toss two people side by side for hours as they start to flounder, and you will have two people who may have started the run mere acquaintances but will walk away old friends, knowing each other on a level that many long term friends may not ever encounter. That was us as I ran in the opposite direction as Adele.

On my own now, I ran my very last out and back point, to the chapel up the slight hill next to the lake. I had been running for over thirteen hours. I was slow, sluggish, and surly but when I saw the cross that hung above the chapel, I couldn't help but be transported back. *How often had I run there, past that chapel, and past that section of lake?* So many times my life had been just breaking apart at the seams. I had lost the baby. My marriage was headed towards divorce. I didn't have any friends. I was alone. I was terrified. Emmett was sick. Emmett was going to have surgery. I was an insomniac. I was full of despair. So many times I had been just barely surviving as I shuffled by that place the cross had been all along. I hadn't ever really paid close attention to it. I never cared. I never saw it as anything more than just mere decoration but that day, I could see it in a different light. I saw the cross and what it represented as clear as day. In the background of my run, it was a reminder of all I have to be grateful for and the beautiful life that is in front of me.

I slowed as I turned around to make my return back to the house, back to my people and my wonderful family waiting for me, and back to tables of food. Adele was not far behind me. This was my final triumphant leg of the journey. I nodded once in the direction of the cross, an acknowledgment of all that I had not seen before and of all the things I could understand now. The cross was out there, watching me and waiting for me. It represented hope, and I could see the different stages of my life in the reflection of that place over the years.

It was funny, but I felt awakened. In that exhaustive daze of feet shuffling after way too many hours of running, I felt honestly and truly alive. Deep within my heart, I could feel the flame burning brighter and stronger. I had the whole world at my hands. It was one of those moments that become hard to explain or put down on paper. It's the overwhelming feeling of possibility. It's a surge of confidence that tells me anything I want to do is possible. I smiled as I felt my legs burst forth with power and my pace bounce back up to what it was when I first set out on that endeavor. I was heading back home with fifty miles under my belt.

I was heading back home with hope in my heart.

#Kathyfacts

Pushing through the pain is not just for running. We push through the pain and exhaustion in everyday life as well. We keep going, somehow, in situations that seem like they will never end.

1.   What is one situation in your life you feel like you are trudging through?

2.   When you feel you have nothing left, who do you turn to? Do you tackle it alone or do you seek out support from your loved ones?

3.   Have you ever been so lost and focused on yourself and your needs at the present moment, you were unable to see the rest of the world?

It's easy to get distracted in our exhaustion. The day in, day out drudgery can keep us from noticing what is around us. If you stop to soak in the world around you, what difference could it make? The pain can dull the rest of our senses. It can cloud our mind and cover our eyes. We can wander around with only the pain for much too long if we let it.

Set aside the pain. Look for the beauty and the possibility of hope in a situation wherever you are. Try to find a positive way to see your circumstances or your place in this life. Find a silver lining. Re-examine the pain. Look past it to see the rest of the world still there before you. There is so much more than just the pain. Revel in the world and the endless possibilities that lay before you.

Chapter 29

One day, I was running in near blizzard conditions. Let the record show, I was safely tucked within the confines of a campground where you must be a member to even enter. It is a place that remains mostly deserted during the harshest of winter days, except for the security guys. I was as safe as one could be given the conditions. I was about halfway into my long run; my socks were all wet, the snow was blowing straight at my face, and I was having a hard time seeing the road in front of me. Little bits of ice pelted me in the face until it started to burn with pain. I was barely getting any traction even with ice cleats strapped to the bottom of my shoes. I was slipping all over the place, moving at the slowest of paces. It was ridiculously hard and I was particularly miserable. It was enough.

Why keep going? It's something I've asked myself time after time while I ran. Why keep going? There's not some sort of superhuman power within me that keeps me from wanting to quit. I'm just like everyone else. It's hard. I'm miserable. Sometimes I want to quit. I want to quit so bad I can taste it. Sometimes, I try to rationalize my way into it and tell myself all the reasons that it's okay to cut it short, to just give up, to go home, and to be done. Why don't I? I'm not sure. There's the obvious: I'm stubborn. A typical first born, Type-A personality that strives for perfection. That can only take you so far. Eventually everyone is faced with the tempting and overwhelming urge to quit and to back down.

Every now and then, I think I've discovered the answer and subsequently dismiss it as rubbish and keep wondering. Why? It's easy to say it's for Emmett. It's easy to say it's for my family. It's even easy to say it's for me. It's good for my soul. It feeds my passion, stokes the fire, and makes me want to go back for more. That's all good and well, but that's not all of it. Sometimes I think I am punishing myself on purpose. I want to demand more out of my body than it feels capable of. I want to keep pushing until I find that breaking point. I want to tear that breaking point down and cross the delicate threshold.

Why on earth would I do that to myself? I can think of many reasons that don't really warrant discussing yet again. The most obvious answer can be found in looking at our life. I want to be tougher. I want to be stronger. I want to prepare myself to be able to handle anything. I want the pain to become my ally. I want it to be my friend. I want to understand it. I want to get comfortable in the pain and run side by side with it. I don't want the pain to control me. I want to tame it like you would a wild animal. I want to be the one in control. I am the wild one. I want the pain to be a part of me. I want to use that deep down desperation that comes from pushing beyond the point of reason in my life. I want to be able to face my deepest fears head on with the assuredness that I am strong enough.

That's not my only driving force but every now and then, that thought pops into my head. I'm doing it on purpose. I want the pain. I want to beat it. I want to bottle it up and contain it and face Emmett with a braver face than I had on before I left. I want to turn the pain into something else. I want to make of it what I want of it.

Just like with the blizzard, I've found myself unable to see the road in front of me. I've been unsure of whether I should go on or just give up and quit. Each time I have to choose, I choose to go on. I choose to find that part of me that remains quiet most days. The deep, hardened part of me that lets my old friend pain in and feels stronger for it, braver for it, and even better for it. When all is said and done, I can go home and see that I have conquered what I once thought I couldn't. I have made it through yet another experience when I wasn't sure I could. If I can do that, I can do more. I can do anything. That's a great thing to grab hold of when you aren't sure about the future. It's a great thing to see that you can be strong in the face of what once threatened to undo you. You can hope for even more from yourself next time. Whatever these motivations may bring, whatever reason there is to go on, we must find our own driving force. The same things that move me won't move you.

Find your force. Find your passion. Unleash it. And own it.

#Kathyfacts

Pain can threaten to bring us to a standstill. Whether the pain is physical or emotional, it can leave you devastated and unsure of how to go on. Often we avoid pain, because it's uncomfortable. We don't know what to say in certain situations, we don't do things that push us past our pain thresholds.

1. Has there been a time you've had to go on despite very physical pain? What did you tell yourself to keep going?

2. Do you tend to face painful experiences head on or do you tend to avoid difficult talks and uncomfortable situations?

3. Are you happy with your current approach to dealing with pain? Why or why not?

Pain doesn't have to be the enemy. When you keep the pain close, you can understand it better. You can even find a purpose inside of it. That doesn't mean you should wallow and get stuck in pain, only that you can make friends with the pain. You can use that pain as fuel to keep going, dig deeper, and do things you never once thought possible. If you choose to let it, pain can be a powerful tool to drive you forward rather than something that makes you want to give up.

If there is pain that follows you around, try taking hold of it. Acknowledge the pain and attempt to understand it. When you understand the pain, you will be less afraid of it. The less afraid of it you are, the better you will be at taming it.

Chapter 30

I can talk myself into or out of nearly anything with such conviction, sometimes those around me believe it's the only way too. In August of 2014, I had just finished six months of long, hard, intense training for my first ever one-hundred mile race and I was thinking about backing out of it.

I had wanted to do one for a while. When my friend Adele announced she was doing the Hallucination One-Hundred in Hell (seriously, Hell, Michigan) and was looking for someone to help crew her, I jumped at the chance. The more I looked at the race and the more I thought about it, the more I wanted to run it myself. I told Adele to forget the crew support; I wanted to run the whole thing. We could do it together. Oh we had such grand plans. I started training promptly after that conversation.

It was hard work, the most miles I've ever put on in a single year. I was blowing up the roads by my house, going through running shoes like they were cheap dollar store flip flops, and eating enough food to put a household of teenage boys to shame. Above all, I loved it. It was fun. It was exciting. It was a long held dream of mine and I was just itching to cross that finish line in a blaze of glory, to learn even more about myself, and what I was capable of by pushing through all of the limits I had set for myself. I'm about to completely switch gears, so hold on while it gets confusing. It's all connected though, I promise.

During my extensive training, we had been seeking a second craniofacial plastic surgeon's opinion for most of the year, looking into options for surgery number four. With our insurance, some office politics and egos, we just couldn't make it happen. We were, in a way, blacklisted. Fed up with going nowhere, Tony called the surgeon's office that had already told us they wouldn't see us weeks earlier to beg for just one consult after all our searching. We only wanted an opinion. It was like the heavens opened up and offered us a gift. Right here, in our hometown, a well-respected craniofacial plastic surgeon had just transferred two weeks prior. He wasn't even listed yet as being employed by the hospital, but he was there, and lucky us, being brand new he did not have a huge list of patients waiting or care that we had been using a different hospital for different parts of Emmett's care. We could see him in a week and a half, compared to the six month wait we were facing then.

I sat in the office clutching Emmett's medical binder. I stared down at my shoes and tried to squelch the hot tears spilling out as the surgeon explained why we should just go with our previous doctor's recommendation of surgery in another five years. We should just wait and hope nothing happened in the meantime. It probably wouldn't anyhow, so it would be okay to wait. This new surgeon had agreed with the long wait too. I lifted my face up to look at my last hope, the one I had prayed would help Emmett, and felt only crushing disappointment roll down my face with my tears. The surgeon seemed startled by my tears and truly affected. I could see it in his face. I heard him say something about "Mom checking out of this conversation," and Tony squeezed my arm. Tony and the surgeon were talking back and forth. Tony's voice grew louder and the words got closer together and came quickly punctuated by frustration. The surgeon was talking a lot but I blocked out his voice. I didn't want to hear it. Yet again, I was powerless to get Emmett the help he needed. *How did we keep ending up in this position? When would enough be enough?*

The problem was Emmett's skull again. It had not healed correctly, just as Emmett's team had initially warned us. He had protruding bones growing in the wrong direction and numerous holes at the sides of his skull where there was no bone to protect his delicate brain. There was one patch of his skull that was nothing but a squishy soft spot. He was like a newborn in fragility, but in the body of a rambunctious three-year-old boy. Sounds terrifying doesn't it?

Emmett was also very accident prone. One of our neurosurgeons called it a lack of spacial awareness. The lesion in his brain is in his spacial center and it affects his ability to determine how close or far from something he is, if he will end up hitting something slightly or plow head first right into it. He's not aware of the space around himself. He runs into doorknobs, falls head first off of couches, trips over nothing in tennis courts, and more. He had already been hospitalized once with a mild concussion. This was more than just some toddler clumsiness, it was dangerous. Every time he hit his head, I cringed. *What sort of damage could he be doing? All it takes is one good direct hit to an unprotected area of his brain and it would all be over.*

We agonized over it. I heard whispers about a helicopter mom from those around me. I shrugged off my initial reaction, which was to let them have it and make them feel bad for their incorrect assumptions about what they didn't understand. It didn't matter anymore. All that mattered was that I kept him safe. But I just couldn't go on waiting and hoping nothing would happen for the next five years. We had already kept him out of preschool for the fear of what could happen. *How long would I need to keep him behind?*

We also desperately wanted to get the surgery over with. He was three, and absolutely beyond words, terrified of the hospital. Appointments consisted of us pinning him down, him hyperventilating, screaming, crying, kicking, and sometimes throwing up because he had become so worked up. He had been legitimately traumatized by his extensive time spent in the hospital, understandably so. We wanted Emmett to have the surgery sooner rather than later in the hopes that maybe he wouldn't remember most of it. In five years, he'd be eight. Recovery would be harder, swelling would be greater, and I was sure he would remember every second of it.

Everyone agreed the surgery was absolutely necessary; they just disagreed on the timeline. Emmett's previous team wanted to wait the five years. We didn't want to wait and hope nothing would happen until then. It was a huge risk with him just walking around in everyday life. We couldn't find a surgeon in network that would agree with us. A world renowned surgeon in Texas that takes second opinions over email and phone believed the surgery should be done right away, but if we went to see him, financially we'd be on our own. Our insurance company wouldn't touch it with a ten foot pole.

All of these thoughts were rattling around in my head when I heard something I didn't understand. Tony's voice had changed. He sounded a little less angry and a little more relaxed. The surgeon spoke up. "You make a really compelling argument. I understand your concerns. If you want the surgery done now instead of later, I will do it now." I wasn't sure I had heard him right until I could feel the surgeon staring at me. I looked up from the hole I had been staring into the floor to see him smiling expectantly at me. I squeaked out a quiet thank you. Tony squeezed my hand tightly and smiled at me. I looked back at the surgeon and started crying, so hard I was unable to get any words out. The surgeon looked at me with concern. "Hey, hey. It's okay," he said. "It's just a surgery. It's not like I'm changing the world here." I managed to get out one sentence before another rush of uncontrollable tears. "You're changing my world." The words hung in the air and filled the room. No one said anything for a few seconds. The surgeon nodded at me and cleared his throat in the quiet room.

It was just two weeks before my one-hundred mile race that we sat in that office and set a date for Emmett's fourth surgery. The surgery would be late September, just three weeks after the race. I was torn. I went back and forth, left and right, and up and down. *Was I selfish to want to do it still? Should I be at home and focusing on tying up as many loose ends as I could before the surgery? I should be devoting my time fully to pre-operative appointments, staying home with him, and taking it easy before the next big challenge, right? I needed to be there for him. People would think I was a cold, callous woman if I went ahead and did this race right before Emmett's surgery.* I was even worried I actually was cold and callous to want to do this race before his surgery. I flipped coins. I prayed. I polled people around me. I looked around and listened for a clue, a hint, or a sign of what I should do. I just wasn't sure. I chastised myself. *What kind of mother was I?*

One night, I had a moment of clarity. What would I expect out of my husband or a family member if they were in this situation? Would I expect them to not do something three weeks before a surgery? Would that mean they loved somebody less? Of course not. I wanted to show my children that you don't quit when the going gets tough. I wanted to be an example for them. I wanted to be that person who someday someone would look at and say "Yes, she's got it right." The more I thought about it, the more I realized I had to do it. I had to do it for Emmett. Each and every mile would be for him. If he could have his head cut open yet again, I could run one-hundred miles. "Easy peasy," as Travis would say. I would still be able go to all of Emmett's appointments. I would still fill out all the necessary paperwork. I would still pack all of our stuff up for our extended stay. I would still run early in the morning before everyone else was awake and I'd still use Saturday mornings for my long run time. I thought back to how I had lost myself with Emmett's diagnosis. How I had refused to live in the wake of fear. I remembered how I refused to do what I wanted to anymore or to enjoy life as I waited for the other shoe to drop. I didn't want to do that anymore. I didn't want to stop living just because I was afraid. I decided to go ahead and run my race.

It was Friday, September 5, 2014. Just thinking about it even now puts a pit back into my stomach after all this time. I was full of nerves, butterflies, excitement, and the promise of what could be for the next day and a half. We had arrived at the campground around 1 pm in a blaze of hot September heat. The heat index was soaring and I was sweating just standing in place. Tony and I had begun to unpack our canopy, chairs, jugs of water, a cooler with snacks, and obsessively labeled Ziploc bags of running supplies all tucked neatly within my storage tote. There were extra clothes, extra socks, extra shoes, an extra headlamp, and more.

The pit in my stomach grew. I felt sick, like I might actually throw up. I surveyed the company I was in and started to panic. These were not my people. I had a good fifty plus pounds on most everybody there. These people were very thin, very fit, earthy, organic eating, super athletes. Looking down at my ample thighs in my size twelve running skirt, I felt like I had a flashing neon sign above my head proclaiming I didn't belong there. *What was I even thinking? Why would I have thought this would be a good idea? What made me think I could do something like this? I wasn't fit enough for something like this.* I was sure I was in over my head. This was serious stuff. I was gearing myself up for a pre-race meltdown of epic proportions. I paced tiny circles in front of our tent and became a ball of uncontrollable nerves.

Then the neighbors showed up. Three guys, Shawn, Alex, and Tin (yes Tin, not Tim), began unloading all of their stuff right next to us. They were friendly, funny, and endearing. Just watching them struggle with their tent made me feel better and lighter somehow. We became fast friends with them and before we knew it, they were putting their stuff under our giant canopy and becoming a part of our crew. They were experienced ultramarathoners, full of all sorts of great knowledge, but weren't intimidating at all. I was instantly grateful for them. Just to have more people right there was calming. We made small talk, told funny stories, and there was good natured teasing. A pre-race jump in pool made me feel even better. By 3 pm, we were standing on the main lawn looking up at a stage listening to race directions and I was feeling sure of myself. I could do this. *I've done much harder things than this. I've trained for the race just like anybody else. I can totally do this.* I met up with Adele at 4 pm on that Friday afternoon and we were off. We would have thirty hours to complete one-hundred miles.

There were no dull moments in the race. The blazing, sickening heat was like running through water. The air was heavy and thick and slowed me down immensely. Luckily, when we made it into the shelter of the trees, it blocked a lot of the sun for us and made it slightly more bearable. Adele and I chatted with those around us and got chased by a possibly friendly raccoon in the middle of the trail. I waved a stick at him and ran for shelter when he started coming after me. Then he took an interest in Adele and a few other runners behind us. It was early evening; I couldn't tell you what time exactly, when I heard the tornado siren. It was long, loud, and disturbing in the eerie silence of the woods.

Here is where some back story helps, or rather five back stories. I am terrified of tornadoes, just absolutely terrified. I've had a lot of run-ins with those awful sirens that unnerve me every single time.

1. The initial fear, I believe, stems from an incident when I was very young at home with my little sister, Jenny, huddled in the corner of our tiny bedroom while sirens went off, afraid we were actually going to die.

2. The movie Twister gave me nightmares for weeks. I could never look at the sky the same way again. I remember hiding in my basement and feeling irrational panic every time it stormed or the wind picked up.

3. One hot summer when I was very pregnant with Travis, I went to the art show in Ann Arbor with my mother-in-law, sister-in-law, aunts, and a few friends. We were standing in the middle of the street when the sirens began going off. I was immediately on the defense. Everybody sat eating their delicious fair food and looking at all the cool things that were nearly impossible to afford. I scanned the crowd to look for people panicking, as they should be, but everyone seemed to think it was an accident. It was a perfectly sunny day, until the wind picked up and the clouds rolled in. Two young women came running from a building yelling that there was a tornado coming. Finally, people started acting appropriately. We ran to the closest building and were shuffled into the lowest floor. I can't even remember what building it was. I was shaking in anticipation and fear. I had been telling my Aunt Mary why I was so afraid of tornadoes and the siren when I began crying like a hormonal, out of control pregnant woman.

4. We had been at the circus for less than an hour with our baby, Travis, when the tornado sirens went off. Everybody said it was an accident and congregated near a tree, of all places where I pointed out that we were about to take down the entire family lineage in one swoop if there actually was a tornado coming. I was antsy and beside myself at being out in the open like that until we knew the siren was for real or not. I was up and out of that circus tent, taking my baby with me, and driving as fast as I could to my in-law's house where I paced back and forth in front of the window checking the sky. As it turns out, it really was just a mistake and no inclement weather had been headed for us.

5. The most frightening encounter occurred back in the day before everyone had cell phones. I was out running about two miles away from home when the sky turned black, the wind picked up, and it started to pour. It felt ominous and I was instantly afraid. I realized I wasn't near any ditches or low spots and had nowhere to go, so my plan was to run home as fast as I could. I ran so fast that I felt like I was going to throw up at any minute. Just over a mile away from

home, it started hailing and pelting me all over stinging my face and arms. The tornado siren rang out through the gusting wind and punishing hail. It lit a fire underneath me. Fear and adrenaline shot through my veins and my legs lost all feeling. I bolted down that street as fast as I possibly could, sure that at any moment I was going to be face to face with a giant whirling funnel of death coming for me. I stared straight ahead and ran with everything I had in me as if my life depended on it, because maybe it very well did.

I came tearing up the driveway to see Tony standing by the door anxiously looking out. Travis was still quite young then and downstairs sleeping safe and sound in his pack and play that Tony had pulled into the middle of the bathroom. I could barely walk down the stairs. Tony had to hold me up as I began tripping over my own two feet with legs that wouldn't work. In true runner fashion, I looked down at my watch and saw the fastest mile I had ever run in my entire life by far– a 6:07 mile. I covered an entire mile in just six minutes and seven seconds. Pride welled up in me despite the circumstances. We sat on the bathroom floor and waited it out where I abruptly started crying, the adrenaline leaving my system and being replaced with a sick feeling.

Let's flash back to the race. There I was, Friday evening. I'd only been running a few hours when I heard the tornado siren. Again, people did not react accordingly in my opinion. Everybody just kept running like it was no big deal. My eyes darted left and right. I asked Adele about it. I asked a few people who we happened upon about it. "No big deal. It's probably nothing," they assured me. I felt sick to my stomach, the feelings of panic and dread setting in. I needed to do something about it. I called Tony. I asked him to find out what was going on. He called me back a few minutes later citing that no one knew anything about a tornado siren there. It was sunny at camp and they had never heard the sirens go off. He asked me if I was sure. *Of course, I was sure!* The sirens had been going off but they had stopped by then.

The race was stationed in this big campground but we were deep in the woods behind the campground. In order to reach one-hundred miles, we would need to run six laps. Each lap was sixteen point seven miles around, so it was easy to be out of reach from our home base rather quickly.

Adele and I kept running, as if there was anything else to do, when it happened again. The clouds rolled in fast and furious. It was dark within a matter of minutes. The temperature plummeted, later the volunteers would tell us it dropped twenty-four degrees when the storm rolled in. I went from sweating profusely and being too hot to shivering in the cold wind as the rain came down in sheets. The wind picked up and was howling all around us. Adele and I were in the middle of the woods all alone when the wind gusts started to get out of control. It roared violently and the tall trees above us bent, creaked, and groaned with the pressure. I suggested we pick up the pace, to get out of there quicker. I wanted to be farther out of those woods and closer to safety. What I really wanted was a road, but all alongside us was a six foot fence with razor wire above it. The property was lined by a medical testing facility and there was no way out. There was no stepping off of the trail and onto the road. The only way out was through.

We ran deeper into the woods and my sense of dread grew. We were running hard and watching the trees above us when the first limb came down. A massive thing right at Adele's foot. It almost hit her. We started to go even faster. The wind shook the whole forest around us and it was like we were in a snow globe. Huge limbs started coming down left and right. Trees fell. The snapping, breaking, and cracking of limbs echoed all around us. Now we were both legitimately afraid, thinking that we could die out there. We were not safe from a tornado in the middle of those never ending woods. We were not safe from the trees themselves. The whole forest seemed like it was caving in on itself and we were right in the middle of it.

I screamed something full of panic to Adele about how scared I was. Adele, a veteran who has seen war and the terrible things that go with it, who has lived with PTSD, assured me that it was a life and death situation. It was okay to be scared. We joined hands and held on tightly to one another. Adele yelled a prayer for our safety that was barely heard over the noise of the storm. I fought the urge to cry and started screaming what I could remember of The Lord's Prayer. "Our father who art in heaven, Hallowed be thy name. Thy kingdom come, thy will be done, on earth as it is in heaven. Give us this day our daily bread. And forgive us our trespasses, as we forgive those who trespass against us and lead us not into temptation but deliver us from evil: Amen." I screamed it over and over, struggling to make my voice carry over the wind.

We ran harder. I stopped to call Tony. In hysterical bits and pieces that I wasn't sure he could even hear, I said my goodbyes. I honestly thought I might die out there. There were too many trees and we were so deep in the forest. "I'm sorry," I wailed. "I'm so, so sorry. This was stupid. I'm so sorry. I love you. Tell the kids I love them. I'm so sorry. I don't want to be here anymore. I want to be done running. I want to be done. I'm so sorry. I don't want to die out here." By the end, I was sobbing thinking of my family without me.

Another huge limb landed near us. That's when it kicked in. I had to go faster. Pure adrenaline was running through my body and every survival instinct I had was on fire, egging me on. I was not about to be hit by a tree. I was not about to call it quits and be okay with possibly being hit by a tree. It both pains and embarrasses me to say I once again abandoned Adele, although this time was not on purpose at all. I sped ahead darting in and out of those trees and jumping over limbs that were littering the floor of the forest. I was sure that she was fast on my heels, but I didn't turn around once and check to be sure. I just bolted forward and kept my eyes half on the trail below me and half on the trees above me for anything incoming. When I finally thought to turn around and make sure she was there, she was nowhere to be found. I yelled for her but got no answer. Now I really was all alone. Adele, who didn't have a phone on her or any way to reach anyone, was even more alone.

The wind died down and the storm started to head out. The rain remained steady and hard, but I could handle the rain. I just kept running and running. I should have been to an aid station by that point, but I was nowhere. The aid station would have water, food, and people. I didn't want to be alone anymore. I wanted people but I was lost. To keep the runners going the right way, there were little orange flags lining the path that should have always been at my right. I was lost in the middle of the woods in the middle of the night with no orange flags in sight. I was all by myself in the pouring rain and darkening night with no headlamp. I was supposed to be back to camp way before it got dark to get my headlamp, lights, and reflective gear. I had to use the dimly lit screen on my dying cell phone a little bit at a time to save the battery. It didn't really matter, because it barely gave off any light at all. I couldn't see below my feet. I stumbled and tripped over everything.

A couple of hours passed with me crying in the woods all by myself on the phone to a helpless Tony who had no idea how to find me or where I was. Once again, I was utterly hysterical, until I saw a flag. Somehow I had stumbled onto the right path, but it was wrong. People were running towards me instead of with me. I stopped the first person who didn't look like a super serious front of the pack runner. I didn't want to be responsible for derailing an elite runner's race. They pointed me back the way they had come, to the next aid station, a couple miles back behind them. Every person I passed, I asked and double checked I was still going the right way because I was so afraid to get lost again. Finally, I saw the lights in the middle of the darkness. It was the aid station. There were volunteers, chairs, food, and something to drink. I had stumbled around for a couple of hours, an extra seven to eight miles, going in some bizarre kind of circle.

I was so happy to see people, so happy the tornado business was done, and so happy to be out of the woods that I just started bawling. A woman there, who would become my most favorite cheerleader, came towards me with arms outstretched, hugged me tightly, and led me to a chair. All the people there were incredibly sweet and helpful as I wept into my running pack. I rambled on in between sobs about being lost and losing Adele, about being hungry and not able to see in the dark, and about the trees falling. They offered to take me back and I laughed through my tears. "No, it's for Emmett," I said, which made no sense to them of course, but I was too exhausted to elaborate. I just needed a few minutes to regroup.

I sat and cried in the folding chair for a good twenty minutes. Runners came through and patted me on the back. They smiled at me and gave the runner's nod in my direction. Such a simple motion, that nod, but it conveyed so much understanding and solidarity. A couple of guys offered a "Pull it together Mama," and reassured me I could do it. I felt loved, cared about, and seen. Yes. I would keep going. Yes. I would finish the race. As runners kept passing me, I saw someone coming from the opposite direction. *No. It couldn't be. Could it? What are the odds?* As the figure came shuffling out of the darkness, I saw the brightly colored tie-dyed pants and breathed a huge sigh of relief. I jumped up so quickly I knocked my folding chair over and yelled "Adele!" I ran to her and we hung on to each other as I cried into her shoulder. "Oh thank God you are here! Oh my God! I can't believe you are here! I got lost! You got lost too! But we both ended up in the same place! I couldn't find you! Oh my God! Are you okay? I'm so glad you are here!" I blubbered and cried some more unaware of what a scene we were making. I saw my favorite aid station worker wipe a tear from her eye and was amazed at how much she had already invested in me while not knowing anything about me. I smiled back at her and then resolved myself to not split up from Adele again. No matter what, I had learned my lesson. Adele took some time to regroup and get herself some food and drink as she had been out there far too long without enough. I called her crew and everyone was immensely relieved we had found each other again and were heading in. We took off down the road again, back towards camp, just four miles away. Thankfully Adele had a headlamp and we could see for our return trip home.

We crashed into camp with pure chaos. My feet were already a mess. Eight hours in soaking wet shoes and socks. There were numerous blisters already. Adele's foot was just one giant blister. We were both mentally exhausted from the ordeal with the storm, losing each other, and adding hours to our race inadvertently. Tears fell freely as we made our way to camp and saw our beloved crews. Each step we took was punctuated by pain because of that first terrible lap when we could not take care of our feet.

Adele, her friend Adam who was pacing us, and I headed out for a second lap. I fought a lot of nausea and the urge to throw up that was constant for the first few miles. Thankfully, Adele distracted me for most of it prompting me to tell Adam all about Emmett and the things I was doing. Adele kept me out of my head and more importantly, out of my rolling stomach. My legs were overly tired, my guess is from sprinting way too fast during the previous lap, and I stumbled and tripped over roots, even with my headlamp. I fell a few times, getting mad at myself each time. At one of the aid stations, we lost Adele. She was dealing with a lot of pain in her foot, so much so that it was changing her running gait. We tearfully hugged goodbye at the aid station and I turned to keep going.

It was barely Saturday morning and still very dark out. I was afraid to head back in by myself. Luckily for me, Adam chose to run me in the remainder of the lap so I didn't have to do it alone, for which I will be forever grateful. Because of my personal detour in the first lap, I was way behind even the slowest of runners by time, but still ahead of the fastest runners at that point by location. I was in the middle of the sixteen mile loop, in no man's land. I was too far behind to catch up to the slower runners and far enough into the loop that the elite runners hadn't caught me yet. The elite runners would eventually lap me and I'd start to see other faster runners go by, but then, it was be just me and the trail. I was happy to have Adam run me in and not go it alone.

When I hit the final aid station that held my favorite volunteer and all the people who saw my first lap breakdown, they cheered for me. They greeted me like an old friend returning home. "One-seventy! All right, so good to see you again. How are you doing? What do you need? How's your friend?" They were so good to me and it renewed my weary spirit.

I took off with my new ultra friends and camp neighbors, Shawn, Alex, and Tin for the third lap. They were way too fast for me and I couldn't keep up with them for more than a couple miles, but the time I did was great. They told me stories, cheered me on, and kept me focused. Eventually, I had to slow down. I thanked them for letting me tag along for a bit, surely still much slower than they were used to going, and bid them farewell. "See you at camp!" they yelled as they quickly disappeared out of sight.

Sometime in what was the actual fourth lap, I began to lose my drive and decided I needed to call Azsure. Azsure was the first grown up friend I made, all on my own. She had been a long time part of the church we had started attending. The first time I met her was on a Saturday morning in the parking lot of our church as a part of the small running group they were getting off of the ground. I was trying to figure out how to say her name without sounding stupid and wondering how on earth anyone could look so flawless first thing in the morning. Seriously. Flawless. During that first run, we discovered that we were nearly the same person. We shared similar life stories, similar milestones, similar past jobs, and nearly identical tastes in all things book, movie, and music related. We became great friends and her uncanny ability to know exactly what I was thinking without me saying a word only propelled the friendship. She was always in my head.

On that early, miserable Saturday morning, separated by hundreds of miles, I longed for Azsure's friendly face and voice that would know just what to say. I whined. I cried. I complained. I freaked out. I told her all about my terrible endeavors and how much

I wanted to quit running. I believe I even threw in some epic "I'm never, ever going to run ever again! I hate running. It's just the worst thing ever," kind of dramatics. She let me go. She let me have my tantrum on the phone without interjecting. Then, ever so logical and able to see through a situation that felt impossible for me to figure out, Azsure presented me with my options of what to do next. She simply asked me to consider what sort of outcome I would truly be okay with. There it was. An Azsure truth bomb blew up. There was only one outcome I was going to be okay with and it was not quitting, especially not after how much I had suffered already to get to that point. I had to go on. I thanked her for her never ending wisdom and on I went; plodding through the thick mud and climbing over the downed trees that blocked off certain portions of my path. It was miserable. Just absolutely miserable. I felt like I was barely moving.

The fifth lap is where it got confusing, because I had been gone for hours, many more hours than I should have been for a lap. Something went wrong yet again. Either I got lost, I ran by our camp without ever stopping, or I got all the way to the end and then turned back the wrong way at the confusing aid station that had people coming and going in two different directions. I don't know what happened exactly. I truly and honestly don't remember. All I knew was I was had to keep running. I was hurting and I wanted to stop so badly I could almost taste it, but I had to keep running.

Not long before I left the woods, I saw a woman wearing a blue CrossWind Church shirt that I knew so well. My church. It looked like my friend Mary. *Ridiculous. I was almost three hours away from home. Why would she be there?* I thought I was hallucinating, but the hallucination kept walking closer to me. I poked at her. Honest to God. I poked her in the arm because I didn't believe she was really real. But she was real. I collapsed in her arms, crying about how happy I was to see her and rambling about how awful the race was. She ran me in to camp for the remainder of my lap.

When I arrived back at camp, I was in really bad shape. The finish line was right there, the volunteer yelled a question. "Finisher? Finisher?" I shook my head no and started crying. Would they know if I just ran through the finish line anyhow and claimed it? Mary helped me change out of my soaking wet, muddy, and sweaty clothes. Then she helped me dress again. Like a mother tends to her children, Mary waited patiently as I whined and cried and helped me do the simplest of tasks. Then, she helped me back into my chair where I hung my head and just cried.

I had two large blood blisters, three different blisters in between my toes, and a huge blister covering the pad of one foot. My feet were so swollen, it was worse than when I was nine months pregnant. I cried in the chair, not sure how I was ever going to be able to go on. Thank God for our new ultra friends. They were brave enough to touch my horrifying feet and nice enough to share their medical kit.

If you want to really know somebody, witness them at their most exhausted state. Tin had dropped down to accept a one-hundred kilometer finish, meaning sixty-two point two miles, instead of going on to finish the one-hundred mile race. However, he had run more than that, settling somewhere just over seventy miles. He didn't want to wreck his legs as he was preparing for a big race just weeks away. He had literally just walked away from the finish line when I saw him. Instead of sitting down, resting, or getting something to eat, there he was crouched down in front of me with Tony, doctoring my feet up. Just the thought of crouching down on my abused legs sent a shiver of pain through me, but yet there he was. Those guys were all heart. They were full of care and concern, doing everything they could to get me back out there for my final lap.

I had talked to the race director about my extra miles and getting lost early on in the race. Before my watch had died, I showed the aid station workers how many miles I had actually run when I hit camp and they wrote down that mileage. My watch had died somewhere around forty miles and so I no longer had proof. The race director told me he'd consider adding them. I thought I was going to finish this one final lap to reach seventy-three miles myself. I had no idea where I actually was. I thought I had already failed in being able to make one-hundred miles in less than thirty hours. I had been beating myself up about it.

My crew all told me I was doing great and that I was so determined and so strong. Their words echoed in my ears and reverberated through my broken down body - they were proud of me. They barely knew me but they were proud of me. My-mother-in-law had brought the boys there to see me but I think I kind of scared them with how out of it I was. Still, I was happy to see their faces and it gave me the extra boost I needed to keep going.

Tony had bought a green running shirt with a giant peace sign that covered the entire front and changed into a pair of cargo shorts. He had been wearing jeans and a button down shirt beforehand. On the front of his shirt was a pacer bib, number one-seventy. It declared to the world that we belonged to each other. Pacer one-seventy for runner one-seventy. He knew I was scared. I was sure I was going to get lost again on my own, and I hated it. I didn't want to do it at all, let alone by myself. I cried tears of gratitude at the sight of him. I was so relieved that I wouldn't have to do it on my own. It's important to note that he wasn't a runner before this. Not at all. The most he'd ever run before that day was three miles on the treadmill many months prior. He doesn't like running. He wasn't trained for anything like that. He could have hurt himself, but he wanted to be there for me. He knew how important it was to me and I think he knew there was no way I'd make it one more lap around on my own.

When my crew got my feet into the shoes, I stood up and nearly fell back over. The pain was excruciating. Every single step was pure agony. The blisters throbbed and my raw skin burned. You know in the summer how you can get a blister in between your toes from flip flops and how much that hurts? Imagine that, plus four more blisters being crammed into shoes that were cramped and heading out for another sixteen miles on them. To say it tortured me would be an understatement. It hurt to stand. It hurt to take a step. The pain throbbed in my feet with every passing second and my mind attempted to shut my body down. I stood up. I started to limp. I cried tears of pain and exhaustion for what I was going to attempt. I gritted my teeth and, ever so slowly, I started shuffling down the dirt path back into the woods for my very last lap.

A group of runners that were already done running and lounging in their lawn chairs stood up as I approached them. They stood and cheered, screaming encouragement "One-seventy – you are pure grit! You are amazing! You can do this!" A thin but muscular girl with spiky hair jumped up and down, cheering and clapping as her friends joined her. I remember thinking how sweet of them it was, but how strange too. *A standing ovation to run?* I asked Tony what he thought it was all about and he just laughed. "You can't see yourself, we can. You know that person who you feel sorry for because you can see they are in tremendous pain and really struggling? You can tell by their face how hard it is for them to go on? That's you. You are the talk of this town. It's impossible to miss it. Everyone can see how much pain you are in, but yet you are still going."

It took a minute for his words to sink in, and when they did, a fresh wave of tears came. *People noticed me?* I had run most of the race completely alone. There were rarely people nearby, though occasionally someone would blow past me like I was standing still, and subsequently give a nod in my direction. I had bumped into a few people at aid stations and at camp, but still I had felt I was on an incredibly painful journey alone for the past twenty-seven hours. People noticed. I really wasn't alone. They were cheering me on, watching me, and rooting for me amidst their own exhaustion. What an amazing group of people I was surrounded by. I felt a twinge of guilt for initially writing them all off as not my people. Clearly they were my people. They were kind, caring, and supportive. They were behind me in both big ways and small. I was not alone out there at all.

With that realization came the longest sixteen point seven miles of my entire life. I cried, sobbed, hallucinated, got sick, cried some more, and just was the most miserable I'd been in my entire life. The whole time, Tony held my hand. He didn't say anything negative, although he'd certainly earned a "You signed up for this," remark as he was stuck out there with me. He did none of that. Instead, he told me stories, he sang songs to me, he tried to make me laugh, and he pointed out all of the roots and trees so I wouldn't trip over them as I had in previous laps. A few times, I saw him flex his hand when he thought I wasn't looking; a sure sign that I was hanging onto him with a death grip. When we made it to the final aid station, I introduced Tony like I was introducing him to family for the first time ever. I wanted them see how great he was. They cheered us on, spoke so much encouragement to me, and gave me the boost I needed to keep going.

The last four miles were the worst. We were dangerously flirting with the thirty hour time limit. If I took too long, it would have all been for nothing. I couldn't let the win go unsung. I had to make it to that finish line before thirty hours. I forced myself to pick up the pace. It was in a word, excruciating. Pain radiated throughout my entire body. I kept whispering to myself over and over "I'm going to make it. I'm going to make it. I'm going to make it." It was an obsessive mantra. I demanded time updates nearly every minute and swung from "Oh my God, I'm going to make it;" to a desperate whiny voice screaming "We're never going to make it. We're never going to get out of this forest!" Back and forth I went from one extreme to the next. *It couldn't be just four miles; it had to have been closer to forty. It was taking too long.* I became more and more desperate. I wasn't sure I was ever going to be out of that forest, and then I heard music. *We were close enough to hear music!* I still had twenty minutes until the official time limit of thirty hours.

The trail opened up and we came out of the clearing and headed down the road into the campground, to the finish line. Tony was walking. I was holding on to his hand, shuffling my feet slowly behind him in a pretend run, and sobbing with pure relief. *I'm going to make it. I'm actually going to make it.* I could see the finish line. People sat in front of their tents and campers, lining the roads and exploded with cheers as they announced over and over "One-hundred mile finisher. One-hundred mile finisher!" You would have thought I was the first place finisher with the amount of noise they were making for me. I was still sobbing. It was that uncontrollable, embarrassing, loud, can't catch your breath, make that weird noise trying to gulp air kind of sobbing. I pushed my feet forward through the pain and through the extreme emotions gripping me. Hand in hand, we crossed the finish line. At exactly twenty-nine hours, forty-four minutes, and forty-four seconds, I was finally done. I was the second to last person to cross the finish line, but I was elated to have crossed that finish line.

Later as I lay in the car, I realized they were wrong. I wasn't really a one-hundred mile finisher. I felt embarrassed and ashamed that I didn't correct them. The next day I checked the results and saw myself listed as a finisher. *Did I actually run one-hundred miles?* I truly couldn't remember. I emailed the race director who checked with the timing company. A week later, my results still stood and I got word back from the race director. It was legit. He said there was no way I could have cheated even if I'd wanted to. A few splits, or times recorded for my laps were missing. Lap two was just not there, even though I know without a shadow of a doubt I was out there running it with Adele and Adam. Lap four was also missing, again, I'm not sure why. Somewhere in between lap four and five, is where I lost track of where I was. Those are the laps where I honestly can't remember what was going on. When I went to run my final lap, I thought it was only my fourth, but it was actually my sixth lap. Six laps meant one-hundred miles. I was obviously still out there all thirty hours running and it wasn't like anyone was going to contest it because I was second to last. I didn't win anything. All I got was a buckle and an immense feeling of accomplishment. All of that suffering was not in vain. I persevered.

My heart soared with pride. I actually made it. I ran one-hundred miles. It was the most awful thirty hours of my life.

And I wanted to do it again.

#Kathyfacts

Determination in the face of unbelievable pain or heartbreak is hard. To keep going when every bone or muscle in your body is screaming at you to stop is a true test of mental strength. Whether it's in running or everyday life, we all have times when we have to push through the pain, keep going despite our circumstances, and face our fears.

1. When have you persevered in the face of many obstacles that could have stopped you?

2. What did you tell yourself to keep going and keep trying?

When you are really pushing through something and trying to keep going, it can be hard to see yourself. Life can feel impossible and can feel like you are failing even though you are up on your feet doing it. Those around you can see the struggle much clearer than you can at times. When others compliment you or praise you for what you have accomplished or done, accept it. If they have noticed your determination and strength, instead of dismissing it, smile and say thank you. Acknowledge yourself and what you can do.

When the journey you are in feels impossible and like you can't possibly take another step, remind yourself of what or who impacts your life the most. Who in your life makes the struggle worthwhile? What in your life do you take meaning and purpose from? Remind yourself of all of your reasons to keep going. The long road ahead is worth it. Sooner or later, the scenery will change. Keep going.

Chapter 31

During the days and months after Emmett's initial diagnosis of Craniosynostosis, Epilepsy, and the brain lesion, people kept telling me how amazed they were that I was still smiling. As multiple seizures raged on and more surgeries were scheduled, people would say things about how strong I was or how they wouldn't be able to handle what I did. They called me brave and inspirational. I would smile in return to these statements. *If only you really knew.* I could say I'm not sure why I pretended and gave a compelling performance of someone I was not to everyone out there, but that's not the truth. I know why. You probably know why too. I didn't want people to know. It's as simple as that. I didn't need help. I didn't want help. Or so I thought. I locked everything up as tight as I could and just pretended. People already thought I was someone I wasn't, and who was I to disappoint them? I didn't want to be the one to tell everyone it was a lot harder than it looked.

I didn't understand then. I was fooling a lot of people, but not everybody. There were a few people who could tell, even when I wasn't up front with the truth. Tony, a close friend, a family member. They knew. They must have seen everything so clearly, I never even had to say anything, but they couldn't do anything to help. There was nothing to say that would make it better or take it away. There was no way to pull me up out of the trenches until I was ready to go myself. I remember being scared that they would think less of me. If I told them how bad it was, the people who knew all along, I was worried they would think I wasn't brave or doing a good job.

Before Emmett's fourth surgery, another extensive operation on his skull, I was terrified once again. I tried to hide it. I attempted to make my peace and talk about fear mixed with hope. The problem was I didn't really believe my own words. I was a fake and a phony. I could string some words together that weren't the truth at all. The truth was that I was heartbroken to my very core to be sending my baby boy off to surgery once again. It hurt deep inside. It made me feel different from everyone around me. I saw the world in different shades of black. Once again, nothing made sense to me anymore.

When I fessed up to the world via a blog post about how scared I was once again, I waited for the backlash. I closed my eyes and braced for impact, waiting for people to take back all those wonderful things they had said about me. *Now they know. Now they could stop calling me inspirational and brave or courageous and amazing. Now they could see me for the coward I really was. I was no different than anyone else.*

The backlash never came, but a huge outpouring of love and support did. I couldn't believe my eyes. People used those words tenfold, over and over. I was overwhelmed with the many emails, comments, calls, and texts over it. *Were they even reading the words I wrote?* It didn't make sense to me. I was admitting defeat and they were calling me strong.

I couldn't see outside of myself and my own impossibly high standards. I couldn't see it from anyone else's point of view but my own, and I am my very worst critic. My inner voice was cutthroat brutal on me, but overly gracious and accepting of others. I thought I was doing such a bad job, I couldn't believe others when they told me differently.

For so long, I had a hard time seeing what other people saw. I guess chalk it up to a lack of self-awareness. I'm ordinary. I really am. I've fallen apart and found God. I've lost myself and run from

God. I've come full circle to trusting what I don't understand and what I hate at times. Then, I've done it all again. It got me thinking about what I expected from myself and what I believed people expected me to do.

I had spent close to three hours running and walking around a track just outside the hospital with a pager in hand while Emmett was in for his fourth surgery. Tony was at my side. My friends Kelly and Kristy were there. Our friend and pastor, Scott, came out to run with me once more, just like during Emmett's very first surgery. My mother-in-law was with me. Others showed up, like my friend and fellow Road Warrior Elizabeth. I was not alone. I was surrounded by my people. It was easy enough to smile and pretend I was fine for the sake of others, but on the inside, everything burned. My soul was on fire. Fear ignited that fire.

When the pager finally went off, we rapidly took off for waiting room. The nurse brought Tony and I back to the recovery room. When I saw Emmett, it took my breath away. The top of his head was swollen. The zigzag incision was right next to the previous full head incision. He was moaning and crying. The drain in his head was bloody. He was full of wires and lines and his monkey shook in his little hand. Tears sprang to my eyes as I stared at him silently. They let me climb into bed with him for transport. I lay down on the hospital bed with Emmett's broken skull nestled against me, staining my shirt red. I had gently put my hands on the back of Emmett's head and saw them shake as I prayed. It took hours for Emmett to wake up from that surgery. When he did, my heart burst and broke at the same time.

I was still lying in Emmett's hospital bed with him, the blood soaked all the way through my shirt by now and my arm tinged pink. I noticed him stirring and shifted my weight to look at him. His eyes were swollen shut and his voice was small, weak, and scratchy sounding, the breathing tube leaving it sore. In a broken voice, the first thing Emmett said when he woke up was "I got hurt." Then tears of blood rapidly slid down his face as he started to cry. I choked back a number of sobs and desperately attempted to get a hold of myself. I could feel the lid about to blow off. If I lost it now, I'd only scare him when he was already scared. I cried as quietly as I could while I wiped away the bloody tears from his face with my shirt sleeve. Blood tears are normal after a major skull surgery but not easy to look at. The sound of his voice kept playing in my head. *I got hurt. I got hurt.* My poor, sweet boy was indeed hurt. Again.

In Emmett's suffering, I have suffered immensely. I have cried with him, for him, next to him, and without him. I have screamed, raged, thrown a tantrum, punched a wall, and more in the throes of my desperation. This suffering is not noble. It is reckless. Fiery. Helpless. What empowered that helplessness were my words. I wrote the things I couldn't bring myself to say. I wrote the words that have been rumbling around in my head for years. I told the truth about the things I had kept hidden. It made a difference.

With those words borne from my stubborn soul, I was able to paint the truth for the world to see. The truth is I am a picture of real life, of struggle, brokenness, and hopelessness. I am a picture of a survivor, a believer, and someone who has overcome things she once thought not possible. I am the product of what God can do. He can take someone quite ordinary like me and make people invested in what I have to say. I don't understand it fully, people caring about what I have to say but I have been gifted the ability to be heard. People listen intently, half-heartedly, or heckle me from the back row and wait impatiently for me to shut up. Regardless of what camp you may fall into, my voice is in the background and I will not cease, not until I have done what I set out to do.

Here is where that stubbornness serves a purpose. In the face of failure, and believe me I have failed in a number of stupendous ways; in a situation that others would give up on; I will still try to move forward. I have stood overwhelmed and unmoving under this burden. I was sure it was too much for me to accept. How could my words do anything for others? How could I make a difference? I'm just me. Still, that fire inside of me wouldn't go out. It urged me on. It pushed me forward. I had to try. These words carry the weight of my heart. They demand to be heard. They demand to be known. I'm not sure what I'm doing with them sometimes; I only know they just keep coming.

The struggle is not picture perfect. We are not picture perfect. We do what we can with what we have at the time. The expectations I put on myself never did me one bit of good when I was in the midst of the heartbreak. I wasn't okay. Not at all. And that was okay. It really and truly was okay. Even when the darkness was looming and I was floating adrift in this world, I was not alone. It felt like it at times, but it was never true. That's what the pain can do, block out all the good in the world. It took some time for me to realize I didn't always have to be just fine.

I am okay with not being okay.

#Kathyfacts

Sometimes we aren't okay. That's a fact. At one point or another, everyone in this world, has not been okay. How we choose to respond to that though can make all the difference in the world. Whether we choose to accept that fact or berate ourselves because of it can have a huge impact on how we work through it.

1. Has there ever been a time you've been able to admit you aren't okay?

2. What enables you to make such an admission? If you haven't been able to admit it, what keeps you from doing so?

3. Do you think your current way of handling challenges in your life is working well for you? What could you do differently?

It's scary to admit the truth. I was afraid of being perceived as unable to handle this life. I was afraid of what people would think of me. I didn't want to let anyone know how much I was struggling. However, once I told the truth, everything changed. I felt better. I feel less alone and more understood.

If there's an area in your life where you are hiding, I challenge you to start telling the truth and owning just a little piece of the story. When you aren't okay, hiding it and pretending you are is a hindrance to your healing. In order to move past something, first you must confront it. I believe acknowledging that I wasn't okay was the first step for me in making things better in my life. Once I could tell the truth about it, I could set out to do something about it. Make the choice to confront that truth.

Chapter 32

On a cold Friday morning, there was a MOPS (Mothers of Preschoolers) meeting at 9:30. Every other Friday, we meet while some lovely volunteers watch our children in the next room, and we have a chance for some time to ourselves. There are guest speakers, crafts, (that I am notoriously bad at. You should seriously see this scarf I tried to make once), short videos, devotionals, games, service projects, and just time to connect with other moms and talk about our week. I had already told my friend and group leader, Kristy, I wouldn't be making it. Emmett was less than eight weeks post-operative from his fourth surgery, which meant he couldn't be running, jumping, or rough housing with other kids. His head was still extremely fragile. I didn't have anyone to watch Emmett if I went, so I decided not to go. Just after 9 am, Tony came home from work sick. He was going to stay home and told me he could stay with Emmett while I left.

I showed up to the meeting a few minutes late and settled in my seat. There was a guest speaker, a professional organizer. She was going to give a presentation on helping us organize and overhaul our lives. Since I am a super nerd and love all things organizing, I was excited to hear the presentation. It was titled "How to Eat an Elephant." I assumed the elephant was supposed to represent life, overwhelming and huge, and seemingly impossible to tackle all areas. Her approach was simple, one bite at a time. I sat there sipping my water, surrounded by other moms, and jotting down a note here and there, when the speaker said something particularly helpful.

My ears perked up at the change in her demeanor and voice. She was talking about recording important information in case of death, divorce, or disability. Her voice sounded more serious than ever as she began to explain. First, she told us how healthy her husband had been. He worked out and even used to run the Fifth Third River Bank Run. Now I was even more invested in this story. She explained that one day after going to the gym; her husband had a grand mal seizure, the same type Emmett lives with. My heart began to beat faster. I could feel it. Something else was coming and somehow I just knew. She went on to explain the results of the MRI her husband had. I was sitting completely still but my heart was pounding wildly out of my chest and my breathing was quick and shallow. *No, it can't be. What are the odds? It's not going to be the same thing.* Then she said it: "A huge mess and tangle of veins." I gasped out loud. Tears started to fall down my face. It really was the same thing. She said something that I have said, word for exact word numerous times. "It was like waiting for a bomb to go off." Their bomb did go off. It bled not long after they found it and her husband was in the ICU. They called family in to come and say goodbye.

I listened as the entire room faded away. I sat forward in my chair, mesmerized. I could feel her desperation in that situation compounded by the recollection of my own desperation I have felt. I could see myself in her. Tears were running down my face steadily as I wiped them away with the collar of my shirt, trying to draw as little attention to myself as possible. My heart ached for her. This woman was a complete stranger, but surely we have felt some of the same things. I was living in her story, pre-bomb explosion. I quietly cried, waiting for the inevitable ending: the serious voice, the death, and the end. This could be my life any day. The sick feeling in my stomach grew.

She continued on with her story. The next step was the extremely risky surgery, the same surgery we can't do for Emmett. Her husband survived surgery. He was rehabilitated. Although he isn't the same as he was before, he is alive. I stifled a sob, but it was no use. I couldn't control it. I felt everything I've felt for Emmett over the past two years come to a head. The fear, the uncertainty, the feeling of waiting for the bomb to go off, and the dread that I will outlive him. That is what it all comes back to. The end. His end. Me outliving him. I had to get up to excuse myself as sobs came out in between short jagged breaths. I wanted to go hug this woman in the middle of her presentation. I wanted to fall to my knees and thank God for this incredible gift. I was so thankful that Tony had come home sick. I was so thankful that this woman was there talking to us and sharing her story about her husband that had nothing to do with organizing.

I cried in the corner of the room away from everyone until I felt I had my composure back and sat down. I couldn't listen to anything else she was saying. I just kept thinking, he's alive, and the tears would be running down my face again. Again and again it resurfaced in my mind. *It's not a death sentence. It's not the end. It might not be the end for Emmett.* I stared at her in a daze for the rest of her presentation. I'm sure it was a very good presentation, but I couldn't hear anything else she said. I was stuck on the hope in her story. The hope that could be in our life. The hope that could be for Emmett. After the presentation, I talked to her privately and we compared notes on treatment and recovery. Tears threatened to spill over at any minute.

So how do you keep the hope? How do you eat an elephant? Maybe it's the same. One bite at a time. One bit at a time. Bits and bites. Little by little, you are working towards what you want. The elephant gets smaller; the hope grows bigger. It takes over, snowballs, and fills your entire being up with hope. For today, tomorrow, and for all of your yesterdays that don't make sense. This was always the way it was going to go. Things went exactly the way they always were going to.

I was almost not there for that presentation. I almost missed the story that gave me hope. I cried the whole drive back home. That hope affected me and rooted itself deep within me. How can I explain it away?

In small acts, in every day acts, in things that get looked over time and time again, I want to find a reason for those things. When I look, I find them.

That's what I want to see. The hope.

#Kathyfacts

It can seem like we are so far away from other people at time. We are surrounded by many others out there that pass through without acknowledgment. There are so many stories around us. There are so many things we have in common even with strangers. When we start speaking or start listening, we are suddenly not alone at all. There are thousands of others who have shared our life experiences.

1. Has there been a time in your life when you were comforted by someone else's story?

2. Do you believe telling your story could help others? In what way?

When we start telling the truth of our stories, which can be messy, embarrassing, and heartbreaking, we are able to better connect with others. That connection, whether we are privy to it or not, can empower and comfort others in their own lives.

Owning my story was the hardest part for me. It took me so long to stand up and tell the truth. I wasn't sure how to do it. I wasn't sure I was going to be able to do it. Once I did, there was a small but significant shift towards the path I am currently on. When I told my truth, others came out of the woodwork with their own truth. I hadn't been alone at all. Attempt to own a part of your story. Tell the hard truth about something you would usually keep hidden. Watch what it can do in your life. Watch what it can do in others. When you are ready, tell your truth. Proclaim it loud and clear for the world to hear.

Chapter 33

I've had people ask me so many times that I have lost track of my answer sometimes. It's beyond the questions of why I run. It's more specifically why I would ever want to run for hours and hours. Why get on a treadmill for seven and a half hours? Why run fifty miles? Why run one-hundred miles? Even other runners view it as a bit extreme. Awesome, but extreme. I've had a mixed bag of reactions to my ultrarunning endeavors. Some people find it terribly unhealthy and think I'm just going to run myself into an early grave. Some people don't get it and think it's long, boring, stupid, and I must be out of my mind. Others think it must be for bragging rights. It must be something I just want to do to cross off my bucket list and move on from eventually. It's more than that.

I can't really pinpoint why exactly. There are a lot of reasons why I love and hate it at times, but nothing easy to understand that can be boiled down into one key point. It's not that simple. It's complicated. It's abstract. It's hard to understand the reason why I do this to myself and my body.

Before I ever had kids or started running, Tony and I were newlyweds. I was happy. I really was. I was happy but something was still missing. I didn't really understand. Everything was fine, but I could truly feel that there was something more that I wanted. I wasn't sure what it was I was seeking. I didn't know if it was a new chapter, a hobby, a different job, a different home, or something else entirely. I started looking for it even though I didn't know what it was.

I started to read a lot more, which was good because I loved to read, but that wasn't it. I moved on, trying again. Maybe I had an untapped talent somewhere within me. I thought, maybe I could draw. Spoiler alert: I couldn't. I got some cheap colored pencils and an old notebook, I just started sketching something. Isn't that how artists are supposed to do it? Just by feeling? I let my hand cross over the paper again and again until I felt my masterpiece was done. When I was finished, I set down my gray pencil and took a long, hard look at it. I was blown away by how terrible it was. What on earth was it supposed to be? Even I didn't know. It was nothing but scribbles and jagged lines each outdoing the other. Thus was the end of my drawing career.

Next I thought about scrapbooking. Yeah, yeah, I know, but that was back when scrapbooking was at the height of its popularity and everyone was always throwing those sticker parties. I went to the local craft store to see what it would take to get myself started. I quickly realized I knew nothing about it or even where to start. There were aisles and aisles of absolutely everything you could imagine. Paper, stickers, punches, scissors, stamps, and pens. There were the "right" kinds of pens to use for scrapbooking followed by the "right" kind of paper. It all lay before me in a giant array of scary. I spent about an hour trying to get myself started with the basics, just a few things, but grew tired and inpatient. I decided that it was way more work than I wanted to commit to. I abandoned my cart and my pursuit of that particular hobby.

I briefly got involved with decoupage, but there were only so many things I could slap glue on. Over and over, I tried various things, trying to find my niche and trying to find something that would help fill the strange void I felt.

In the span of that year of looking, I had put on ten pounds. I still had nothing that really stuck and nothing that was my own. I eventually gave up looking for a hobby. I thought maybe that was just what life was supposed to be like when I grew up. I was missing direction. I was missing a purpose. I thought there should be something more, but maybe I was wrong all along. Maybe I wasn't meant to do anything but merely exist.

It was about that time that I looked in the mirror, highly dissatisfied with my reflection. Oh sweet, naive twenty-two year old me. How I would give away every possession I have to be the same size as that twenty-two year old girl that saw nothing good in her reflection. It was summer and the red bikini I had worn the year prior on our honeymoon felt a little too small. I decided it was time to lose a little bit of the weight I couldn't stop obsessing over. I didn't have any exercise equipment. I had always hated working out. I didn't know of any gyms close by and I didn't really want to have to deal with other people. I decided on running. How hard could it be?

It only took a few miles to realize that was it. No need to search any further, that was the thing I wanted to do. It was something that made me feel, strangely, even more like myself. It didn't feel new, though of course it all was, but somehow it felt old and familiar. Correction. Old and familiar, and also excruciatingly hard. Still, it was as if I were returning home. It was a sigh of relief and a deep exhale that made me feel truly happy.

It's almost laughable how I was concerned back then my other hobbies weren't cost effective. I could have bought out that entire book store and craft store and still have spent less than I have on running these past twelve years. Running is practically the third child in our family nowadays. We spend a small fortune on enough running shoes and clothes to outfit a small village. We spend more on food for just me than entire families rack up. Don't even get me started on the gadgets and electronics and extra stuff that one requires when running outside all four seasons at all hours of the day.

It didn't matter though because I had found it. No amount of money, no amount of time spent, no amount of pain, no amount of toenails lost; nothing could measure what I had gained. I had found what I was looking for. A purpose. A point. A reason. An untapped talent somewhere in me. Always hungry for more.

Now that I had found this reason, this thing that filled what was missing, where would it stop? When was it going to be enough? Would it ever be enough? The answer was no.

I ran for hours beyond what I thought I could. I pushed myself harder than I felt I could stand. I walk a fine line of love and hate during the throes of a long race. Each time though, I have come out of it knowing more about myself than when I started. I know more about what I'm capable of and know more about what I can do. I know how much I can endure, how much I can suffer, and how much better life is out there. I see in color when I'm running. Full blown color that surrounds me. The world comes to life below my very feet. Okay, maybe that sounds corny, but maybe that's true. No. Not Maybe. It is true. It's very true for me. The world is at my fingertips when I'm out there. I'm not sure how or why, but it taps into a part of me that wants and needs more. When I'm running, I find it: the more. See? I told you it didn't make sense. It's not easy to find the right words that can make you feel the way I feel when I run.

It seems so simple to say running saved me. Running brought me to God. Running brought me out of depression. Running steadied my marriage. Running gave me hope. It's so overly simplified. It leaves out so much of the in-between. The story that matters. The pieces that never fit together before. The in-between is where I live, though. That's where change happened. That's where the transformation took place, day after painful day, until I emerged, a different human being. Like stepping foot into an exotic, foreign country, I took notice of my surroundings for the first time. I saw things I hadn't bothered to see before. I was seeing it with new eyes and with a new appreciation.

So what's out there? Maybe it's the connection with nature. Maybe it's about me. Maybe it's because God lives outside. I can feel Him out there on my favorite trail, watching over me. Maybe it's because, at the height of my exhaustion and pain, I finally feel alive. It awakens my senses to be living my life out there. Not sitting inside on a couch somewhere watching someone else do it, not reading stories about all those amazing adventures, but outside doing it for myself. Outside making my own adventures. Making my own stories. Leaving my mark on this place. It's about running, but it's about so much more than that. The air outside is full of hope. I stockpile it greedily until I can get back out there. To bask in it, to breath it in, to see it, and feel it.

That hope lives in me now.

#Kathyfacts

Finding something you are passionate about can be intimidating and hard to pinpoint. Not everyone feels like they have a cause or a driving force behind what they do, but I believe everyone is passionate about something. You just need to find it. You need to figure out what makes you feel alive and pursue it.

1. What are you passionate about? Why?

2. If you don't believe you have a hobby or a passion in this life for something, are you willing to step out of your comfort zone and try something new?

3. Do you think pursuing hobbies are worthwhile investment in yourself? Why or why not?

I believe we all should have at least one personal pursuit. One thing that is just for you. Not a job, a project in your home, something for your children, or a family member. Something just for you. Maybe that seems really selfish or maybe you already have a lot of just-for you-pursuits. Wherever you may fall, know that pursuing a passion will greatly enrich your life.

If you feel like you don't have a passion within you, what are you willing to do to find it? Start today. The more different things you try, the more likely you are to find what moves you. Find something that you truly enjoy and invest time in it for yourself. You are worth that investment.

Chapter 34

In February of 2015, my friend Adele was organizing her first Upward Spiral Event, a twenty-four hour indoor run to raise awareness of mental health issues, bullying, suicide, and depression. I had originally thought I would aim for eighty miles during this run. Eighty miles seemed reasonable to me. I could walk a bit, take a few extended breaks, maybe a half hour nap, and chat with friends. It would still be a lot of running but it would also be a lot of fun.

I changed my plans a bit at the Fellow Flowers Declare it Day. Declare it Day is a gathering of friends where we set goals, say them out loud, and celebrate the journey ahead. Adele had made such a compelling case on how one-hundred miles would be possible. I felt a little sick to my stomach when I proclaimed I wanted to run one-hundred miles in less than twenty-four hours. Simply running one-hundred miles was hard enough, and then I had to go and put a time limit on it. Of course, since I said it, I'd have to do it. I wouldn't be able to back out of it after I'd told a room full of people.

When I went back home and talked to Tony about it, he thought it was perfectly doable and not at all as unobtainable as I had worked myself up into believing. Just over four miles an hour sounds doable and easy enough, until you really get into it. You must factor in bathroom breaks, switching shoes or socks, eating, drinking, outfit changes, dealing with blisters, upset stomach, fatigue, and just the general weariness that can settle in after being awake and active for twenty-four hours straight. The clock doesn't stop running just because you have stopped running. All those extra minutes spent on other things add up quickly but I was committed to following through on it.

When I sat down the next day to write, I saw that I was one page away from one-hundred pages in this book. It was like a sign. I finished out the final page so that my book stood at exactly one-hundred pages and vowed not to touch it until after the race. One-hundred miles for one-hundred pages; it was poetic.

On race day, I showed up an hour prior to the start. I needed to get ready still and set up my spot. What we've dubbed the "ultratote" was in my hands. Nothing makes the tote ultra really. It's just a heavy duty tote with some stickers on it and my entire running closet packed neatly inside of it. Still, it sounds cooler to call it the ultratote.

The race was taking place inside a local high school's field house. It was a two-hundred meter track. That meant eight laps around equaled one mile. I would need to make eight-hundred laps to reach one-hundred miles. Eight-hundred laps! Over and over I'd go in an attempt to meet my goal. One of the obvious perks was I couldn't get lost, the bathroom was twelve steps away, and I was never far away from all of my gear, food, and water.

This would be my second one-hundred mile race but I was anxious about my time goal. I was already worrying I had overextended myself with this audacious declaration.

At 3 pm, we started running. I was nowhere near as nervous as I had been a year prior, when I first set out to run one-hundred miles in a campground with the sun beating down on me. I felt surprisingly calm. Adele and I ran the first few hours together. We talked, laughed, and caught up on each other's lives before we went our separate ways. Around and around that tiny track I went, two-hundred meters at a time. Hours passed as I got slower and slower.

It wasn't look before I started asking myself all of those same questions. *Why do I put myself through this pain?* Make no mistake about it; running for one-hundred miles involves a lot of pain. *Why do I do something I know will make me cry? Make me hurt? Make me hobble slowly? Make me doubt myself? Make me feel desperate? Why do this to myself? Why do I do something that brings about so many knots in my muscles? Why do*

I do something that causes me to lose toenails? Why do I do something that inevitably ends in taping something up? Why all the pain? I don't enjoy it but then I think again longer and harder and wonder, maybe I do enjoy it. I keep doing it.

What I like is not always about the pain itself, but defying that pain. I like outrunning it. I like the fact that I can grit my teeth and not give up when every cell inside of my body is screaming at me to stop. I like that I am in control. I like that I can push my body to do what my mind says. My body says no more, but my body isn't in control, I am. I decide when enough is enough. I don't give up even though I want to stop. I keep going even when want to sit down and rest. I don't give in even when I want to take a nap. It's kind of like mental toughness training. I see it. I know what I want. I know what needs to be done if I'm going to succeed. I choose what needs to be done instead of what I want. I believe it helps me to be stronger in my everyday life when I'm facing another kind of pain, like watching Emmett suffer. I am stronger because I know I have to do what needs to be done, not just what I want. I can endure it because I must and because I have no choice. There is no room for self-pity in ultrarunning. Well, there is, but it won't take you very far. I hone that skill to use for other areas of my life.

Evening had come and I was starting to struggle when some friends showed up to keep me company. We watched their kids run just ahead of us on the track and they made me laugh even in the midst of my rising exhaustion. My friend Kristy, a non-runner, showed up and helped me log some of my fastest laps of the entire day. We laughed as we ran circle after circle. She didn't even seem like she was getting winded. Her husband Alex ran around the track in jeans and our friend Andy ran around the track carrying multiple children. It was only about five hours into the race when they showed up, and it left me feeling rejuvenated and ready to settle in for the long night ahead.

When they left, it was just me again and I got to work, hoping to reach my goal by employing my strategy. My strategy was to hit a certain amount of laps per hour. When I first started, I needed to hit thirty-four laps an hour. I would be on pace to run one-hundred miles in twenty-four hours, as long as I could run at least thirty-four laps each hour. In the beginning, when I wasn't tired, I'd hit my thirty-four laps before the hour was up. Even though I didn't have to keep running, I kept going. I was "banking" those extra laps so that when I slowed down and couldn't run thirty-four laps in an hour, I had more of a cushion to fall back on. As fatigue set in, I stopped running after my thirty-four laps in an hour and started to walk as fast as I could for the remainder of the hour. I wanted so desperately to sit down, rest, and take a break, but instead I persisted, slowly and steadily around that track to gain even more laps. That would be my only saving grace once I hit close to hour twenty. I continued this methodical approach around the track with two phones, a lap counter, and Tony making a hash mark on a piece of paper keeping track of every lap I'd run so far.

Sometime around midnight, which is not just a song I love, but the time I started falling apart, someone came to save me again. My friend Jacci showed up and sent me crying again at the mere sight of her happy face. Her perkiness and general light woke me up a bit and I started to make much better time each lap around. I was barely making my thirty-four laps each hour and with her help, I was able to bank a few more once again. She ran with me in the middle of the night, for almost three hours. She hadn't been able to run more than about three miles prior to this race because of an injury, but there she was, circling that track with me. No doubt, we were both going too fast for it to be comfortable but she never complained, not even when I was sure her knee was bothering her. She just kept going and kept me going.

When she left, Tony returned to running and walking with me, but he had already been running with me a lot. It was obvious that wasn't going to be able continue for much longer. He was going to run himself into the ground. When all was said and done, he'd covered over seventeen miles with me. It's important to note once again, he was still not a trained runner. He just keeps finding himself in these crazy situations and forges ahead for me, to help me do something that is important to me. How lucky I am to have someone who sees it as so much more than just a silly race. I think the reason my long runs have become so important to him is because, like me, he sees it as an extension of myself. He no longer sees just a race or just a bunch of miles. He sees me, this person who has to run, who has it deep in her bones, and needs to be out there. He knows that it's not a separate entity that exists alongside of me but rather a passion that lives inside of me. He understands that my weeping in pain makes me feel alive to the very core of my being. He understands that when I am feeling exhausted and defeated, by continuing to run, I am and doing the strongest, most extreme thing I can fathom.

Around 2:30 am, I hit fifty miles and started throwing myself an epic pity party. *I was not going to be able to continue for another fifty miles. It was too fast. I was dead on my feet.* I was crying and felt desperation rising up within me, and it was way too early for that. I sat down in my lawn chair and covered my face with my hands, feeling sorry for myself and feeling angry that I ever agreed to this. That I ever thought I could do it. *It was too ambitious of a goal. I just didn't have it in me to do this for another twelve hours.* Tony allowed me a five minute meltdown before he kicked me out of the chair and pushed me back out to the track. I glared at him and started shuffling around the track.

Misery ensued for a few hours. I no longer had a lead, I had fallen behind my laps needed per hour, and I was now starting to use my extra cushion of laps. I didn't care. I didn't want to run anymore. It didn't matter if I made one-hundred miles. I told Tony I didn't want to know how far I had gone or how far I had to go still. I'd click the lap counter on my end and we could compare, but he was not to tell me how far I had gone. I was really struggling, feeling down, and questioning whether I should just stop and go home. Who would blame me? It was an impressive fifty mile time. I was happy with it. I could call that good enough and just be done with it.

It was close to 5 am and I was trying to think of a way I could get out of this whole running thing when I spotted a bright orange feather boa standing in the doorway. There stood the most amazing sight. My Fellow Flower crew members: Susan, Nancy, Jennifer, and Meagon. I had been friends with a few of them on Facebook for a bit. We all represent Fellow Flowers and do what we can as ambassadors for something we believe in so deeply. I had just met them for the very first time a couple weeks prior during a Fellow Flowers Declare it Day party where I told them about my race. Some of them were from an hour and a half away. They got up in the middle of the night, put on their Fellow Flowers gear, feather boas, crowns, and sunglasses. They brought inspirational signs, adorned themselves in flowers, and showed up for me in a big way. Just the mere sight of them sent me into tears as I covered each one of these poor women in my sweaty runner hugs.

We took a few fun pictures and then were off to run. With all of them there, I felt alive and renewed, and like I really could do it.

These amazing women believed in me. I'm not sure why they believed in me, because I doubted myself. I didn't know them that well, but yet there they were, in the middle of nowhere in the middle of the night, for me. This is the power of Fellow Flowers and the people who stand behind it. Some of the most loving, caring, supportive people I've ever known wear flowers in their hair. The movement attracts a certain type of person to it. It's the type of person who you wish you knew. The type of person who restores your faith in humanity. These are the kind of women who are Flowers.

With so many friendly faces by my side, I not only caught back up, but started banking laps once again. I was running faster than I had in hours and more importantly, I was feeling really good. Their positive energy gave me a second wind and I was suddenly unstoppable. There were no more pity parties and no more tears. There was only laughter and stories. There was hope being found and miles being covered together with friends. I was speechless by their presence, and if you know me well enough, which you should at this point, you must know that doesn't happen often. I always have something to say.

Morning brought more and more people out to the track. I was slowly shuffling by in a daze when Amy, my fellow Road Warrior, and Coach Joann showed up. I got a few lessons on my poor running form, how to fix it, and a quick leg massage for my calves that were screaming at me. My knees were throbbing from the constant state of turning on that track, but not much could be done for that.

Not long after the Road Warrior crew arrived, my saving grace came waltzing in. Abbie. She was wearing a Fellow Flowers shirt and a flower in her hair. She wanted to run with me. Again, I didn't know her all that well either. We had been Facebook friends for a while and I kept up with her life and vice versa through regular updates. She was a friend of a friend. We had been introduced through our mutual friend, Liz, at a get together for mothers of children with special needs. When I realized Abbie was a distance runner too, we hit it off even more. She was standing right in front of me, all fresh faced and ready to help the mess I had become.

I'm not sure what time she got there, but I hadn't quite had my final meltdown. She showed up and she didn't leave again until I had crossed that finish line in triumph. I would guess it was a good six to seven hours that she led me around the track. My cheering section began to fill up and she stayed right with me. Lap after lap, she was there urging me to go on, filling up my water, retying my shoes for me, making me eat when I felt too sick to eat, and reminding me to do simple things that my mind was no longer capable of comprehending.

Sometimes when you run long, your mind goes to this other place. It's happened to me a handful of times, but it still can be very confusing. One minute I am running and the next I'm not sure if I really am or not. I'm somewhere else. It's a strange place when you are there but not really. You can see things happening, but you can't quite grasp the fact that you are doing them. It feels like a dream, like it's not real. In the last few hours of that race, I wasn't sure if I was actually running. I wasn't sure if I was actually there. It was like a scene from *The Wizard of Oz*. "I had this dream and you were there and you were there too." It didn't make any sense. I'm not sure what exactly brings on this state of mind. Sleep deprivation, extreme exhaustion, or self-preservation maybe. I was aware I had slipped into this state, citing something about how I felt like I wasn't really there. Abbie, my lifeline, convinced me I really was there and even better, I really was going to run one-hundred miles.

I can still see her purple shirt blurring next to me. Her face staring into mine, looking for signs that I was going to just pass out, or maybe just signs that I really was still there. "Eyes open, head up," I could hear her say. It was just one of many reminders I would need as my eyes begged to close. I could hear the people behind me, so familiar and so distant but I couldn't quite place them. I was circling that ridiculous track for reasons I couldn't remember anymore. *What was the point? Why was I still running?*

When we came around the bend I saw four women in matching shirts walking towards me. My first reaction was annoyance. They were going the wrong way and I was way too tired to move out of their way. If we weren't going to collide, they were going to have to move themselves, because I wasn't interested. I had it in my mind to bowl right through them, but then confusion came. Every two hours, we were supposed to switch directions on the track. *Had it been two hours already? Was I supposed to be going the other way around the track right now?* No. We had just switched directions. These people were in the wrong and in my way, so I just kept going.

As I got even closer and their faces came into view, I was even more confused, but it didn't matter. I started sobbing at the faces of my friends walking toward me. Kristy, Kelly, Jacci, and Becci, all wearing matching purple shirts. I didn't even notice anybody taking pictures or standing around watching, although extensive documentation was made and I can see now the spectacle we made. The front of their shirts had a footprint on it that said "Team Kathy." They were all there standing in front of me; friends who had become family. Friends who had seen me pace in long hallways, cry in hospital rooms, lose my mind in a slow and steady descent, and struggle to bring my head back above water. Friends who had stood by me when I lost my faith, when I lost the will to fight it, and when I just sat in the deep, dark pit. Friends who refused to let me sink all alone.

I saw my tumultuous journey of the past few years staring back at me in the face. I saw my triumph and defeat, and pain and secrets in their eyes. They had seen it. They had heard it. They had absorbed it. They were there then and they were there now. I sobbed into my shirt, overcome by the exhaustion and love that I felt. I enveloped them in a sweaty hug and cried even harder when I saw the back of their shirts proudly proclaimed they were a "Division of Team Emmett." Team Emmett was still faintly on my arms in marker. Once I pulled myself back together, it was time to run again, and I set off with my people behind me. Matching shirts, matching strides, and matching hearts.

The last hour was probably the longest. My friend and fellow Road Warrior, Kelli, showed up with a group of kids she mentored from a programmed called No Surrender. Kelli sang Gavin Rossdale songs to me as she had many times before. "Let's go Kath-y," was being chanted behind me along with the rhythmic clapping like an old cheer. Each time I passed the start/finish line I cried, wanting desperately for it to be the last lap. I got angry. I got whiny. I elbowed poor Tony in the side for saying we were almost there. I got desperate and started crying so hard I couldn't catch my breath. Now I needed to be instructed to breathe because I was on the verge of hyperventilating.

It was kind of like a scene out of *Forest Gump*, or so they told me. I couldn't really see the whole thing from where I was, but my friends and family assured me it was amazing. I was slowly plodding along the track and the crowd of people running and walking right behind me kept growing and growing. Round and round I went until I thought I would just drop dead right there. Tony was walking with me, trying to push me to stand up straight despite the hunched over hobbling train wreck that I had become. When he finally told me it was the last lap, all I could do was cry.

The last curve before the finish, Emmett ran out onto the track ahead of me. Travis ran with me for just a minute, but I was moving way too slow for such an energetic six year old. I hobbled past the table with the super enthusiastic announcer, a woman who had remained motivating, supportive, and positive for twenty-four hours straight, no matter how often I passed her. I threw my head back and cried in sheer relief at being done when they told me there was a finish line to cross. I broke the orange tape, probably the only time in my life that I will ever cross a finish line first. Twenty-three hours and fifty minutes, by the skin of my teeth, I did it under twenty-four hours.

There is a power to be found in holding onto hope.

#Kathyfacts

I have been so unbelievably lucky and blessed to have people who constantly show up for me. I've said before how surprised I've been each time and that's true. I am not playing at being humble. I am genuinely surprised by how many people are willing to cover me in love and support in my life. Not everyone has that, which is unfortunate. Without friends, nothing I do and nothing I have would mean as much. If there aren't people to laugh and cry with, to celebrate and grieve with, my experience feels less real. Less important.

1. Who are your people? The ones you can always count on?

2. Have you ever pushed yourself out of your comfort zone to show up for others?

Life is better with others. I believe and know that to be true. Some of the most wonderful friends I have are because I risked putting myself out there. I was scared to make a new friend all on my own. I didn't know about that quiet woman at church. I wasn't sure about the woman around the corner that was always waving and smiling at everyone. I was hesitant about running and training for a long race with a woman I barely knew. Yet, all of these people I took a chance on, that took a chance on me, were a blessing. They showed up for me, supported me, cheered me on, and became a part of my people.

If you don't have people, there is no time like the present to find some. Take a chance on a runner in your training group, a coworker, someone at the park, a woman from church, or an old acquaintance. You are going to have to step out of your comfort zone to build a group. It will take time, trial and error, and probably a bit of frustration but it's worth it. It is so worth it.

Chapter 35

Sometimes, when I'm running really early in the morning or late at night, I can lose track of where I am. Everything looks different in the dark. Everything blends and blurs together in a shadowy landscape that looks entirely the same all over the place. I usually don't panic. It takes me a minute or two to get my bearings after turning one way or another. Then I can just vaguely make out the dim outlines of parks, houses, a lake, and other telltale signs.

I'm not sure what it is about running at night. It's kind of like running in the rain; it's good for the soul. At times, it's spooky, at least for me. I'd like to pretend I'm brave and sensible, but out in the dark all by myself, sometimes I hear things that maybe aren't there. I see shapes off in the distance and my mind runs ahead into wondering about the kind of people who would be lurking around in the moonlight, and it's not good. Never mind, I am one of those people running around in the moonlight and I know I've scared a few neighbors more than a time or two.

When I run in general, I like to get all philosophical. This happens twice as often when I run in the dark. I don't know why. Everything just sounds better when I run. I'm convinced these amazing thoughts mid-run are just brilliant and I've somehow unlocked and uncovered the secrets to life. Maybe that's part of the reason I love running so much. Not the only reason, of course, but a small part. Running makes me feel more. Everything else in front of me is cleared away and I'm left with only my own thoughts. That can be scary and liberating all at the same time.

During the day, like many others, I'm usually thinking about twenty-five different things at any given moment. *I need to call the surgeon's office. Did I send in Travis' permission slip? I need to wash my favorite shirt so I can wear it for Saturday's long run. Did I start the dishwasher or just think about starting the dishwasher? I need to make a list of everything I need to get at the store today. Am I really out of chocolate chips already? When is the surgeon's office going to call me back? I should probably call again. I wonder if Tony cashed that check yet.* You get the picture.

When I run, all of that clutter, all of that constant background noise ceases to exist. It's like I can breathe again. That's what I mean when I say free. Running makes me feel free. I am a real, live person. I am my own person for just a few hours, and they are the most glorious hours, most of the time. In the quiet, dark hours, when there is nothing to even look at, I am even further reduced to living inside of my head. In the day, there are other distractions constantly taking place, random people doing random things and surroundings to take in. In the dark there is nothing. It's like a sensory deprived box. There is nothing but shadows. In that dark place, the world has never looked so beautiful. Granted, I can't make out much of it, but there is so much that just finally looks right cloaked in mystery.

I'm always talking about the lake. Its part of my favorite route, a scenic little place with great meaning to me. I have regularly run by that lake over seven years. That's how long it took me to notice my makeshift cross. Off in the distance, two telephone poles appear close together and look like a cross standing tall over the lake. In the early light of dawn or the dimly lit evening light, all I can see is the outline of the cross. In broad daylight, I can clearly see it's just two telephone poles, but in the darkness, it becomes more.

I think that's kind of like life. Everything becomes more in the darkness. People, places, and things are more beautiful when you struggle to see them. In the darkness, we become more too. We are shaped and molded when we can't see the road in front of us. When everything looks the same and there is nothing to distract us from our own heads, we are forced to look closer. You can find hope in the darkness and it will be ten times sweeter than hope found in the light. You can persevere in the darkness and it will carry you further than if you were to have an illuminated path guiding your way.

I even think I have better running form in the dark, but maybe that's because I can't see myself all hunched over and slack jawed. I like to imagine I look much stronger than I actually do when I run. That's kind of the beauty of being in the dark. You notice things you may have never noticed before in the light. It all feels different. It's richer, sharper, and truer. Even in the darkness, there is more to see if you really look. At first everything is just black. It is pitch black with no end in sight. Once your eyes get used to it and can focus again, you can make out shapes, objects, and things in the distance. It's like you are seeing the world for the first time. Yes, that's a bit heavy on the symbolism, but do you get my point?

At first, when I was tossed into this new world with Emmett and his diagnosis, everything was pitch black. I didn't dare move one single inch because it was so scary. What if something bad happened? I didn't know where I was going. I couldn't see a thing. Why not just stay put and wait for the light? As my eyes adjusted to the darkness, I could make out more of the landscape before me. Soon I was brave enough to start going in the direction I thought would be best. Sometimes I turned back around and went the other way, only to turn around and head right back in the same direction I had come from. Some days, I lost ground, and that was okay too. That was part of it; learning to see in the dark. Learning to be okay with not having the answers. Making peace with not knowing what will happen to Emmett. Letting go and trusting God that this is what needs to happen. It was devastating to watch him suffer but I couldn't do anything about it. There was nothing to do but ride out the storm, and so I did.

I continue to do so with the hope and assuredness that it is not all for nothing. I hold onto that hope, even when I can't see the rest of the world and everything is dark and scary.

The beautiful darkness that surrounds us is filled with hope.

#Kathyfacts

Often, we can fear the darkness. There are a lot of unknowns and uncertainty in the dark. Whether it is the literal darkness after sundown or a figurative darkness where you are struggling, it can be hard to push through that darkness and see light again. It can be easy to get derailed and wander off in the wrong direction in the dark.

1. What's the most beautiful thing you have seen in the actual darkness?

2. What's the most beautiful thing you have seen during a painful struggle in life?

3. Do you tend to avoid the darkness in either sense? Why or why not?

In the darkness, I believe we are presented with what maters the most. It can allow you to focus on the big picture. Hope, possibility, and a bit of fear lurk in the darkness but it can be beautiful if we start paying attention to it. When we focus only on the fear, we lose the beauty that is there. The fear can block out everything else. It can be crippling and confusing, forcing us into circles that lead nowhere.

When we look up from the fear, we can see more of our surroundings. We can see the hope that there is in this life. We can find possibility in situations that seemed impossible. Get comfortable in the dark. Turn out the lights, sit in your backyard after sunset, and look for things that appear more majestic in the dark. While you are there, mull over the darkness that has been a part of your light. Consider how you could shine light on it and change.

Chapter 36

On June 20, 2015, the third anniversary of Emmett's first surgery, I set out to run one-hundred miles. It would be my third one- hundred mile race, but I was nervous because it was the middle of summer; it was hot and sticky. I would be running this race all on my own, through the campground near our house. It was my very own race that I had made in honor of Emmett.

I woke up on Friday, June 19th at 5:15 am. I didn't have to be up until 6 am, but I couldn't sleep. I drug myself out of bed and started my pre-run routine. When I got to the pile of clothes that I would start out this run with, I was transported. I stared at the white shirt and pink letters with a kind of disgusted fascination. I had bought it special for that day three years prior. Three years before, when I stared at this same exact shirt that proudly proclaimed me as unstoppable, I felt like a fraud. I didn't feel unstoppable, I felt afraid and nauseous and like running away. But that was then and this was now. As I put the shirt on, I knew I had grown into it. I truly believed what it said. I say that not with arrogance or conceitedness or to pat myself on the back, but to remind myself. I am unstoppable. I have seen worse. I could do this. I could survive anything. I could not be stopped. I would keep going. Somehow, some way, I would. And with that in mind, I finished getting ready and took off running, full of determination.

When attempting to run one-hundred miles, time ceases to exist. It's just me and my legs fighting against my mind. As far as running goes, the first ten hours were pretty uneventful. Friends came to keep me company and decorated my home base camp with all kinds of signs. I wandered around in the huge campground for a few hours, before deciding on a five mile route so as to never be too far away from my people, and so I could be easily found.

I ran and I ran and I ran. It got hot and I ran. Things hurt and I ran. I got really tired and I ran. I got cranky and I ran. I got discouraged and I ran. I got blisters and I ran. I wanted to stop running and I ran. I just kept going. That's how you run one-hundred miles. There is no secret. You just keep going. You shut off everything else and just keep going. If my previous races had taught me anything, it was that once I started crying, I wouldn't be able to stop. The dam would break and I would never be far from dissolving into hysterics at a moment's notice. So I worked hard to keep myself together, to not lose it. I focused on my mind, shutting down all the cant's and negative thoughts threatening to spill over. I held it together, willed the emotions back in until I was ready for them. I told myself things I wasn't sure I really believed, but forced myself to adhere to them.

I hit fifty miles in a bit over twelve hours. My friend Adele showed up to run me into the dark night and early morning. She ran with me and occupied my mind, kept the impending doom from setting in, and gave me a welcomed and happy distraction. Round and round the five mile loop different people went with me. A group of friends sat around a campfire all night long, not sleeping, and taking shifts running with me. Kristy. Alex. Becci. Jay. Andy. Tony. I was never alone. These are my people. They show up for me time and time again.

Highlights of the night include hysterical laughter with friends, high fives from groups of kids on golf carts, being scared of a bug zapper, and blinding everyone around me with my super-powered headlamp.

Somewhere around 3 am, it took a turn for the worse. I was sitting on a fence, eighty miles under my belt, feeling sick to my stomach and fighting back the tears with every fiber of my being. Tony was standing next to me, urging me onward and upward, but under the cloak of night, my resolve wavered and I couldn't help but cry. *It was too long. It was too far. I was too tired. It was too dark. It was going to be dark forever. I didn't want to do it anymore. I couldn't do it anymore.* I don't remember what exactly Tony said, nor does he as we were both sleep deprived, but it was tough love. A "Get up and get your butt going right now because you don't get to stop here," kind of sentiment.

Whatever it was, it pushed me to stand back up on feet that felt like they were on fire. The pain blocked out everything else. All I could feel in each step was how much it hurt. Nothing else registered, just the burning pain in my feet. A very long and very dark night ensued. A darkness so encompassing, I didn't think I would ever see the light again. I was convinced that was it. When dawn finally broke, I felt hope. The sun rose again and it with it came my spirit. I could breathe easier in the daylight. I was not doomed to run in the darkness for the rest of my life. I had run out of the darkness, both literally and figuratively.

My friend Liz, a woman and mother I admire greatly for her loving heart, all she does for the Cystic Fibrosis community, and for the way she preserves in the face of the unknown, showed up to run in the early morning with me. My friend Kelly, who I have nicknamed "Unikitty" came and kept me company in the morning hours. I call her Unikitty because she is notoriously positive and upbeat. Kristy, the non-runner that ends up running all the time with me, went nearly twenty-five miles over the course of a day and half. She was just there through all of it. How lucky could one person possibly be to have all of these amazing people there for me yet again?

When it was finally June 20th, the day of Emmett's first surgery three years after the fact, I allowed my mind to go back. I saw myself on that treadmill, tears streaming down my face silently, my teeth gritted in sheer effort, and a crushing despair that filled me as I waited for that blasted hospital pager to ring. Waited to hear that my baby boy had lived. Waited to hear that I could stop running. Waited to hear that everything was going to be okay. I waited and I ran, a terrified mother trying to convince herself how brave she was. I could still feel it as I ran three years later.

Sometimes I am still that mother, trying to convince myself I am actually brave when I feel anything but. Yet, as my home base came into sight, one-hundred miles within my grasp, I felt the brave rise up. I did not cry. I smiled and sighed with intense relief as I crossed my finish line holding Emmett's hand. I was victorious. I really felt unstoppable. In previous races, I felt like I had merely survived one-hundred miles. It was a brutal assault to my body and senses. This time, I felt like I did more than just survive, I thrived. I remembered the reason I was doing it. I used it to power through what I thought I couldn't. I finished and I smiled. After running for twenty-seven hours and thirty-eight minutes, I really did run out of that darkness.

While I was running, I told a handful of people about Craniosynostosis in person. I told even more online. I ran to honor Emmett's journey, and I did. I ran to remind myself I can do hard things, and I did. I ran to make a difference, and maybe I did or maybe I didn't. What I do know is that I have done something and that is better than nothing.

We can leave hope behind for others.

#Kathyfacts

I will be the first to admit, there have been times, when I have gotten stuck in my story. I have been caught up on one page for way too long. I've been unable to see that an entire chapter still lay before me because I was too busy obsessing over what had happened on this one page. I had been sure I wouldn't be able to move forward. One foot in front of the other wasn't going to work for me. Of course, I was wrong. It took me some time, years even, to realize I had no choice but to go forward.

1. Have you ever gotten stuck on an event?

2. If so, how did you decide it was time to move forward once again?

3. Why do you think we forget there are entire chapters still waiting for us at times?

Running has been a very simple way for me to move forward. I used it as a physical means of literally moving forward, one step at a time on the road. I have also used it as a measuring stick of my progress. Because running is tied to my very soul and Emmett, I have been able to watch the process of running move me forward in this life. I've seen my coping skills grow stronger and watched in awe as I began to actually process events, thoughts, and feelings, rather than hiding from them and pretending they didn't exist.

Look ahead at the chapters that wait for you. If you've been stuck on one page for too long, I urge you to take the scary step of not looking back. Turn the page and go forward in your story.

Chapter 37

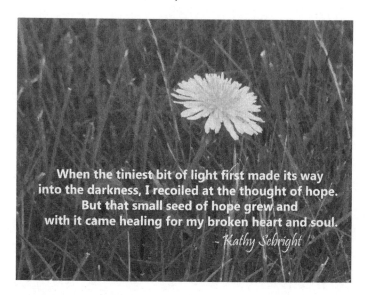

When the tiniest bit of light first made its way
into the darkness, I recoiled at the thought of hope.
But that small seed of hope grew and
with it came healing for my broken heart and soul.
— Kathy Sebright

Two of my worlds collided at the end of 2015. The stories seemed completely unconnected at first but they were intertwined deeply and subtly until it all became so clear, I couldn't ignore it any longer.

I've mentioned Fellow Flowers numerous times, but it's important to explain why it matters and what the flower are all about. It's about community. It's about looking within for the reasons you run and hopefully finding a flower that puts it into words eloquently. I've loved Fellow Flowers ever since Emmett's very first surgery. I read their statement cards. I read the meanings behind the different colored flowers. I loved the idea. I loved the way their words conveyed so much more than just running. I loved what they were doing. I loved absolutely everything about it, except I never bought a flower for myself. It never really fit. I never really felt like any of the flowers were for me, until the Silver Lining flower.

I use the word hope a lot. It's my power word. It's part of my mantra. I write it in sentences. I use prayers. I mention it in everyday conversations. Hope. It's the essence of my life. I have rings, knickknacks, magnets, journals, decorative rocks, small picture frames, necklaces, worry stones, cups, and more all with the word hope on them. I have to have almost anything I see with the word hope on it because it speaks to me so powerfully. I was attached to the word long before Emmett, but it became even more powerful and important to me later on in life when hope seemed to have left me for good. Through every trial and every heartbreak, hope was always there in some way, shape, or form.

One day, I was mindlessly scrolling through my Facebook feed when I saw the announcement for the new flower. It was the Silver Lining flower. I clicked the link to check it out and with the first word, the screen blurred into unrecognizable letters before me. This is, word for word, the Fellow Flowers statement card for the Silver Lining flower: "Hope. Braving the journey. Learning to heal. Finding the courage to be vulnerable. I can – I will make it, and I'll be better because of it. I will take it on, take it in, let it hurt…and let it go. This is my story, and I decide how it ends. Because picking up the pieces doesn't mean I'm broken." Tears streamed down my face and I knew this was it. This was my flower. The words on that statement card stuck to my ribs until they became a part of who I was. They became intertwined with my soul.

After I bought the flower, I wore it to every race. I clipped it on my purse for doctor appointments. I hung it from my rear view mirror on long drives to the hospital. I put it on my shoe while out on the trails I love so much. I wore it on my wrist on nights I went out. It was a symbol of hope. It was a symbol of me. Many women have different colored flowers for different moods or different situations but I could not. This was the only flower for me. I was loyally attached to it in many ways. It was my flower and my hope. When the petals began to tear and the flower broke down from so many miles, I tucked it lovingly away in my hope chest to keep forever. That flower was important. It had been with me through some very rough times. Then, I bought another one.

That second flower went everywhere with me, as the first had. It took me through my first, second, and third one-hundred mile runs. It took me on my seven hour and twenty-six minute anniversary treadmill run. It took me through Emmett's fourth and fifth surgeries. Maybe that makes me a little too sentimental, being so attached to an inanimate object, but that inanimate object was with me through crying, screaming, running, and giving up. It was there while I was hopelessly defeated and when I had power roaring from within me. When I faltered, I only needed to look at the flower and remember that there was still hope.

Emmett's fifth surgery came less than three months after his fourth skull surgery. Emmett had cracked his head on the side of a door and the delicate skin of his head had detached from his skull and filled up with fluid. The battered skin on his head had been cut, pulled down, stretched back up, and stitched together many times leaving room for a pocket to fill up with fluid. The surgeon needed to cut him open once again to drain it and check for infection. I was heartbroken. *Not again.*

After that fifth surgery, we learned it would be an ongoing battle. His scalp was refusing to attach to his skull. This meant his delicate scalp was (and still is) just draped over his skull. It never bonded with it and reattached. One hit, just right, could land him back in surgery, for the rest of his life. His scalp may never, ever attach to his skull, meaning it will always be extremely fragile. I just wanted something to go right for him. Yet another thing to worry about.

Things started taking a turn for the worse for me personally. My insomnia came back in a very big way. For about three months, I began sleeping no more than four hours a night. I was just awake. I couldn't go to sleep. If I woke up in the middle of the night, which I almost always did, my mind was just instantly on, like someone flicked a light on. I'm not sure when exactly it was that I could notice a difference, but it crept up on me once again. The view wasn't as beautiful anymore. I didn't notice things that used to make me want to stop and take them in. Food didn't taste as good anymore. I didn't want to eat anything, not even my favorites. I didn't want to run. I didn't feel like it and just couldn't find the will to care. I gained a good bit of weight within a short amount of time and, as much as I tried to be okay with it, I looked in the mirror and hated my reflection. I berated myself for doing this to myself every time I tried to squeeze into my favorite jeans or caught a glimpse of my rounding face. I became volatile. I was crying over nothing rather suddenly. I was screaming at Tony and losing my cool over small and insignificant things. I couldn't write anything. The words just wouldn't come.

Then it got worse. I began sleeping less than two hours a night, not just one night, but every single night. I didn't sleep for more than two hours a night for almost three straight weeks. There was no reprieve.

I became a zombie. The walls started to crumble. I was unstable. I was forgetting things, forgetting words, and stuttering frequently. I started hallucinating. I was seeing and hearing things that weren't there. I even swore Tony and I had conversations that never happened. I was spinning out of control but I didn't know how to stop it. I was so sure I couldn't tell anyone. I just kept trying to get a handle on it myself, but I was scared. I was terrified I really was going crazy. Something was very wrong with me.

I could be thrown into a sheer raging panic over the littlest of things and then cry hysterically over something I couldn't even put words to. I could also sit unmoving and not really absorb events around me. More often than not, it was this that filled me. A blanket of deadness cloaked over my soul. I couldn't laugh. I couldn't feel joy. There was no more hope. There was nothing. The whole world had gone dark. Someone had turned out the lights. I was no more. There was only me pretending.

Close friends and family could see a difference in me, but didn't know what it was. I could see a difference in me. Tony didn't think I should drive because I was on the verge of having some sort of real psychotic break. I couldn't pray. I didn't want to go to church at all, but did only occasionally out of obligation. I was sure that this time, God had truly abandoned me. This was it. There was no one but me in the darkness.

One day, Tony and I were fighting in the car about running late to church. I was burning with rage and didn't understand it. I screeched at him, my voice becoming shrill and hysterical. I know exactly what I said, something I had been feeling building in the past few nights. I pulled at the door handle and screamed at the top of my lungs, "I just want to make it stop. I'm going to jump out of this car right now! I want to die!" The door automatically locks in my car when going over fifteen miles an hour, and because of this, when I pulled at the handle, it didn't unlock. I cried in frustration about not even being able to do that right, without realizing why I couldn't open the door. When we pulled into the church parking lot, I composed myself and went in there smiling and pretending that everything was fine but I knew I had let something slip that couldn't be unheard. I could tell from the way Tony was looking at me that now it was real.

The next day I went to see a friend. I knew had struggled with depression and anxiety. We talked a little bit about it and I asked a few questions about her treatment and what she did. I was very vague and left out a lot of details. I focused mostly on insomnia, extreme exhaustion, and my behavior that I couldn't seem to control because of it. I never mentioned the incident in the car. I never mentioned the letters I had written to my family. I never mentioned how hopeless, bleak, and alone I felt, even at that very moment. The following day while Tony was at work, I texted him the question that would change my life. "Will you call the hospital for me?" Two days later, I was admitted to a mental health institution for eight days.

The first day I was there, I sat on a brown sofa in the community room. I couldn't look up from my feet. I couldn't make eye contact with anybody. I was dead inside. I felt like a failure. I hated myself. *How did I ever end up there?* I was given multiple medications. I amassed a team with a case manager, doctor, chaplain, art therapy director, and therapist. I went to classes to learn about coping skills and my behavior. I attended group therapy. For the first two days, I said practically nothing to anyone. On the third day in group therapy, I had a breakdown and a breakthrough. Sitting in group therapy class, I saw the big picture. The instructor noted that I looked visibly upset and asked if I wanted to say anything. I shook my head no as tears ran down my face. Then I blurted out a sentence of incoherent words until I was sobbing hysterically in front of that group of strangers sitting in a circle. I was sobbing and gasping for air. Someone brought me Kleenex and someone else patted my shoulder while I cried until I couldn't cry anymore. When I opened my eyes, I saw my bag on the floor next to me with my Silver Lining flower clipped to it. Hope. It was still there.

After my admission to the group, I felt a small but significant change. I was still here. No matter how deep and dark it felt, I was still here. There was still more I wanted out of this life. I took notes in every single class. I did all of my "homework." I talked more and more. I opened up about the last of what I had been hiding. I told the truth and indeed, it set me free. I took my meds as prescribed. I started sleeping. I wrote in my journal furiously; I filled an entire notebook in a matter of days. I practiced deep breathing. I stopped being so awful to myself. I stopped screaming and raging over nothing. I kept crying at strange times without any provocation, but they told me that was healing and I should just do it. So I did. I saw my doctor. I started meeting with a therapist weekly. I kept the momentum going. Something had to be different. This was it.

Three short weeks after my stay, Fellow Flowers was hosting their first ever retreat called "Rock, Retreat, Run." It was held in Arizona and promised four days of sun, inspirational speakers, running, yoga, mountain climbing, connection, cocktail parties, and more that culminated in the reveal of their thirteenth flower. Tony had already bought me tickets for Christmas. My flight was scheduled. My hotel room was secured. I was good to go, except I didn't want to go. Everything was still raw and fresh. I still wasn't sleeping like I was supposed to. I wasn't sure how to act around others yet. I had taken off my pretend mask and refused to put it back on, but I didn't know how I was going interact with a group of women on vacation having fun. I was going to be the outsider. I felt small and broken.

I decided I was going to sell my ticket. I had concocted a good reason I was going to need to miss it and sell it for half price to ensure it went. I wrote everything out for the Facebook page, but I couldn't bring myself to post it. Tony had told me over and over not to give up the ticket. He told me to go. He told me I needed to go. That it would be good for me. I wasn't sure at all. I could see that when I went to offer it up for sale. I wasn't sure about going or not going, so I decided on a whim to go.

When I arrived at the hotel in sunny Arizona, before I even brought my luggage to my room, I looked at the schedule of events. That was where I saw the open microphone session. I was overcome with the need to share my story. Standing right next to the schedule of events was Tori, one of the founders of Fellow Flowers. I decided to make my move. I talked to her in a jittery, probably somewhat incomprehensible fashion, about the open session and told her that I wanted to participate. I went back and forth in my head about whether I should or should not share what had just happened, never quite deciding if it was a good idea or a terrible idea.

The first day I was there, I lost my beloved Silver Lining flower; the only flower I had was gone. That was the item I was going to bring to another session where I needed a meaningful object. That was what I was going to hold up; that beaten down, falling apart flower that had been well loved and traveled so far with me. I had intended to keep it with my previous Silver Lining flower. I had an idea brewing for what to do with my retired flowers. But now it was gone.

Being overly attached to it, I devoted a big chunk of my time to looking for it, to no avail. I retraced steps. I tore my room and luggage apart. I put in an inquiry with the lost and found department. Others joined me in looking. I looked for it on three different days but came up empty handed. I bought another in its place but left it in my room for some reason.

The first night, Mel and Tori, the founders of Fellow Flowers, unveiled the "Say Yes Manifesto." The words were perfect and seemed to reach into my heart and squeeze tightly. The giant "Say Yes" poster was on the wall and they invited everyone to write down why they could have said no to coming but said yes instead. When my friends from the retreat were elsewhere, I walked over to the poster on wobbly legs. I quickly looked around and then picked up a marker. My hands shook so badly, the handwriting didn't look like my own. With my heart pounding out of my chest I stood back and looked at my work. "Because 3 weeks ago I was in a mental institute and wanted to die. Today I want to live." I walked quickly out of the room with the enormity of what had just happened. I told the truth, even if it was only on paper anonymously. It was big. I could feel it welling up inside of me and threatening to spill out. I continued to play my part for the next day and a half, if a little less enthusiastic and bubbly than I normally am.

On Saturday morning, after we had climbed Camelback Mountain, I attended the session where I had intended to speak. Mel and Tori were inviting people to share what flower they connected to most and a bit of their story. I raised my hand and my heart thumped out of my chest. I held the microphone in my sweaty hands and realized I had made a grave mistake. *This was not a good idea. This was a terrible idea.* I started talking about Emmett instead of telling the truth about my hospital stay and what was going on. In bits and pieces that I'm sure didn't make sense to people unfamiliar with my life, I rambled about my son being sick and a long treadmill run.

Suddenly, without my permission, the words came out. In the middle of one story, I did a complete one-eighty and started another. I announced I would not cry and summarized what had happened, where I had been just weeks earlier, and sat back down. I still did not cry, but I could not think straight. For the rest of the session, I fought the urge to run out of there. *It was a mistake. I want to leave. I shouldn't have said anything. I need to go. Now.*

As soon as the session was over, I bolted out of the room and into the bathroom. I had started crying and was gathering piles of Kleenex before I intended to hide in a bathroom stall. My tears gave way to sobbing. The demons had been unleashed and before I knew it I was sobbing. Loudly. Brokenly. Openly. It echoed in the empty bathroom. The darkness that had filled my soul for so long was pouring out and I was so lost that I couldn't even move from where I stood.

That's when help came waltzing in. Women who had just happened to walk in the bathroom surrounded me. There were arms around me, hands squeezing mine, heads on my shoulders, and people holding me. I was crying so hard my eyes were tightly shut and I didn't know exactly who was there. I hung my head and sobbed with reckless abandon until I could barely breathe. It hurt everywhere inside of me, but these women were not afraid. They were not taken aback at the intensity. They surrounded me with love, support, and flowers while I was transported back to that day where I had lost it in group therapy.

It was the same, and yet it was so different this time. This was not the same as the fear I had felt the first time. This was power. This was healing. I cried because I had done it. I had owned my story. Fully. Completely. I had told the truth and it was okay. I was still okay. Those beautiful, caring women held me until I was done crying. I stood back up and felt better, lighter even. I looked at the raging mess I was in the mirror and a smile crept over my face. I let it hurt and I let it go. I felt stronger and braver. I felt hope surging from within. I didn't know before that point if I'd ever feel hopeful again and there I was, the power from that hope bursting forth so brightly I could barely contain it. I was going to be okay. I really didn't know if I would before then. I felt a wave of reassurance wash over me. A different woman walked out of that bathroom. It wasn't a mistake to stand up and speak. It was a good idea. It was the right thing to do. I owned it. I unleashed the hold it had on me.

After that morning, I didn't bother looking for my Silver Lining flower again. I sat at the pool and had a long conversation with another Fellow Flower friend, Nikki. She told me how poetic it was that I had lost my flower there on the very first day. She said she always saw the Silver Lining flower as a transitional flower. You could pick up the pieces but sooner or later, you would be done with that part of it. You would have all your pieces and need to decide what to do next.

I had never thought of it that way. I never believed I would be done picking up the pieces. I had thought I was irrevocably broken and shattered beyond all repair. It was a long, hard journey to realize that I wasn't. I picked up some of those pieces but I also left others on the ground beneath my feet, refusing to go back. I held all of those jumbled pieces in my bleeding hands and shook with fear as I held that microphone and made the simple decision to speak truth that would reignite the spark of hope.

That very night, Fellow Flowers unveiled their thirteenth flower, the Wildflower. I gasped out loud when I heard it. These are the words spoken in honor of the Wildflower: "Free spirit, rebel soul. Shows up, loves hard. Here to make a difference. Willing to fall, determined to rise. A beacon; an undeniable light radiating through cracks of imperfection. Seeks adventure and meaning, not approval. Grows in the places unexpected...making the world beautiful. Unapologetically, her. She belongs among the Wildflowers. Run free. Run on the wild side." I smiled through a few tears that had escaped. I have used some of those phrases and sentences, word for word in the past. This was it. I was done picking up the pieces. I wasn't broken. I wanted and needed to move forward. I wanted to let the light show through all of those cracks of imperfection. I wanted to make a difference with my words and with this life I was given. In the brilliant words of Fellow Flowers:

This is my story, and I decide how it ends.

#Kathyfacts

Joy and suffering. Hope and desperation. Faith and fear. They seem like strange companions, but they have been intertwined in my life deeply. They have been side by side, pushing me forward, pulling me back, and holding me in this eloquent, heartbreaking dance. I thought being brave meant pretending I was okay. I thought admitting the truth meant I was now a failure. At first, I didn't understand how powerful and brave it was to tell the truth. I let go of my head strong notions about who I was and who I should be and just was me.

1. What is bravery to you? Is it strong and stoic? Or open and vulnerable?

2. Do you own your story or are you still running from it?

3. Is there a particular piece of your story that you haven't come to terms with yet? Why?

Owning your story sounds both simple and abstract. What does it mean to own your story? How do you even do it? Telling your truth is hard. When you tell the truth, when you admit to what you've kept buried for much too long, the burden lifts. I had to own the fact that I desperately needed real help, that something was so wrong I couldn't do it on my own. The more you own your past, the more at peace you are able to become with your future. It changes everything. You must make the choice to move on with your life. You must make the choice to heal. To learn from it. And to be better because of it.

Epilogue

What's the point in sharing all of this? Did I really need a book to map out all of the highlights, low points, and running adventures of my entire life so far? Maybe. Maybe not. If you take nothing else away from this book other than I'm unlucky and like to run a lot, I want it to be this. There is always a reason to keep going. No matter what. No matter how helpless it seems. No matter how dark the night. I know that the hopelessness can invade your body like a sickness. I know the crushing way it can sit on your shoulders. I too have heard that voice in the back of my head tell me it will never, ever get any better, but it can. It will; if you want it to; if you choose to let it. If you choose to see it, there is hope. I promise there is.

Whether you find God, find running, find hope, or just find that you spent a lot of time reading this first attempt at writing that you wish you could get back, I don't really know. I don't know what is going to happen for you, for me, or for anyone. The only thing I can do is tell you what I wish I had known from the beginning, but I guess that would take away from the journey of it all and the importance of becoming who I am through the struggle. Either way, please know that you are braver than you think. So many times I couldn't believe that. I didn't think I could do it. I didn't think I was going to make it. I curled up into a ball on the floor and wanted to give up. I locked myself in the closet and cried until I couldn't cry anymore. I wasn't brave. I was so sure of it, but I was wrong. I was brave. I still am brave. You are too. If you believe it.

No one can say with any certainty what they will do when a crisis hits. If you had asked me before any of this, before any one single crisis, I would have given a thousand different answers. Nowhere in those answers would have been the truth or what really happened. Bravery extends what you think it can't. Bravery pushes you out the door. Bravery stares you in the face when you don't want to see it. People have said so many things about me: good, bad, outright lies, and amazingly overgenerous words. For so long, I could only believe the bad. I could never believe the nice things people said about me because I knew the truth. I knew I was suffering in secret. I knew I was a big fake, a pretender, and a fraud.

I had to face that fear because it was slipping out despite my best efforts to mask it. It was like I had forgotten how to breathe all that time and now finally I could again. No matter how hard I tried to hide it, it seeped out around the edges, out of the corner of my red, bloodshot eyes, from the top of my messy, unbrushed hair, to the bottom of my feet that stomped harder and harder with each step. I tried to hide it. I tried to tuck it away and not let anyone see. That was what bravery was, right? I was so sure bravery was about sucking it up and pretending you were fine. Gritting your teeth, like I do so often in running when it gets hard and refusing to back down. Bravery, to me, was all about sheer grit. I was so wrong. That can be brave too, but that kind of bravery is isolating. It cuts you off from the rest of the world.

A friend told me she referred to those years for me as the dark days. When I was there but really wasn't. When conversations went in one ear and out the other. When I couldn't focus on anything. When I couldn't do anything but weakly smile and tell the world I was just fine. How scary it was to admit defeat. To hang my head in shame. To label myself as a wreck for whatever reason I thought. A harsh critic to my pain and suffering, I demanded more than was possible from myself. I cracked under that pressure. I crumbled, and out of those ashes I found hope. I found me. I found strength and power lurking just under the surface. I held my head high and cried those tears. I didn't want to hide anymore. I didn't want to be all alone anymore. I didn't want to push the rest of the world away because I was in pain. I wanted to live. I wanted to laugh. I wanted to hope.

So I did. I ran into it. Down the long flat road that runs past my house. Down the dusty hilly trail that knows my name. Past the lake that holds my tears. I ran and I decided I was going to be brave. I was going to tell the truth. I was going to find help. I was going to pray again to a God that I was still angry at. I ran and I justified my behavior. I ran and realized I never needed to in the first place. I ran and I let go of the things people have said and done to me. I ran and I filled my lungs up with gratefulness and the beauty of my surroundings. I sweated out the toxicity in my system. I inhaled hope. I exhaled hope. I became hope.

Now it's all good and fine to wax poetic a bit. Where is the underlining, defining, reoccurring theme? You may have already guessed. Hope. It was always there. Always. Under a blanket of fear. Cloaked in pain. Trembling under my anxiety. It was in the faces of my children. It was in the hands of my friends. It was in the tears of my family. I was surrounded by such love and compassion and people who could hold onto hope for me until I could do it for myself. They were the keepers of my hope.

This is my life. It's a collection. A tapestry. The good and bad. It all goes together. Without the bad, there wouldn't have been the good. Within the bad, there was good. Try as I might, I can't wish for a different outcome or a different life. This is my life. It's not better or worse than before, just different. It took time. It took hard work. It took faith, but eventually I found it. Hope. In the long run.

There is always hope in the long run. Always.

The End
is only
the
beginning

The Family Update

These present days find me more at peace in my life than I'd ever been before. I've made a conscious decision to leave the past behind me, not to forget it but to learn from it. I have learned, grown, and broken free of what threatened to break me. I am still running for hours on end, writing whenever I get the chance, leaning on my faith, and feeling incredibly blessed by my life. I have also started speaking in order to share my hope with others. It's too important to keep to myself.

Tony is still working hard for our family. He remains a strong and steady constant. He is an amazing father to our children and the most supportive husband I could have ever asked for. He continues to push and encourage me even when I'm scared. To this day, he insists he is "a non-runner" and has sworn off any additional double digit runs with me. Although, faced with watching me struggle through another brutal race, I believe he'd be out there in a heartbeat.

Travis keeps growing and amazes me daily. He loves reading to Emmett and continues to take care of him. Travis entered a writing contest and won with his book *My Favorite Hat*. He also single handedly illustrated the book *Crayons on my Toesies: Colored by Craniosynostosis*. If you ask Travis, he will tell you he wants to be a writer and a runner, just like Mom. He still proclaims Emmett is his best friend and my heart swells with pride for the person he is becoming.

Emmett is doing great. There haven't been any additional surgeries at the time of this writing and his skull seems to be healing well, even though the scalp remains unattached. Emmett is thriving in preschool. He can count, write his name, and learned his colors this year. All of these milestones are completely breathtaking to me because I remember when we didn't know if it would ever be possible. Emmett is running around full of light and laughter. His joy and his smile are infectious and full of hope.

And they lived happily ever after. Or something like that.

What is Craniosynostosis?

Craniosynostosis is a birth defect of the skull that causes one of the sutures in a baby's skull to fuse prematurely. This changes the natural progression of skull growth. Symptoms of Craniosynostosis include an unusual shaped head, a hard, raised ridge along the affected suture, and a soft spot that closed too early.

Craniosynostosis can inhibit brain growth and can cause intracranial pressure, seizures, eye problems, developmental delays, and more if left uncorrected. If you think your child or a child of someone you know has been affected, please speak to your doctor or ask to see a pediatric craniofacial plastic surgeon.

There are many resources and avenues for support available to families dealing with Craniosynostosis. Below are just a few.

Cranio Care Bears: http://craniocarebears.org

CAPPS: http://www.cappskids.org

Cranio Angel Network: http://www.cranioangelnetwork.com

Causes and communities near and dear to me

~Broken but Priceless Ministries is an online ministry catering to those that deal with a chronic illness or are caretakers of a loved one with a chronic illness.
http://www.erinelizabethaustin.com

~Cranio Care Bears is a nonprofit organization that lends support, knowledge, and sends free care packages all over the world to children undergoing surgery for Craniosynostosis.
http://craniocarebears.org

~Fellow Flowers is a community that honors and celebrates the reasons why women run.
http://fellowflowers.com

~Michigan Runner Girl is a community dedicated to nourishing the Michigan Runner through inspiration, information, and motivation.
http://michiganrunnergirl.com/

~Heart Strides is a charity that gives the gift of running, through a pair of free running shoes, as well as support to mothers of children with special needs or those who are critically ill.
http://www.heartstrides.org

~I Run 4 Remembrance is a running group to honor those that have passed. You can run in remembrance of someone's loved one and help keep their memory alive. This run is for you Brextin.
http://www.whoirun4.com

Coming soon

Kathy is currently working on the upcoming children's book *Crayons on my Toesies: Colored by Craniosynostosis*. The book aims to help younger children understand what Craniosynostosis is and what to expect before and after surgery.

The book was originally written in 2012 as a small gift to her three year old son Travis to help him understand what was happening with his brother Emmett. It was decided as a family to pursue the endeavor and publish the book in the hopes of comforting other children in a time of great stress. The book is a labor of love from the entire family and is due out fall of 2016.

Romans 5:3-5 (ESV)

[3] Not only that, but we rejoice in our sufferings, knowing that suffering produces endurance, [4] and endurance produces character, and character produces hope, [5] and hope does not put us to shame, because God's love has been poured into our hearts through the Holy Spirit who has been given to us.

About the author

Kathy Sebright is a writer, speaker, mother, and runner in a small, rural Michigan town. She loves her family and friends, God, the woods, chocolate, and laughing until she cries.

Kathy writes for the pure love of writing and tries to pursue hope, bravery, and light with each word. She writes for The *Huffington Post and Broken but Priceless Ministries*. She also has been published on numerous on-line sites as well as printed publications.

You can learn more about Kathy, help with her mission to serve others, inquire about speaking engagements, and more at www.kathysebright.com. You can also email Kathy directly at contact@kathysebright.com.

Finding
Hope
in the
Long Run

Kathy Sebright

Made in the USA
Middletown, DE
05 June 2016